The Missing Martyrs

The Missing Martyrs

Why There Are So Few
Muslim Terrorists

Charles Kurzman

OXFORD
UNIVERSITY PRESS

OXFORD
UNIVERSITY PRESS

Oxford University Press, Inc., publishes works that further
Oxford University's objective of excellence
in research, scholarship, and education.

Oxford   New York
Auckland   Cape Town   Dar es Salaam   Hong Kong   Karachi
Kuala Lumpur   Madrid   Melbourne   Mexico City   Nairobi
New Delhi   Shanghai   Taipei   Toronto

With offices in
Argentina   Austria   Brazil   Chile   Czech Republic   France   Greece
Guatemala   Hungary   Italy   Japan   Poland   Portugal   Singapore
South Korea   Switzerland   Thailand   Turkey   Ukraine   Vietnam

Copyright © 2011 by Oxford University Press, Inc.

Published by Oxford University Press, Inc.
198 Madison Avenue, New York, New York 10016

www.oup.com

Oxford is a registered trademark of Oxford University Press

Library of Congress Cataloging-in-Publication Data
Kurzman, Charles.
The missing martyrs : why there are so few Muslim terrorists / Charles Kurzman.
    p.   cm.
ISBN 978-0-19-976687-1 (hardcover : alk. paper)
1. Terrorism—Religious aspects—Islam.   2. Terrorists—Psychology.
3. Terrorism—Prevention.   4. Islam—21st century.   I. Title.
BP190.5.T47K875   2011
363.325'12—dc22
2010039083

1 3 5 7 9 8 6 4 2

Printed in the United States of America
on acid-free paper

CONTENTS

Chapter 1. Why There Are So Few Muslim Terrorists   3
Chapter 2. Radical Sheik   25
Chapter 3. Thoroughly Modern Mujahidin   59
Chapter 4. Liberal Islam versus Revolutionary Islamism   92
Chapter 5. Uncle Sam versus Uncle Usama   128
Chapter 6. Predicting the Next Attacks   169

Acknowledgments   205
Notes   207
Index   243

The Missing Martyrs

CHAPTER 1

✿

Why There Are So Few
Muslim Terrorists

The rental car rolled onto the sidewalk behind the registrar's office and drove slowly down the brick path between a dining hall and the English Department, a few steps from my office. "Beyond Time," an upbeat German dance song, played in the car's stereo. The driver, Mohammad Taheri-Azar, had just graduated from the University of North Carolina three months earlier, so he knew the campus well. Beyond the dining hall was a plaza known as the Pit, where students were hanging out at lunchtime on a warm winter day in early 2006. Taheri-Azar planned to kill as many of them as possible.[1]

He brought no weapons except a knife, some pepper spray, and the four-wheel-drive sports utility vehicle he had rented in order to run people over without getting stuck on their bodies. When he reached the Pit, Taheri-Azar accelerated and swerved to hit people as they scattered out of his way. His fender clipped several students, and several more rolled over his hood and off the windshield. One of them happened to be a graduate instructor on his way to teach the university's course on national and international security. Taheri-Azar turned left at the end of the plaza, hit another couple of students in front of the library, then sped off campus just beneath my office window.

On Franklin Street, Taheri-Azar slowed down and merged into city traffic. He drove a mile to the east, down the hill that gave Chapel Hill its name, and thought about heading for the highway. Instead, he pulled over in a calm residential neighborhood, parked, and called 911 on his cell phone. "Sir, I just hit several people with a vehicle," he told the operator. "I don't have any weapons or anything on me, you can come arrest me now." Why did you do this? the operator asked. "Really, it's to punish the government of the United States for their actions around the world." So you did this to punish the government? "Yes, sir." Following the operator's instructions, he placed his phone on the hood of the car and put his hands on his head as police officers arrived.[2]

Before leaving his apartment that morning, Taheri-Azar had left a letter on his bed explaining his action more fully, along with a computer memory card "so the police could have an electronic version":

> Due to the killing of believing men and women under the direction of the United States government, I have decided to take advantage of my presence on United States soil on Friday, March 3, 2006, to take the lives of as many Americans and American sympathizers as I can in order to punish the United States for their immoral actions around the world.
>
> In the Quran, Allah states that the believing men and women have permission to murder anyone responsible for the killing of other believing men and women. I know that the Quran is a legitimate and authoritative holy scripture since it is completely validated by modern science and also mathematically encoded with the number 19 beyond human ability. After extensive contemplation and reflection, I have made the decision to exercise the right of violent retaliation that Allah has given me to the fullest extent to which I am capable at present.
>
> I have chosen the particular location on the University campus as my target since I know there is a high likelihood that I will kill several people before being

killed myself or jailed and sent to prison if Allah wills. Allah's commandments are never to be questioned and all of Allah's commandments must be obeyed.[3]

From prison, Taheri-Azar wrote that "I turned myself in so that the American public would know exactly why the attack took place—with the higher goal of encouraging them to force the United States government to leave all Islamic territories in the Middle East to take care of themselves and hence unoccupy the territories of Israel, Saudi Arabia, Iraq, and Afghanistan by completely removing any military presence of United States forces from those territories and any other Islamic territories not mentioned, including those in Africa."

Nine people suffered broken bones and other injuries that day. Fortunately, Taheri-Azar didn't kill anybody, though the toll might have been higher if Taheri-Azar's earlier plots hadn't fallen through. Initially, he planned to join insurgents in Afghanistan or Iraq but was discouraged by visa restrictions on travel to those countries. Then he looked into joining the air force and dropping a nuclear bomb on Washington, D.C., but he realized that his eyesight was too poor to qualify to be a military pilot. Turning closer to home, Taheri-Azar considered shooting people randomly at the university—his letters from prison indicate that he thought about targeting the dining hall where I often eat lunch.

In the weeks before his attack, Taheri-Azar test-fired a laser-sighted handgun at a nearby shooting range but was told that he couldn't buy it without a permit. Taheri-Azar could have purchased a rifle on the spot, if he had completed some federal paperwork, but he had his heart set on a Glock pistol. Later, at his apartment, he started to fill out the permit application—then gave up when he found that he would need three friends to attest to his good moral character. "The process of receiving a permit for a handgun in this city is highly restricted and out of my reach at the present," Taheri-Azar complained in the letter he left on his bed for the police. Months later, in prison, he rationalized his decision. "The gun may have malfunctioned and acquiring one would have attracted attention to me from the FBI in all likelihood, which could have foiled any attack plans." Taheri-Azar could be the only terrorist in the world ever deterred by gun-control laws.[4]

Taheri-Azar's incompetence as a terrorist is bewildering. Surely someone who was willing to kill and die for his cause, spending months contemplating the attack, could have found a more effective way to kill people. Why wasn't he able to obtain a firearm or improvise an explosive device or try any of the hundreds of murderous schemes that we all know from movies, television shows, and the Internet, not to mention the news? And once Taheri-Azar decided to run people over with a car, why did he pick a site with so little room to accelerate?

Even more bewildering is the fact that we don't see more terrorism of this sort. If every car is a potential weapon, why aren't there more automotive attacks? Car bombs have been around since the 1920s, when the first one was detonated on Wall Street in New York City, but they require a fair bit of skill. Drive-through murder, on the other hand, takes very little skill at all. People have been killing people with cars ever since the automobile was invented, and the political use of automotive assault was immortalized in a famous film, *The Battle of Algiers* (1966), which shows two Algerian revolutionaries driving into a bus-stand full of French settlers. Yet very few people resort to this accessible form of terrorism. In the United States, for example, out of several million Muslims, it appears that Taheri-Azar was the first to attempt this sort of attack. He was followed by two possible copycats. In addition to cars, plenty of other terrorist weapons are readily available. One manual for Islamist terrorists, published online in 2006, listed 14 "simple tools" that "are easy to use and available for anyone who wants to fight the occupying enemy," including "running over someone with a car" (number 14) and "setting fire to homes or rooms at sleep time" (number 10).[5]

If terrorist methods are as widely available as automobiles, why are there so few Islamist terrorists? In light of the death and devastation that terrorists have wrought, the question may seem absurd. But if there are more than a billion Muslims in the world, many of whom supposedly hate the West and desire martyrdom, why don't we see terrorist attacks everywhere, every day?

Islamist terrorists ask these questions too. In their view, the West is engaged in a massive assault on Muslim societies and has been for generations. This assault involves military invasions, political domination, economic dependence, and cultural decadence, and is reaching new heights of aggression each year. Islamists offer a solution: the establishment of Islamic government. Revolutionary Islamists offer a strategy to achieve Islamic government: armed insurrection. Terrorist revolutionaries offer a tactic to trigger insurrection: attacks on civilians. These attacks are intended to demoralize the enemy, build Muslims' self-confidence, and escalate conflict, leading Muslims to realize that armed insurrection is the sole path to defend Islam.

But Islamist terrorists worry that things haven't worked out as planned. Acts of terrorism have not led Muslims to revolt. Leading terrorists wonder aloud, Why aren't more Muslims resisting the onslaught of the West? What more provocations do they need before they heed the call to arms?

The world's most notorious Islamist terrorists have all denounced their fellow Muslims for their passivity. Usama Bin Ladin of al-Qaida, the global terrorist organization, frequently sounded this theme. "Each day, the sheep in the flock hope that the wolves will stop killing them, but their prayers go unanswered," he declared in May 2008. "Can any rational person fail to see how they are misguided in hoping for this? This is our own state of affairs." Bin Ladin and Ayman Zawahiri, the number two leader in al-Qaida, have tried to infuse their statements with a triumphal, inspirational tone, but their disappointment shows through. "There is no excuse for anyone today to stay behind the battle," Zawahiri lectured in a video released on the Internet in 2007. "We continue to be prisoners restrained by the shackles of [mainstream Islamic] organizations and foundations from entering the field of battle. We must destroy every shackle which stands between us and our performing this personal duty."[6]

An al-Qaida recruitment video from 2008 opens with this lament:

My brother in Allah, tell me, when will you become angry?

If our sacred things are violated, and our landmarks are demolished, and you didn't become angry;

If our chivalry is killed, and our dignity is trampled on, and our world ends, and you didn't become angry;

So tell me, when will you become angry?...

I saw death erected above our heads. And you didn't become angry. So be frank with me, without embarrassment: to which ummah [religious community] do you belong?

If what you suffer, what we suffer, doesn't make you want revenge, then don't bother.

Because you're not ours, nor one of us, nor do you belong to the world of man.

So live as a rabbit, and die as a rabbit.[7]

You are scared like a rabbit, al-Qaida tells Muslims. You are not human if you fail to join us. Other terrorists have issued similar insults in their attempt to goad Muslims into revolutionary activity. "What is wrong with the Muslim Ummah today?" the Pakistani militant group Harakat ul-Mujahideen complained on its website. "When the Kuffar [non-Muslims] lay their hands on their daughters, the Muslims do not raise even a finger to help them!" The local al-Qaida affiliate in Saudi Arabia declared, "We are most amazed that the community of Islam is still asleep and heedless while its children are being wiped out and killed everywhere and its land is being diminished every day, God help us. Islam is the faith of unity and cooperation, and it commands us to assist Muslims whether they are oppressors or oppressed.

Oh, brother in religion, why have you quit supporting Islam and its people?" Abu Musab al-Suri, a widely read strategist of Islamist revolution, called it "regrettable" that so few Muslims, only one in a million, have committed themselves to jihad. Mulla Dadullah, an Afghan Taliban commander, quoted a statement of the Prophet Muhammad in a video interview released by al-Qaida in 2006: "This is what the Messenger (peace be upon him) mentioned about the weakness of the Muslims against the non-believers in the last days. 'In those days, you are numerous, but you are like the scum of the flood, and the cause of all that is the love of this world and hatred of death.'" This sums up the terrorists' main challenge: too many Muslims are "scum" who love this world and refuse to risk martyrdom.[8]

Proponents of violent jihad have insulted and guilt-tripped their fellow Muslims for decades. Sayyid Qutb, the Egyptian revivalist who inspired a generation of Islamic movements, went so far as to declare in the 1960s that "the Muslim community has been extinct for centuries." Today's Muslims do not deserve to be called Muslims, he insisted, because they have veered from the principles of Islam. Only a revolution that establishes Islamic government will entitle Muslims to call themselves "believers."[9]

Qutb's exhortations treated revolutionary jihad as a collective duty of the community of Muslims. By the 1980s, however, Islamist militants had honed their religious judgments to a finer point. "Today, jihad is an individual duty of every Muslim," wrote Abd al-Salam Faraj, chief ideologue of the group that assassinated Egyptian president Anwar Sadat in 1981. This obligation cannot be fulfilled through peaceful means, he asserted, but only through "confrontation and blood." Abdullah Azzam, one of the chief organizers of the pan-Islamic jihad against the Soviets in Afghanistan, called participation in this battle—actually going to fight, he specified, not just sending money—an individual duty that is "incumbent upon every Muslim on earth until the duty is complete and the Russians and communists are expelled from Afghanistan. This sin weighs on the necks of everybody." In 1998, Bin Ladin and colleagues used similar language in declaring war on the United States: "The ruling to kill the Americans and their allies—civilians and military—is an individual duty for every Muslim who can do it in any country in which it is possible to do it."[10]

These revolutionaries do not mind being called terrorists. Azzam defined his activities in these terms in a speech in the 1980s that was included in an al-Qaida recruitment video in early 2001: "We are terrorists, and terrorism is our friend and companion. Let the West and East know that we are terrorists and that we are terrifying as well. We shall do our best in preparing to terrorize God's enemy and our own. Thus terrorism is an obligation in God's religion." Bin Ladin adopted the same approach. "If killing those that kill our sons is terrorism, then let history witness that we are terrorists," he told an al-Jazeera reporter soon after 9/11. Many Islamist revolutionaries continue to identify themselves as *irhabiyun*, Arabic for terrorists. One of the myriad "poems for jihadists" circulating on the Internet repeats over and over, "I am a terrorist. I am a terrorist." Al-Muhajiroun, a British group that allied itself with al-Qaida, declared that "whoever denies that terrorism is part of Islam is *kafir* [that is, not truly Muslim]." An al-Qaida booklet in early 2008 noted that the term "terrorist" is used as an insult against Muslims. Nonetheless, the author concluded, "A fighter [*mujahid*] in the path of God, seeking to exalt the word of God, is indeed a terrorist toward the enemies of God who seek to eradicate the religion [of Islam] and occupy its sacred places, for he terrorizes and scares them and strikes fear in their hearts to prevent their misdeeds and repel them from Muslim lands, for terrorism is a goal, even a duty, of Muslims, because it is among the causes of victory over the enemies." Not every Islamist revolutionary accepts the label of terrorist, but enough do to justify our use of the term.[11]

For several decades now, Islamist terrorists have called it a duty for Muslims to engage in armed jihad—against their own rulers, against the Soviets, and later against the Americans. Tens of thousands have obeyed, perhaps as many as 100,000 over the past quarter century, according to U.S. government estimates of the size of terrorist groups. This is a significant number of potentially violent militants, even if most of them received little serious training and subsequently dropped out of the militant movement. At the same time, more than a billion Muslims—well over 99 percent—ignored the call to action. This is typical for revolutionary movements of all sorts, of course—few revolutionaries ever manage to recruit more than a small portion of their target populations. Leftist terrorists such as the Weathermen in the United States, the Red Army Faction in West Germany, and the Red Brigades in Italy were even less successful at recruiting, even at their height in the 1970s and 1980s. Among terrorist groups, the most effective recruiters tend to be territorially based movements such as the Irish Republican Army, the Basque Homeland and Freedom group ETA, or the Palestinian group Hamas, whose military wing is said to have grown since its takeover in Gaza to approximately 1 in 100 residents. Global Islamist terrorists have managed to recruit fewer than 1 in 15,000 Muslims over the past quarter century and fewer than 1 in 100,000 Muslims since 9/11.[12]

Recruitment difficulties have created a bottleneck for Islamist terrorists' signature tactic, suicide bombing. These organizations often claim that they have waiting lists of volunteers eager to serve as martyrs, but the scale of these waiting lists appears not to be very large. Al-Qaida organizer Khalid Sheikh Mohammed made this point unintentionally during a 2002 interview, several months before his capture by American and Pakistani forces. Mohammed bragged about al-Qaida's ability to recruit volunteers for "martyrdom missions," as Islamist terrorists call suicide attacks. "We were never short of potential martyrs. Indeed, we have a department called the Department of Martyrs." "Is it still active?" asked Yosri Fouda, an al-Jazeera reporter who had been led, blindfolded, to Mohammed's apartment in Karachi, Pakistan. "Yes it is, and it always will be as long as we are in jihad against the infidels and the Zionists. We have scores of volunteers. Our problem at the time was to select suitable people who were familiar with the West." Notice the scale here: "scores," not hundreds, much less thousands—and most of them were not deemed suitable for terrorist missions in the West. After Mohammed's capture and "enhanced interrogation" by the Central Intelligence Agency—using methods that the U.S. government had denounced for decades as torture—federal officials testified that Mohammed had trained 39 operatives in all for suicide operations and that the 2001 attacks involved only 19 hijackers "because that was the maximum number of operatives that Sheikh Mohammed was able to find and send to the U.S. before 9/11." According to a top White House counterterrorism official, the initial plans for 9/11 called for a simultaneous attack on the West Coast of the United States, but al-Qaida could not find enough qualified people to carry it out. Mohammed's claim that al-Qaida was "never short of potential martyrs" seems to have been false bravura.[13]

Since 9/11, with al-Qaida and its allies under pressure all over the world, the scale of terrorist recruitment has been further reduced. During five years of Taliban rule, 10,000 to 20,000 recruits passed through terrorist training camps in Afghanistan, according to U.S. officials. Since 9/11, the scale of terrorist training has dropped by 90 percent. The largest concentration of terrorist camps in the world, in the frontier regions of northwestern Pakistan, has trained fewer than 2,000 militants. The biggest single camp in the region consisted of approximately 250 recruits, who were featured in a "graduation ceremony" covered by Pakistani television stations that had been invited by the local Taliban. Other

Taliban have spoken of an early camp, disbanded in late 2002, that trained as many as 200 militants. However, U.S. and Pakistani intelligence officials say that most of the camps in the region consist of only one dozen to three dozen men. If the camps were any larger, they would be easy targets for American satellite surveillance and missile attacks. In Somalia, another site of terrorist training, intelligence officials place the number of foreign fighters at even lower levels, from a few dozen to a few hundred in total.[14]

Islamist terrorists have found it especially hard to recruit in the United States. Al-Qaida's leaders have encouraged American Muslims to attack the United States from within, and the American government has identified the possibility of domestic Islamist terrorism as a serious threat. In early 2003, for example, Robert Mueller, director of the Federal Bureau of Investigation, told Congress that "FBI investigations have revealed militant Islamics [*sic*] in the US. We strongly suspect that several hundred of these extremists are linked to al-Qaeda." ("Islamics" is a law-enforcement term for Muslims.) Alarmists outside of government have implied that the number of Muslim terrorists in the United States is even larger, perhaps in the thousands. However, all of these estimates must be regarded as exaggerations. By the U.S. Department of Justice's own accounts, approximately a dozen people in the country were convicted in the five years after 9/11 for having links with al-Qaida. During this period, fewer than 40 Muslim-Americans planned or carried out acts of domestic terrorism, according to an extensive search of news reports and legal proceedings that I conducted with David Schanzer and Ebrahim Moosa of Duke University. None of these attacks was found to be associated with al-Qaida. A month after Taheri-Azar's attack in Chapel Hill, Mueller visited North Carolina and warned of Islamist violence "all over the country." Fortunately, that prediction was wrong.[15]

To put this in context: out of more than 140,000 murders in the United States since 9/11—more than 15,000 each year, down from 24,000 in the early 1990s—Islamist terrorists accounted for fewer than three dozen deaths by the end of 2010. Part of the credit for this good fortune is due to the law-enforcement officers and community members who have worked to uncover plots before they could be carried out. But the number of disrupted plots is relatively small—fewer than 200 Muslim-Americans have been involved in violent plots since 9/11, most of them overseas—so credit for the low level of violence must be due primarily to the millions of Muslims who have refrained from answering the call to terrorism.[16]

Of course, more terrorists may still be in hiding, or under surveillance, or deported or jailed for other offenses. There is no way to know how many—so there is no way to debunk paranoid fears about massive secret threats. In any case, even a single violent plot is too many, and I do not doubt that a small group of committed people can change the world, to paraphrase the adage that is often attributed to anthropologist Margaret Mead. Islamist terrorists are likely to continue to kill and maim thousands of people around the world each year for the foreseeable future.[17]

However, terrorism accounts for only a tiny proportion of the world's violence. Every day, according to the World Health Organization, approximately 150,000 people die, all around the world. The U.S. government's National Counterterrorism Center calculates that Islamist terrorism claims fewer than 50 lives per day—fewer than 10 per day outside of Iraq, Pakistan, and Afghanistan. By way of comparison, approximately 1,500 people die each day from civilian violence, plus an additional 500 from warfare, 2,000 from suicides, and 3,000 from traffic accidents. Another 1,300 die each day from malnutrition. Even in Iraq, while it was suffering the world's highest rate of terrorist attacks, terrorist bombs caused less than one-third of all violent deaths. In other words, terrorism is not a leading cause of death in the world. If we want to save lives, far more lives would be saved by diverting a small portion of the world's counterterrorism budgets to mosquito netting.[18]

Yet terrorism dominates the headlines far out of proportion to its death toll. Terrorists are grimly successful at attracting public attention. Of the thousands of violent incidents that occur around the globe each day, the world media efficiently sifts for hints of terrorist motivations, then feeds these incidents over the wire services and satellite networks to news consumers who may not realize how rare terrorism really is. In this way the media are accomplices to terrorism. They bring the perpetrators' message to vast audiences; without these audiences, the terror would only be felt locally. Indeed, if a terrorist act occurred and nobody heard about it, it would be a failure. The media is just doing its job in reporting terrorist violence—if a terrorist act occurred and journalists didn't cover it, we would consider the media to have failed. But the result is that media consumers, ordinary folks who try to keep up with world affairs, get a skewed picture of the prevalence of terrorism.

Even without incidents of violence, mass media stoke fears of terrorism by reporting hugely inflated estimates of alleged threats. These stories, often citing unnamed government officials, create the false impression that "sleeper cells" are ready to wreak havoc. In the United States, Fox News has made a name for itself by repeatedly trumpeting alarming information such as "a growing body of evidence pointing to the presence of suspected members of terrorist sleeper cells operating on U.S. soil" and secret reports that "Mexican drug cartels are teaming up with Muslim gangs to fund sleeper cells right here in the U.S. and abroad." None of these allegations has been borne out by judicial investigations. Fearmongering about Islamist terrorism is not limited to the United States. India, for example, has also experienced media frenzies, such as the flurry of baseless stories about a suspected "terror hub" in Karnataka state, where "operatives have infiltrated into the region and are acting as sleeper cells, spreading messages [and] brainwashing youths." No terrorism ever emerged from these so-called sleeper cells.[19]

The media's fascination with terrorism coincides with terrorists' interest in the media. Media-savvy terrorists such as Bin Ladin admit that they use news coverage for recruitment. That is why Bin Ladin granted interviews to international reporters in Afghanistan, despite prohibitions by Taliban leader Muhammad Umar: he considered it the most efficient way to reach a global audience of potential conspirators. (On tensions between the Taliban and al-Qaida, see chapter 3.) Bin Ladin explained to an Arab journalist that international media—especially Arab satellite television channels—unintentionally helped recruit militants by broadcasting news of the Palestinian uprising and Islamist activities around the world. Yet Bin Ladin's media strategy was controversial even among other terrorists, two of whom wrote to Bin Ladin in 1999 to inquire whether he had "caught the disease of screens, flash[bulb]s, fans, and applause," according to e-mail stored on a computer in Afghanistan that was later purchased by American reporters. Another al-Qaida official complained that Bin Ladin was "obsessed" with media attention. After al-Qaida's training camps in Afghanistan were overrun by U.S. and allied troops in the fall of 2001, electronic media became even more central to Islamist terrorism. Instruction manuals that had previously been distributed in photocopies in Afghanistan are now digitized and posted on the Internet. One pamphlet from 2003, itself distributed online, listed "electronic jihad" as one of 39 ways to participate in the struggle: "the Internet [is] a blessed medium that benefits us greatly by making it possible for people to distribute and follow the news. It also allows us to defend the mujahidin and publicize their ideas and goals." Even hostile news coverage may make terrorists look appealing to some viewers (see chapter 2 on "radical sheik"). Scholarly discussions of terrorism, too, may indirectly help recruit potential conspirators. Taheri-Azar, for example, learned about al-Qaida's ideology at his university library.[20]

Mohammad Taheri-Azar grew up in Charlotte, North Carolina, where his parents settled after emigrating from Iran when Mohammad was a toddler. In his "meditations" from prison, as he called them, Taheri-Azar wrote that he had been outraged by the foreign policies of the U.S. government since the Gulf War of 1991, when the United States and its allies liberated Kuwait from republican Iraq and returned it to the al-Sabah monarchy. Taheri-Azar was seven years old at the time. In the following years, he was "secretly happy to see U.S. interests attacked as I grew up, seeing the Oklahoma City Bombing [1995], the Columbine High-School massacre [1999], the 1993 World Trade Center bombing, etc." In high school, he was more interested in fast cars and raunchy videos. In the summer of 2001, he graduated and moved to Chapel Hill for college.

"The 9/11 attacks revived my anger towards the U.S. government because it distressed me to see the nineteen hijackers lose their lives this way because of the military decisions of the United States and Israel in the Middle East since the 1950s," Taheri-Azar wrote. "I decided then and there that I would most likely engage in some attack of my own against U.S. interests." At that point, according to Taheri-Azar's account, he was not particularly religious. In fact, he had had no religious education of any sort. "It is dangerous to raise a child without a religious upbringing, as my parents did," Taheri-Azar later reflected. "As long as the child perceives that they won't be caught by their parents, the school, or the police, the child is likely to perform all kinds of mischievous actions." It was not until 2003 that a friend introduced him to the Quran. For two years they read it together and increased their observance of pious rituals.

Incrementally, Taheri-Azar began to combine his hatred of U.S. government policies with his newfound interest in Islam. In the summer of 2004, he decided to drive his car more carefully, in keeping with the methods of Pakistani terrorists he read about in the *Atlantic Monthly*: "The trained martyrs, called the 'armored corps' of jihad, return to their homes and jobs to live normally until summoned. While they wait, they are under strict orders to shun beards and traditional clothes; to maintain a neat, inconspicuous appearance; to have their documents (real ones issued under fake names) in order and to carry them at all times; and to do nothing illegal or out of the ordinary. They are forbidden even to run a red light." In the summer of 2005, "on a leisurely visit to Davis Library" at the University of North Carolina, Taheri-Azar discovered the ideology of al-Qaida. He found it in an anthology of writings about terrorism and guerrilla warfare compiled by one of the United States' most respected experts on terrorism, Walter Laqueur, a Jewish refugee from Germany whose parents perished in a Nazi death camp. The chapters by al-Qaida so captivated Taheri-Azar, according to his account, that he "decided to become less open about my religious views," even with the friend who had introduced him to the Quran. Taheri-Azar read further, including books about Timothy McVeigh, who was convicted and executed for bombing a government building in Oklahoma City, and the sarin poison-gas attack that killed 12 subway riders in Tokyo in 1995. "After reading these books I decided that I wanted to join an insurgency force in Afghanistan or Iraq as soon as possible." He changed his phone number and shut off almost all contact with his family, who didn't see him again until they visited him in jail.[21]

Taheri-Azar was a volunteer to the cause of revolution. Nobody recruited him. No organization welcomed him. No comrades swore him to a bond of solidarity. Taheri-Azar encountered Islamist terrorism solely through the prism of the global media, but that was enough to convince him to sacrifice his life.[22]

It didn't matter that his knowledge of Islam was limited and extremely confused. Taheri-Azar apparently didn't know the difference between Sunni and Shia Islam, or that al-Qaida and other Sunni militants would consider him non-Muslim because he is Shia. Taheri-Azar called Muhammad Atta of al-Qaida his "role model," but he willed his belongings to the theocratic Shia government of Iran, which al-Qaida and its allies repeatedly deride. He also asked to be transferred to Iranian custody, "since Iran hasn't declared war on an Islamic country"—an odd claim, since Iran fought a bloody war in the 1980s with Iraq, one of the Islamic countries that Taheri-Azar wanted to liberate from U.S. occupation. Taheri-Azar knew no Arabic, and in his handwritten letters from prison he misspelled al-Qaida as "al-Quaeda." The "e" is a legitimate English transliteration of Arabic script, but the "u" is simply wrong—it appears to come from Microsoft Word's auto-correct function, which Taheri-Azar apparently trusted more than any Islamic source. Taheri-Azar drew his Quranic justifications from an English edition translated by Rashad Khalifa, who was assassinated in Arizona in 1990—a murder that Khalifa's followers blame on militants linked with al-Qaida. Taheri-Azar endorsed Khalifa's emphasis on the significance of the number 19 in the Quran, a view that many Islamists consider to be heretical numerology. His prison letters listed his favorite songs and albums; Islamist militants frown upon Western music as frivolous or sinful. In other words, Taheri-Azar knew next to nothing about the Islamist ideology that he was willing to kill and die for.[23]

If terrorists like Taheri-Azar can be recruited through the Internet and books and news media, then why aren't there more attacks? What is stopping people? Chapters 2–4 propose three explanations. One is that much of the support for Islamist radicalism is symbolic, not strategic. Al-Qaida and Bin Ladin may be "sheik" in the way that Che Guevara and Malcolm X are chic—objects of youthful pop culture more than inspirations for revolutionary militancy. Even among militants, al-Qaida faces competition from local Islamist rivals such as the Taliban and Hamas, who object to al-Qaida's global agenda. More broadly, al-Qaida faces competition from liberal Islamic movements, whose combination of democratic politics and cultural conservatism is far more popular among Muslims than the revolutionaries' antidemocratic violence. Anxiety over their unpopularity has divided the revolutionaries: some have responded by converting to liberalism, while others have turned to ever-more-heinous attempts to purify their societies through violence.

Chapter 5 looks at U.S. foreign policy in light of the failure of Islamist terrorists to mobilize Muslims around the world. One aspect of al-Qaida's strategy has been to provoke the United States, and to a lesser extent other Western countries, into committing atrocities that will galvanize support for Islamist revolution. Critics of the U.S.-led "war on terrorism" worry that this strategy is working. But it may be that changes in U.S. policy don't matter much for most Muslims. Distrust of the U.S. government's intentions may run so deep that new policies are discounted and dismissed even before they begin. I propose that a more reasonable yardstick for the success of U.S. policy in Muslim societies is the fate of the liberal Islamic movement in those countries. U.S. actions ought to be judged by the extent to which they assist or undermine those movements.

Finally, chapter 6 examines what to expect from the study of Islamist terrorism. Expertise on the subject is hard to come by, not just because few scholars in the West read Arabic and other languages of Muslim societies, but also because these scholars are under attack by right-wing think tanks for being terrorist-coddling ideologues, whose failure to anticipate the disasters of 9/11 demonstrates their bias and cluelessness. At the same time, government agencies frequently invite Middle East and Islamic studies experts to help them predict and prevent terrorist attacks. These are unreasonable expectations. Both the condemnation by the think tanks and the invitations by the government seem to imply that social scientists can predict the future actions of tiny cells of highly committed radicals. This has never been true. Although some social scientists may brag about their predictive models, revolutionary violence is inherently unpredictable. The best that we can do is try to understand it as it happens, because even the terrorists can't tell us what is going to happen next.

The bad news for Americans is this: Islamist terrorists really are out to get you. They cannot be deterred by prison sentences, "enhanced" interrogations, or the prospect of death. They consider the United States to be their mortal enemy, and they would like to kill as many Americans as possible, in as dramatic a way as possible. The more I look at their websites, watch their videos, and read their manifestos and discussion boards, the more I realize that these are a brutal and inhumane bunch. It is worth taking them seriously.

The good news for Americans is this: there aren't very many Islamist terrorists, and most of them are incompetent. They fight each other as much as they fight anybody else, and they fight their potential state sponsors most of all. They are outlaws on the run in every country in the world, and their bases have been reduced to ever-more-wild patches of remote territory, where they have to limit their training activities to avoid satellite surveillance. Every year or two they pull off a sophisticated attack somewhere in the world, on top of the usual daily crop of violence, but the odds of their getting lucky and repeating an operation on the scale of 9/11 seem like a long shot, since no other attack in the history of Islamist terrorism has killed more than 400 people, and only a dozen attacks have killed more than 200.[24]

Still, the fear of terrorism persists, wildly out of alignment with the rate of terrorist violence. In one recent survey, 15 percent of

Americans said that terrorism was the greatest threat to the United States—a higher percentage than for any other threat. (Six percent considered "the economy" as the greatest threat, and 5 percent listed "Barack Obama.") Politicians in the United States and many countries fan these fears, or cater to them to avoid appearing "soft" on security issues. The U.S. government spends $170 billion a year on the Global War on Terror, compared with less than $25 billion for the fight against HIV/AIDS, which causes 7,000 deaths every day. I am not suggesting that funding should necessarily follow a one-to-one ratio with casualties, but a mismatch of this magnitude seems like an indication of panic.[25]

This panic does not match America's image of itself as the land of can-do pragmatism and "the home of the brave," as our national anthem describes us. Disproportionate fear of terrorism is prolonging a state of emergency that limits civil liberties, skews budget priorities, and projects force excessively around the world. Exaggerated fear of Islamist terrorism has stoked suspicion of Muslims, to the point that some Americans object to the very presence of Muslims and mosques in the United States as a sinister plot to impose Islamic rule—as though this tiny minority might somehow convert or subjugate the 80-plus percent of Americans who are Christian. Panic over terrorism has led some Americans to compromise their belief in the freedom of religion, when it comes to Islam, and to hedge our foundational judicial principle of innocent until proven guilty.

This book aims to reduce the panic by examining evidence about Islamist terrorism—the actual scale of it and the reasons it is not more widespread. The book presents evidence from the terrorists' websites, in Arabic and other languages, and from interviews with young Muslims around the world. It also presents findings from surveys in Muslim communities, election results, and other indicators of public opinion. At the end of the book are detailed notes where you can check my sources and compare them with the sources presented in alarmist writings, most of which are based on fear and ideology more than serious research.

Let me be clear, though. I have no intention of whitewashing the potential for violence of small groups of Islamist revolutionaries. There will be more terrorist attacks, and some of them could be successful in killing hundreds of people, perhaps even thousands. Last year, Faisal Shahzad almost succeeded in an attack of this scale, filling a vehicle with explosives and parking it just off Times Square in New York City. As with the terrorist who drove through campus in Chapel Hill, incompetence saved the day—Shahzad used faulty firecrackers as his detonator. We may not be so lucky in the future. But even if they succeed in killing thousands of us, attacks like these do not threaten our way of life, unless we let them.[26]

As the trauma of 9/11 recedes, Americans will come to realize that—for all its faults and dangers—the world today is the safest it has ever been. Life expectancy has risen in recent generations to the point where people commonly see their grandchildren grow up. There have been fewer wars in the past decade than at any time in modern history. Terrorism kills fewer people now than it did in the 1980s. All this could change overnight, and I am not suggesting that the world turn a blind eye to the threat of terrorism. I am suggesting that we treat this threat on the scale that it deserves.[27]

On September 11, 2001, Mohammad Taheri-Azar and I were both in Chapel Hill, North Carolina, far from the events that made the day historic. Taheri-Azar reports that he was pleased by what he saw on television that day, because America finally reaped what it sowed. I have my own 9/11 story. That morning, my godfather went to work, as usual, in a building across the street from the World Trade Center. As he arrived, he saw smoke on one of the towers, then on the other, and when the south tower started to come down he ran. Clouds of dust from the devastation enveloped him as he fled miles on foot to his home. If 9/11 reminded

Taheri-Azar of the Gulf War and other recent events, it reminded my godfather of an earlier trauma. He was a child in Holland when the Nazis occupied the country and forced his family into trains. He survived years in concentration camps. New York was a refuge for him after the liberation of Europe, and now the refuge itself was under attack. In our conversations since that day, he has wondered whether 9/11 signaled a new era of violence on the scale of the Nazi holocaust. This book is an attempt to understand why that hasn't happened.

CHAPTER 2

✧

Radical Sheik

In the hour before the south tower of the World Trade Center came down, the world tuned in to watch. Television networks all over the globe interrupted their regular programming with live updates from New York and Washington. It was mid-afternoon in the Middle East. Al-Jazeera, the most successful television station in the region, was among the first to broadcast live from New York. Before either tower collapsed, al-Jazeera reported that one of the airplanes had been hijacked. By the end of the day, al-Jazeera reported from Afghanistan that al-Qaida might be responsible.[1]

Yasmin (not her real name) was leaving school in Cairo, Egypt, when she heard the news on the radio. Her initial reaction was satisfaction. "In the first instants, I thought, okay, somebody broke America's ego," Yasmin recalled in an interview at an upscale café with a pan-Asian theme. Yasmin was no fan of Islamist revolution. In fact, she hated al-Qaida, which she considered a bunch of "extremists." The group is "violent, fundamentalist, conservative. I don't agree with their ways, their ideas. I don't sympathize with them at all." She had no desire to see Islamists come to power. She came to her interview wearing a fashionable business suit with her hair loose—a look that Islamist revolutionaries would ban if they ran the government. At the same time, Yasmin had mixed feelings about America that affected her reaction on September 11. "The U.S. is the superpower since the fall of the Soviet Union. It is the indisputable power, the economic power—which is okay, this is no problem." Unfortunately, she felt, Americans had become overbearing. The United States' dominance generated "the idea that we are powerful, we don't care about anything outside of our borders." America suffers from "a high ego," she continued. "If I know a person, even a friend, and he is always arrogant, he should learn a lesson that this is not how things should be all the time." On September 11, despite her Westernized outlook and her hostility toward terrorism, her first response was schadenfreude, a guilty feeling of pleasure in the pain of others. Only as she watched the coverage on television and started to appreciate "the human losses" of the day did she regret her initial response.[2]

Yasmin's gut reaction, the feeling that the United States got its comeuppance on September 11, was not unique. Many others— people who had no sympathy for the goals of Islamist terrorists— reported similar sentiments. "To tell you the truth," wrote one Arab on an Internet chat room on September 16, 2001, "at the beginning when we heard of the attacks we were happy, but when we saw how many people died we stopped being happy." Sadik al-Azm, a prominent Syrian intellectual who is hostile to Islamist movements, has struggled to understand his "shameful response to the slaughter of innocents." His first reaction, he wrote, involved an emotion called *shamateh* in Arabic, which is analogous to schadenfreude. It is not a pleasant emotion, and Islamic scholarship considers it sinful. "Yet it would be very hard these days to find an Arab, no matter how sober, cultured, and sophisticated, in whose heart there was not some room for *shamateh* at the suffering of Americans on September 11. I myself tried hard to contain, control, and hide it that day." Perhaps, he speculated, it was spurred by "bad news from Palestine that week; the satisfaction of seeing the arrogance of power abruptly, if temporarily, humbled; the sight of the jihadi Frankenstein's monsters, so carefully nourished by the United States, turning suddenly on their masters; or the natural resentment of the weak and marginalized at the peripheries of empires against the centre, or, in this case, against the centre of the centre?"[3]

Arabs and Muslims were not the only ones to admit such feelings. A French literary scholar confessed to "a troubling sort of pleasure as she watched the collapse of the twin towers." A group of Greek soccer fans burned an American flag and jeered during a moment of silence for the victims of 9/11. Russian politicians told television audiences, "We're sorry for the Americans, but not for America." British conversations exhibited an "undercurrent of schadenfreude" involving an "instant deflection of rage from the perpetrator to the target": "What do you expect, given American foreign policy? They had it coming to them. We have to have a more complex view of where terrorist rage comes from. Americans will just have to learn why the world hates them so much." Muslim sympathies for the attacks of 9/11 were particularly newsworthy because they seemed to indicate a potential for future attacks. Scattered images of Palestinians and others celebrating on September 11 not only suggested an inhumane response to tragedy but also a pool of supporters and recruits for further terrorism. Gallup polls in seven Muslim-majority countries in late 2001 and early 2002 found that 4 to 36 percent of respondents believed the attacks of 9/11 were justifiable. If this was representative of the world's 1.5 billion Muslims, then more than 100 million Muslims considered the attacks justifiable. That would mean a lot of potential terrorists.[4]

But there are nowhere near 100 million Muslim terrorists. As discussed in the last chapter, fewer than 100,000 Muslims have been involved in Islamist terrorist organizations over the past quarter-century, less than one-15,000th of the world's Muslim population. Sympathy for Islamist terrorism rarely translates into

Islamist terrorist activities. In fact, most of the respondents in the Gallup poll who said that 9/11 was justified were not Islamists at all. Two-thirds of them followed movies, television series, or game shows; they were more likely than other respondents to read art books and novels and to favor "living in harmony with those who do not share your values." These are not characteristics of Islamists. The country expressing the most support for 9/11 in the Gallup samples was Kuwait, the oil-rich city-state whose independence had been restored by the United States military 10 years earlier. In 1991, Operation Desert Storm ended months of Iraqi occupation and handed the country back to its king. It struck some people as strange that a republic like the United States would put a monarchy back on the throne, but the move seemed popular with Kuwaitis at the time. A decade later, more than a third of the country considered the attacks of 9/11 to be justified, if Gallup's respondents were representative. These opinions did not translate into a surge in Kuwaiti terrorism. According to U.S. government-sponsored data, Kuwait has generated very little terrorism.[5]

Similar findings emerged in subsequent surveys by the Pew Global Attitudes Project. Support for terrorism does not appear to be associated with support for revolutionary Islamist ideals. In 2002, the Pew surveys found a huge range of respondents—from 7 to 73 percent in 14 countries with significant Muslim populations—stating that "suicide bombing and other forms of violence against civilian targets" are sometimes or often justified "in order to defend Islam from its enemies." (By way of comparison, 24 percent of Americans considered "bombing and other types of attacks intentionally aimed at civilians" to be sometimes or often justified, according to a 2006 survey. A majority of Americans have consistently believed that bombing civilians in Hiroshima and Nagasaki during World War II was justified, and the U.S. government's Cold War doctrine of mutually assured destruction envisioned massive civilian casualties.) More than half of the Muslim respondents who supported attacks on civilians also said they considered it a good thing that foreign movies, television, and music were becoming more widely available, the same proportion as among respondents who did not approve of violence against civilian targets. These are not Islamist revolutionaries.[6]

The following year, the Pew survey asked people directly what they thought of Usama Bin Ladin. In nine Muslim-majority countries, disturbingly large percentages expressed confidence in Bin Ladin "to do the right thing regarding world affairs." It is possible that some respondents interpreted "the right thing" to mean turning himself in to stand trial, but more likely this question reflects some positive sentiment toward the al-Qaida leader. In many of the countries surveyed, a majority reported confidence in Bin Ladin: 55 percent of Indonesians and Jordanians, 58 percent of Moroccans, 62 percent of Pakistanis, and 77 percent of Palestinians. Yet this support did not translate into ideological affiliation with Bin Ladin. Most of the respondents who had confidence in Bin Ladin also expressed support for Western-style democracy—a departure from revolutionary Islamists' hostility toward democratic procedures.[7]

Why would Muslims who oppose Bin Ladin's ideology say positive things about him and his violent activities?

In 1970, the American author Tom Wolfe coined a phrase to describe nonrevolutionary people who claim to support revolutionary causes: "radical chic." Wolfe applied the term to wealthy white hipsters who threw an expensive party on behalf of the Black Panthers, a militant African-American organization, but the term caught on more widely. By the early 1980s, newspaper headline writers had discovered the pun "radical sheik," playing on the Americanized pronunciation of the Arabic honorific, *shaykh*. In recent years, several conservative journalists have attached this label in the same mocking spirit as Wolfe to liberal non-Muslims who allegedly support Islamist terrorism because it is the latest fad in anti-Americanism.[8]

For Yasmin and many other Muslims, "radical sheik" involves expressions of sympathy for Bin Ladin and his ilk as heroes of anti-imperialism and Islamic authenticity—without actually wanting these revolutionary movements to succeed. This sort of symbolic endorsement does not translate into support for revolutionary goals or potential collaboration with terrorism.

The epitome of radical sheik may be the Bin Ladin T-shirt, which apparently sold well in several Muslim-majority countries for a time after September 11, 2001—despite the fact that an Islamic government as envisioned by Bin Ladin might ban human images as un-Islamic and ban T-shirts as a form of Western cultural imperialism. The Bin Ladin T-shirt is a self-undermining statement, and it is difficult to imagine an actual Islamist terrorist calling attention to himself by wearing one. "Young people are wearing T-shirts with Bin Ladin's picture on them just the way people used to wear pictures of Che Guevara," a student in Saudi Arabia told a *New York Times* reporter in 2004. "It's simply because he is the only one resisting."[9]

The Che analogy is appropriate. For decades, left-leaning American and European youths have taped Che posters to their dorm-room walls without lifting a finger to overthrow capitalism. Che's image is now consumed like any other fashionable commodity by people who care little for his ideology of armed socialist revolution. Even some Islamist terrorists are Che fans: Shamil Basayev, the bloodthirsty Chechen revolutionary, carried a picture of Che in his breast pocket. (Basayev also loved the movie *Braveheart* and wanted to die crying "Freedom!" like Mel Gibson.) Similarly, many devoutly Christian African-Americans embrace the iconography of Malcolm X despite his critique of Christianity as the religion of white slave-owners. The symbol of resistance is detached from content.[10]

Expressions of radical sheik can also be found on Internet discussion forums, where some self-identified Muslims express support for Bin Ladin while distancing themselves from the ideology of Islamist revolution. In September 2002, for example, a participant in an Urdu-language bulletin board defended al-Qaida after a violent incident in Pakistan. "I say destroy all of America!!" she wrote, in a posting that included a logo for a song by the English rock band Coldplay and a thumbnail picture of herself with her hair uncovered. On an Arabic-language website in 2005, a participant whose icon showed a trendy male portrait—clean-shaven, a strand of hair stylishly tousled over his forehead—beseeched God to protect "our shaykh, the warrior Usama Bin Ladin." On a Turkish discussion board, a Muslim who identified himself as a Sufi wrote, "He [Bin Ladin] is a terrorist? If he is a terrorist, then I would like to be a terrorist (!) too, God willing"—notwithstanding al-Qaida's hostility toward Sufi Islam.[11]

This phenomenon predates 9/11. When al-Qaida bombed U.S. embassies in Kenya and Tanzania in 1998 and survived a missile attack by the United States on its base in Afghanistan, Bin Ladin became a symbol of resistance. "Now, anyone who stands up to the U.S. becomes a hero," a Muslim leader in London told a journalist. The carnage of September 11 only reinforced this image for some young Muslims in Britain who "see Osama Bin Laden as a bit of a hero," according to Dawood Gustave, a Muslim youth worker interviewed by the BBC in 2005. "It's not because terrorism is an Islamic thing, or that they want to see it happen. It's about defiance. Tupac [Shakur, the late hip-hop star] is not enough anymore—it's about doing this to the powerful—giving the finger to the West and authority." Aki Nawaz, a British Muslim rapper and activist, helped cross-fertilize the worlds of pop music and Islamist revolution with a 2006 album that included syncopated samples from Bin Ladin (in Arabic) and Che (in Spanish) over funky world beats. "What makes one a symbol of resistance and the other a terrorist?" Nawaz wrote in a manifesto that accompanied the album. "It is nothing new in history for empires to be challenged and destroyed." Nawaz was not trying to encourage terrorism, he explained, but rather to encourage listeners to examine their ideological assumptions and prejudices. To my knowledge, none of Nawaz's fans has ever been detained for terrorist activities. Taheri-Azar, the Tarheel terrorist, listened to German dance music as he committed his attack, but in general, Islamist terrorists are more likely to listen to martial music or lyrical *nasheeds*—traditional Arabic songs—that al-Qaida and other organizations have updated with themes of martyrdom and struggle. Islamist revolutionary music can be quite upbeat, but it is a far cry from funky.[12]

Some scholars and government officials speak of the "cool factor" that certain young Muslims associate with Islamist terrorism. Indonesian students considered Bin Ladin "pretty cool in some ways," according to an Australian who spent the fall 2001 semester studying in Yogyakarta. A British Muslim airport worker explained to a court in London that she posted poems online under the name "Lyrical Terrorist" "because it sounded cool." According to Harvard terrorism specialist Jessica Stern, "Jihad has become a global fad, rather like gangsta rap. It is a fad that feeds on images of dead children. Most of the youth attracted to the jihadi idea would never become terrorists, just as few of the youths who listen to gangsta rap would commit the kinds of lurid crimes the lyrics would seem to promote. But among many Muslim youths, especially in Europe, jihad is a cool way of expressing dissatisfaction with a power elite whether that elite is real or imagined; whether power is held by totalitarian monarchs or by liberal parliamentarians."[13]

Radical sheik disassociates terrorist symbols from terrorist activities, just as the global popularity of gangster rap removed the music from its origins in African-American gangs. Tamer Nafar, a Palestinian rapper in Lod, Israel, came to love gangster rap as a teenager in the 1990s through the albums of Tupac Shakur, the African-American rapper and actor who was murdered in 1996. "We [Palestinians] are the black people of, yani, the Middle East," Nafar told an interviewer. "Yani" is a pause word in Arabic, comparable to young people's use of the word "like" in English. "Tupac, when he said, 'It's a white man's world,' spoke to me, because I live as an Arab in a Jewish world." Nafar hung a poster of Tupac over his bed, next to a poster of Che, and launched his own group, Da Arabian MC's. DAM (the acronym means "blood" in Arabic) became the biggest Palestinian rap act in Israel. (There are several.) "Who's the terrorist?" Nafar demanded in his most famous song, rapping in Arabic with an African-American cadence. "I'm the terrorist?! How am I the terrorist when you've taken my land?... You're a democracy? Actually it's more like the Nazis! Your countless raping of the Arabs' soul finally impregnated it, gave birth to your child. His name: Suicide Bomber. And then you call him the terrorist?" These lyrics were calculated to enrage Jewish Israelis, whom Nafar identified with Nazis, terrorists, rapists, mass murderers, and thieves. Nafar blamed Palestinian suicide bombers on Israel and at the same time denied that these murders were terrorism. But for all his anger and gangster-rap style, Nafar has never engaged in violence. Instead, he has played for free at peace rallies.[14]

Some Islamist terrorists are pleased to see signs of radical sheik. In Yemen, former al-Qaida member Abu Jandal told a reporter proudly about young Arabs who "admire Usama Bin Ladin ... [and] love al-Qaida, but they do not carry its ideology." In Britain, al-Muhajiroun, a group that celebrated the hijackers of September 11 as "The Magnificent 19" also hailed the potential radicalism of Muslims "who do not agree with what took place on 9/11" but who "do not deny the sacrifices made by Sheikh Usama Bin Laden and the Mujahideen and their unflinching heroism against the terrorism and atrocities of the US and UK in Afghanistan and Iraq."

In this view, "jihobbyists"—a term coined by counterterrorism expert Jarret Brachman—might one day develop into revolutionaries.[15]

Other terrorists resent Muslims who claim to support Islamist revolution but never actually participate in it. A young British Muslim of Pakistani origin berated such poseurs as *munafiqun* (hypocrites). "They say and say that they are Muslims but they just play at it." A book on the subject of identifying hypocrites noted scornfully, "The hypocrites do not participate in jihad, and they also prevent others from doing so." Ayman Zawahiri of al-Qaida condemned his former Egyptian comrades in arms who now live in comfortable exile in Europe, "hot-blooded revolutionary strugglers who have now become as cold as ice after they experienced the life of civilization and luxury." "How can you dare say that you love the religion of Allah and you know well that the enemy has desecrated the book of Allah and you do nothing? When you know that they have flushed the Quran down a toilet and you don't pick up your weapon and fight for the sake of Allah?" wrote Anwar al-Awlaki, a Yemeni-American revolutionary whose online videos inspired several American Muslim terrorists. "Do you need a bomb to drop on your house to give you a reason to get up and fight? It will be too late by then."[16]

The difficulty facing Islamist terrorists, like all revolutionaries, is how to convert radical sheik into actual recruits. No doubt there are examples of young Muslims being drawn into violence through the appeal of revolutionary "cool," though I haven't found anybody admitting to that yet. Revolutionaries tend to explain their actions through commitment to their faith, not popular culture. Far more commonly, radical sheik leads to fashionable youth culture, not terrorist training camps. French scholar Amel Boubekeur has identified this phenomenon as a "post-Islamist" spectacle. Young Muslims attend religious lectures and Islamic pop concerts, "waving their arms in the air, lighting lighters, asking for autographs, and crying out 'takbir'—that is, Allahu Akbar (God is great)—to encourage the performers on the stage." These youths are searching for "the ambience of a 'cool' Islam, freed from the stigma of the 'old' Islamist rhetorics," according to Boubekeur. They are not interested in an Islamic state, much less in revolutionary violence. A former militant in France complained to Boubekeur that at Islamic lectures, "everyone is well-dressed, is there to be seen," not to be devout.[17]

Even more problematic for the terrorists is that they seem to lose by winning. Part of their strategy has been to engage in dramatic acts of violence in order to polarize society and force Muslims to choose sides. An influential statement of Islamist terrorist strategy recommended continual escalation of tension that will "drag the masses into battle": "We must make this battle very violent, such that death is a heartbeat away, so that the two groups will realize that entering this battle will frequently lead to death. That will be a powerful motive for the individual to choose to fight in the ranks of the people of truth in order to die well, which is better than dying for falsehood and losing both this world and the next." This strategy has backfired. The more that terrorists target Muslims, the less popular the terrorists become. In Jordan, for example, suicide bombers attacked a wedding reception in November 2005, killing more than 50 people, including the fathers of the bride and groom. The following spring, a Pew survey found the proportion of its Jordanian sample saying that violence against civilians is never justified had jumped to 43 percent, from 11 percent the previous year. The portion of Jordanians who considered al-Qaida a legitimate resistance organization dropped from 67 to 20 percent, according to the Center for Strategic Studies in Amman. In Morocco, the proportion expressing confidence in Bin Ladin dropped from 50 to 26 percent after the Casablanca bombings of May 2003. Similarly in Pakistan, where attacks increased 10-fold between 2005 and 2008, the proportion opposing violence against civilians doubled from 35 percent in 2004 to 69 percent in 2006, and then rose again to 75 percent by 2008. In Britain, Muslims' admiration for "organisations like Al-Qaeda that are prepared to fight against the West" went down to 7 percent after the London bombings of July 2005 (3 percent of non-Muslim Britons expressed the same admiration), as compared with 40 percent of British Muslims who said in fall 2001 that Bin Ladin was justified "to mount his war against the United States." In Iraq, where tit-for-tat communal violence after the U.S.-led invasion of 2003 escalated into civil war, large majorities of all major groups (Kurds, Sunni Arabs, and Shia Arabs) continued to support democratic government, and declining segments of each group desired an Islamic state, according to surveys conducted by sociologist Mansoor Moaddel and colleagues. Instead of converting radical sheik into committed militancy, terrorist violence appears to turn shallow support into open hostility.[18]

Zuhra (not her real name) was at home in the Punjab region of Pakistan on 9/11. An aunt living in the United States called to say that she was all right. She heard nothing about al-Qaida involvement at that time, and her first thoughts were sympathy for the casualties and amazement that such violence could occur in the United States, which she associated with security and order. In her hometown, by contrast, there had been considerable communal violence, with some of the worst offenders allied with Islamist terrorists. Among the earliest groups to affiliate with al-Qaida in the 1990s were Pakistani militants who targeted Shia Muslim Pakistanis more often than Indians or Westerners, killing hundreds through assassination of community leaders and bomb attacks on religious ceremonies. (Shia militants killed many Sunnis as well.)[19]

Zuhra's home region was the site of considerable sectarian violence. Though herself Sunni, she viewed al-Qaida and its allies as an abomination. These people are "extremists" who "say that murder is jihad," she said contemptuously. She had no sympathy for Islamic government of the Taliban sort. "I don't think that our religion permits us to enforce such sharia law as imposed by the Taliban," she told my research assistant Ijlal Naqvi. It was not that Zuhra was indifferent to Islam. She wore a tight headscarf and a lightweight, loose overcoat, her usual modest garb, which she considered a religious duty. A woman should wear "proper dress," she explained. "She can wear pants, but not so tight that her organs are prominent, and not a tight shirt." Women's hair should be covered, she said, because it is a private part of the body, not for public display. This interview was conducted at a university in Pakistan where headscarves are common—on university campuses in Turkey, by contrast, Zuhra's outfit would be illegal, because headscarves are banned at schools and government offices. "There should be Islamic rule, because we are Muslims," Zuhra said. "But not like al-Qaida's rule." Islam is a religion of moderation, in her view, and leaders should be selected democratically. If the voters are devout, then they will select representatives who will govern in accordance with their beliefs. That is the sort of Islamic state Zuhra envisions.

At the same time, Zuhra acknowledged that Bin Ladin appears to be larger than life. "I'm not saying that he's supernatural, but his character is somewhat supernatural. A human being can't be like this." Many Muslims have expressed such views since 9/11—the idea that Bin Ladin could not have engineered an attack on the world's greatest superpower from one of the world's least developed countries without some sort of *baraka*, or divine blessing. One story posted on Arabic-language Internet bulletin boards attributed Bin Ladin's effectiveness to a vision he had when he was nine years old. In this dream, an angel supposedly told Bin Ladin that he would play a major role in a titanic clash with the West. Islamist revolutionaries responded to the story by posting warm notes of appreciation. But the story also touched the hearts of some non-Islamists as well. We know this because some of the most favorable responses to the story were posted by people whose online icons included images that Islamists would never choose. One enthusiastic response, for example, featured pictures of a woman with flowing black hair and a male model with blond highlights. Another positive response showed a woman with long hair, pouty lips, trendy sunglasses, and an off-the-shoulder blouse. Another included a photo of a bare female leg with an anklet bracelet and polka-dot shoes. "Hallelujah," wrote someone whose signature icon was a blond female with a bare midriff. "Niiice information," wrote someone whose signature icon was a photo of several unscarved women at a party. This is radical sheik in action—people who are impressed by Bin Ladin but do not share the conservative Islamic mores that Bin Ladin and other Islamists hope to enforce.[20]

Unlike Yasmin, whose secular worldview was so strong that she opposed democratization for fear that her fellow Egyptians would elect an Islamic regime, Zuhra and these dream posters adopt Islamic frames of reference, such as the long heritage of premonition through dreams. According to an eyewitness account, the Prophet Muhammad is supposed to have foretold such visions: "When I am done, there shall remain naught of the glad tidings of prophecy, except for true dreams." Many Islamist terrorists believe that they have experienced such dreams. In a videotaped conversation with Saudi visitors in the fall of 2001, Bin Ladin himself apparently said that dreams about airplane attacks on America were so common at al-Qaida camps that "I was worried that maybe the secret would be revealed if everyone starts seeing it in their dream." Anthropologist Iain Edgar has collected media reports of dream premonitions by Islamist terrorists, including Richard Reid, the "shoe bomber" who tried to ignite his explosives-filled sneakers on a trans-Atlantic flight in late 2001. In an e-mail to his sister, Reid said he dreamt that a pickup truck passed him by instead of giving him a ride. "I now believe that the pickup that came first was 9/11 as it's true that I was upset at not being sent." A few apocalyptic texts have suggested that contemporary events signal the imminent coming of the messiah, or even that the leaders of the Taliban or al-Qaida might themselves qualify as the messiah (though Bin Ladin did not encourage this belief, which might strike many Muslims as blasphemous).[21]

Devout Muslims who share the terrorists' appreciation for dream prophecy do not necessarily share their violent strategy. A case in point is one of the world's largest Islamic movements, the Tablighi Jamaat, which was established in India in the 1920s and is currently headquartered in Pakistan. The founder of this movement, Muhammad Ilyas, told his pupils that he was invited to form the Tablighi movement through a dream, and more recent followers also cite dreams as premonitions of their commitment to the cause. The Tablighi Jamaat insists on a rigorous interpretation of Islam that involves precise obedience to rituals of devotion, everyday behavior, and even garb. Tablighi men avoid Western-style clothes and wear beards at least "one fistful" long. Tablighi women are encouraged not to work outside of the home, if possible, and to wear full *hijab*, including the *niqab* over their faces. If this sounds like al-Qaida or the Taliban, the parallel ends there. Tablighi leaders rarely get involved in politics, much less revolutionary politics. This position is both principled and strategic, as historian Yoginder Sikand has noted in his study of the group. The principle lies in the preference for other-worldly goals over this-worldly activities such as influencing policy or conquering the state. The strategy lies in the innocuous, legal cultivation of pious Muslims who might, some day in the future, be proper members of a fully Islamic polity. Ilyas himself, while rejecting present-day mobilization, told his more radical critics that he was "preparing soldiers for your *junud* [armies]. I am training these people in such a way that they will serve your and our interests alike." Sikand quotes a more recent Tablighi activist as writing that the movement "is preparing the minds of thousands of its participants" to give not only "time and money but also their lives in the cause of Islam," should circumstances warrant it. At that time, Tablighi members will emulate Imam Husayn, "who drank the nectar of martyrdom in the field of Karbala"—a Shia reference that will hardly endear the movement to Sunni Islamists. In any case, the Tablighi Jamaat has consistently argued that conditions do not warrant militancy of any sort, and they have earned the ire of Islamist revolutionaries for insisting that the path to an Islamic society is based on personal transformation rather than political change. The result, a revolutionary magazine recently charged, is a huge waste of energy spent training millions of Muslims to be "weak."[22]

The Tablighi Jamaat's annual meetings are some of the world's largest congregations of Muslims—more than a million followers gather each year in Pakistan and Bangladesh—and a number of terrorists have used these meetings as cover for their own recruitment and coordination. Members of the Harakat al-Ansar, a militant Pakistani group that has since been banned, used to attend Tablighi meetings regularly, according to one of the group's leaders. Muhammad Haydar Zammar, a Syrian-born German who allegedly recruited some of the 9/11 hijackers to al-Qaida, joined the Tablighi movement, according to his brother, and news reports indicate that a variety of convicted terrorists studied with Tablighi Jamaat before moving on to militant training camps. These linkages have led some observers to call the movement a security threat. If it is a front or a gateway to terrorism, however, it is a remarkably inefficient one—the number of Tablighi members who have engaged in violent activities is a tiny proportion of the group's millions of dedicated members.[23]

Alternatively, the Tablighi Jamaat may be seen as part of the crowded ideological field that terrorists face as they compete for

Muslims' support. On one side are secularists who do not want the government to implement Islamic law. These number a fifth to a half of the population in various Muslim-majority countries polled by the World Values Survey. On another side are liberal Muslims, many of whom believe that Islamic government is important, but that such a government, as they understand it, would follow democratic procedures. This current encompasses about half of the population, even in Saudi Arabia, where the majority in a recent survey sample agreed that democracy is the best form of government. Liberal Islamic currents are sometimes dismissed as tiny minorities with little popular support, but survey evidence suggests the opposite: that there is a large unmet demand for democracy in Muslim societies that is blocking the spread of revolutionary ideologies. (Chapter 4 discusses this further.)

Some of these liberal Muslims go so far as to deny that the terrorists can even be called Muslims. For example, Maher Hathout, a prominent Muslim-American activist in California, acknowledged that the hijackers of 9/11 considered themselves Muslim, but said their violent actions run contrary to "every fiber in Islam." By virtue of having committed such acts, he concluded, the hijackers could not possibly be Muslims. In effect, this denunciation is a sort of liberal *takfir*—a nonviolent inversion of the terrorists' practice of declaring their ideological opponents to be apostates (and hence eligible for murder). Islamist terrorists have pronounced *takfir* on millions of people—a splinter group in Algeria declared the entire Algerian population to be *kuffar* (non-Muslims) in the 1990s—and have murdered thousands of them. In a handful of high-profile but less violent cases in Egypt and several other countries, nonrevolutionary Islamists have used the practice of *takfir* to have their opponents' marriages annulled, taking advantage of sharia family laws introduced by secular leaders seeking to bolster their religious credentials. The liberals' version of *takfir* has no military or judicial goals. It is intended only to express the view that revolutionary violence is anathema to their understanding of Islam, though it adopts the same language as the perpetrators of revolutionary violence—in effect, attempting to excommunicate Muslims who disagree with them.[24]

The Tablighi Jamaat and other pietist movements comprise a further set of ideological competitors that reject political mobilization in favor of a hearts-and-minds strategy, arguing that it is improper to implement Islamic law before people are ready to accept it willingly. Another example from the pietist movement is the network of groups labeled "Wahhabi" by their opponents and supported by the Saudi kingdom in Arabia. These groups share the goal of a universal Islamic state, but their methods are generally evangelical, not violent. Whatever one's opinion of the highly conservative mosques and student groups subsidized by the Saudis, very few of them engage in politics, much less political violence—at least in the West (in Pakistan and other places, some Saudi-sponsored groups engage in sectarian violence against Shia Muslims). Terrorists routinely denounce pietists for their apolitical stance. Bin Ladin was especially harsh toward the Saudi dynasty, which he hoped to overthrow (in which case the country would no longer be called Saudi Arabia). The Saudi regime "has desecrated its legitimacy through many of its own actions," including its "bloody confrontation" with politically active Islamists, Bin Ladin wrote in his declaration of jihad in 1996. He continued on this theme for the next 15 years.[25]

Terrorists are also isolated among political Islamists—that is, movements seeking to establish an Islamic state. Most of these movements have decided, for a combination of pragmatic and ideological reasons, to seek power through peaceful means. The largest network of political Islamists is the group of organizations that grew out of the Muslim Brotherhood of Egypt. Most of these organizations abandoned revolutionary violence a generation ago and now run candidates in parliamentary elections, with party platforms that pledge allegiance to democracy and limit jihad to peaceful definitions (aside from destroying Israel). Political scientist Carrie Rosefsky Wickham has called this process "auto-reform"—the realization that Islamist policies are more likely to be implemented through a commitment to participatory politics and responsive governance than through violent upheaval. These groups now meet in an informal international federation called the Muslim Communities Union, which is modeled on the Socialist International, the Liberal International, and other global political groupings. At periodic conferences of the Union, branches of the Muslim Brotherhood come together with the Jamaat-e-Islami parties of Pakistan and Bangladesh, the Islamic parties of Iraq and Malaysia, the Society for Peace in Algeria, and the Justice and Development Party of Morocco. The Justice and Development Party of Turkey might have joined, too, but it was preempted by its marginal conservative rival, the Felicity Party, which has hosted several of the Union's conferences. Islamist terrorists are aghast at these developments. "Fie on moderation, politics, the presidency and the cabinet," Zawahiri told an interviewer in 2007. "I thank God for the bounty of extremism, militancy, and terrorism and everything else we are labeled with."[26]

Almost all of al-Qaida's Islamist competitors denounced the attacks of 9/11, publicly and in no uncertain terms. The shaykh of al-Azhar University in Cairo, the oldest and most respected Islamic seminary in the world, said the terrorists "will be punished on the day of judgement." Yusuf al-Qaradawi, the Qatar-based religious scholar and satellite television personality, signed a statement encouraging Muslims to bring the perpetrators to justice: "All Muslims ought to be united against all those who terrorize the innocents, and those who permit the killing of non-combatants without a justifiable reason. Islam has declared the spilling of blood and the destruction of property as absolute prohibitions until the Day of Judgment." The heads of Hamas, the Muslim

Brotherhood in Egypt, the Jamaat-e-Islami in Pakistan, and more than 40 other Islamists movements issued a pronouncement on September 14:

> The undersigned, leaders of Islamic movements, are horrified by the events of Tuesday 11 September 2001 in the United States which resulted in massive killing, destruction and attack on innocent lives. We express our deepest sympathies and sorrow. We condemn, in the strongest terms, the incidents, which are against all human and Islamic norms. This is grounded in the Noble Laws of Islam which forbid all forms of attacks on innocents. God Almighty says in the Holy Quran: "No bearer of burdens can bear the burden of another"
>
> (Surah al-Isra 17:15).

Some of the Islamists who denounced the attacks of 9/11 have encouraged the murder of civilians in Israel. They consider Israeli civilians, even children, to be integral to the government's military activities and therefore legitimate targets and not "innocent" in the same way as American civilians. Al-Qaida leaders pounced on this distinction to condemn their Muslim critics: "[Y]ou will truly be surprised by those who rule that the martyrdom operations in Palestine in which civilians fall victim are among the highest forms of jihad, and then rule that the martyrdom operations in America are wrong because of civilian deaths. This inconsistency is very strange! How can one permit the killing of the branch and not permit the killing of the supporting trunk?" Al-Qaida's consistency, targeting anyone who stands in the way of Islamist revolution, is much less popular than the inconsistency of mainstream Islamist leaders, who continue to excuse civilian targets in Israel—as well American military personnel in Afghanistan and Iraq—but draw the line at civilian targets in the United States or in Europe.[27]

Zuhra, the university student in Pakistan, represents the huge bloc of pious Muslims who abhor terrorism. "Why are you asking all these things?" Zuhra objected at the end of her interview. "Why especially the topic of the U.S. and al-Qaida, these sort of issues are selected by you people to take the views of Muslims? There are a lot of other matters" that are far more important, such as discrimination against Muslims, poverty, and other social issues. She hated terrorism as much as anybody in the West would, and she also resented having to explain her opposition to a Western audience that, in her view, too often equated Muslims with terrorism.

On a ferry crossing from Asia to Europe, Murat (not his real name) and three of his friends, university students with part-time jobs, dressed in cheap but trendy jeans and jackets, kidded each other about Turkish soccer clubs and an ostentatious watch that one of them had recently bought. I introduced myself as a sociological researcher studying young Muslims' views of Bin Ladin and other terrorists. "He doesn't exist," Murat said immediately. "How could a person in a cave in Afghanistan have planned such an attack as 9/11? He is an American creation, a mask that America uses as an excuse to invade Afghanistan and Iraq." If Bin Ladin exists, he is "probably sitting in a garden in America sipping scotch this very minute." What about his anti-imperialist rhetoric? "It is all a show," said a second youth. "We hate America and we hate Bin Ladin. They are the same." Do any of your friends consider Bin Ladin cool, like Che Guevara? "No," said a third youth, who had been quiet throughout the conversation. "This is not our version of Islam here in Turkey." But there have been violent incidents in Turkey, too, by groups claiming affiliation with al-Qaida, no? "Yes, they bombed a British embassy building and a British bank, plus some other things, but they must be American-controlled too. Turks wouldn't do that on their own. Americans support the PKK"—a Kurdish Communist terrorist group—"and they support the Turkish military to go after the PKK. Americans play off both sides against each other." The fourth youth in the group said nothing. He appeared to be recording the conversation on his cell phone while pretending to listen to something on it. He looked at me suspiciously, as though I were a CIA agent plotting the next secret American operation. Two months later, armed assailants opened fire at the American consulate in Istanbul. I wonder if he considered the United States responsible for that too.[28]

Conspiracy theories such as these are common in Muslim communities. During my dissertation research on the Iranian Revolution of 1979, I interviewed numerous Iranians who were certain that U.S. president Jimmy Carter had replaced the monarchy with the Islamic Republic, notwithstanding the disaster that this transition posed for Carter's political career, notwithstanding Carter's efforts to maintain the shah in power, and notwithstanding the massive general strike by Iranians who had actually overthrown the shah. All of that was seen as inconsequential. Reality always occurs "behind the curtain," according to a popular Persian phrase. In part, this sensibility comes from the experience of conspiracies. The French and the British actually made a pact to divide up the Middle East after World War I. The United States actually plotted to overthrow the elected government of Iran after World War II. Israel actually built a nuclear arsenal and arrested the scientist who leaked the news. And Muslim societies, too, are full of plots—alliances manipulated and betrayed, oppositionists co-opted or secretly sponsored. But conspiracies exist everywhere. Muslims are no more likely to be suspicious of appearances than anybody else. Americans, myself included, may be possible exceptions to this generalization—many of us pride ourselves on taking things as they appear rather than speculating about fantastical hidden realities, though this worldview may be retreating under the weight of Watergate, *The Matrix*, Internet scams, and conspiracies like 9/11. I, for one, still want to see evidence before I will give credence to a conspiracy theory, but perhaps I'm just naive. Perhaps conspiracies specialize in destroying evidence of the sort that I would consider conclusive. Perhaps things really aren't what they seem.[29]

Many Muslims share Murat's belief in a hidden hand manipulating the specter of global terrorism. Surveys in a dozen Muslim-majority countries and four Muslim minority communities found only two places—Azerbaijan and Nigeria—where a majority of respondents believed that Arabs had carried out the attacks of 9/11. A popular alternative scenario holds that Israel was behind the attacks—43 percent of a recent sample in Egypt and 31 percent in Jordan agreed with this theory, which emerged immediately after September 11 and got significant play in Arab newspapers. American conspiracy theories, by contrast, tend to focus on the United States, not Israel. In a 2006 survey, 36 percent of Americans, including a majority of young adults, said that it was likely that "people in the federal government either assisted in the 9/11 attacks or took no action to stop the attacks because they wanted the United States to go to war in the Middle East." A year later, 62 percent of an American sample felt it was likely that "some people in the federal government had specific warnings of the 9/11 attacks in New York and Washington, but chose to ignore those warnings."[30]

The various conspiracy theories have started to annoy al-Qaida. "How do you refute conspiracy theorists who claim that 9/11 was an act carried out by elements within the Israeli government?" somebody asked Bin Ladin's second-in-command, Ayman Zawahiri, in an online question-and-answer session that al-Qaida sponsored in early 2008. Zawahiri was not interested in absolution. "These suspicions are baseless," he responded. "The Lebanese Hizbullah's television station, al-Manar, was apparently the first to broadcast these suspicions from the Internet with the clear aim of spreading this lie that Sunnis were not the heroes who struck America as America had never been struck before. Then the Iranian media adopted this lie and repeat it to this day, for the same purpose, perhaps inspired by al-Manar television. Iran's purpose is clear: to cover up its collaboration with America in the invasion of Muslim lands in Afghanistan and Iraq." Hizbullah and the Iranian government are Shia institutions, and al-Qaida is hostile to Shiism, which it does not consider a legitimate branch of Islam. In addition, Hizbullah's leader Hasan Nasrullah has become the most popular figure in the Arab world over the past several years, thanks in large part to his attacks on Israel. According to surveys in six Arab countries in early 2008, reported just a few days before Zawahiri's Q & A, Nasrullah's popularity had more than doubled that of Bin Ladin. Al-Qaida may view him as a rival.[31]

Anti-imperialist, anti-terrorist attitudes comprise a significant portion of Muslim respondents in various surveys. They may share the terrorists' opposition to Western influence, but that commonality draws them away from terrorism, not toward it. Political scientist Shibley Telhami has conducted annual polls on this subject in six Arab countries since 2005. "When you think of Al-Qaeda, what aspect of the organization, if any, do you sympathize with most?" his surveys ask. A quarter to a third of respondents consistently answer that it "confronts the U.S.," as compared with less than 10 percent who sympathize with its efforts to create an Islamic state. Another survey in Egypt, Indonesia, Morocco, and Pakistan found that a quarter of respondents "oppose al Qaeda's attacks on Americans but share many of its attitudes toward the U.S." Similar numbers said they opposed the attacks and did not share its attitudes toward the United States; fewer respondents said they supported the attacks.[32]

For Murat and his friends on the ferry in Istanbul, and for many Muslims, al-Qaida is not a powerful organization on the verge of precipitating a mass movement, but rather a pathetic charade. As Middle East expert Gary Sick suggests, refusing to accept Muslim participation in 9/11 may be "a healthy form of denial," a way of distancing themselves from acts that they consider so heinous that they do not believe that their co-religionists could have been responsible. "That may be small consolation for observers outside the Muslim community, who found such stories absurd to the point of obscenity from the very beginning, but it does at least acknowledge the discomfort of virtually all Muslims with the events of 9/11." According to the Pew Global Attitude Project's survey of 2006, Muslims in 10 countries who doubted that Arabs were responsible for 9/11 were more likely to condemn suicide attacks on civilians in defense of Islam than respondents who didn't express doubts.[33]

Conspiracy theories are possible in part because so few Muslims have ever met a terrorist. Islamist terrorists are so rare—fewer than 1 in 10,000 Muslims—that if every single one of them bragged to a thousand acquaintances about their militancy, they would reach fewer than 10 percent of all Muslims. Of course, few terrorists are so reckless as to tell a thousand people. The one terrorist I've met was extremely cagey, even though he lived in comfortable retirement with little chance of extradition and imprisonment. His name was Dawud Salahuddin, an African-American convert to Islam, and he had assassinated an Iranian opposition figure in Maryland in 1980. I met him—at least I think it was him—for breakfast in Tehran in 1999. I was in Iran for an academic conference, and I happened to check in to a small hotel where Salahuddin was staying. The desk staff was shocked to have *two* Americans there at the same time, since American visitors are so rare in Iran, and insisted that we meet for breakfast. The staff told me that the other American at the hotel spoke little Persian and that his main social interaction was haranguing the staff for new American movies on the hotel video system. At breakfast, I asked the man what had brought him to Iran, and he said he had come to study ancient herbal remedies. I didn't believe him. It seemed to me anybody who cared so much about Iranian medical traditions would have managed to learn the local language. But I didn't have any other explanation for his presence in Iran—I did not remember news of the assassination, Salahuddin's escape from the United States to Iran, and his trial and conviction in absentia, though I later realized that I was living only a few miles from the murder site at the time. I listened to Salahuddin rant for half an hour about the failings of Western medicine and then excused myself from the table as politely as I could. Two years later, I saw him again—in the movies. Salahuddin appeared in a major Iranian film, *Qandahar*, playing the role of an African-American expatriate. Suddenly my strange breakfast in Tehran seemed even stranger. Salahuddin later gave interviews to the Western press in which he admitted to the assassination and distinguished it from the indiscriminate violence of al-Qaida. "The religion allows you to kill people, but it's very strict about whom you can kill," he told American journalist Ira Silverman. "From a religious point of view Muslims are forbidden to kill civilians and noncombatants. It is something that I have always been very careful about."[34]

Al-Qaida and other Islamist terrorists are even more secretive than Salahuddin. One of the qualifications for membership, according to a document captured and translated by the British police, is "keeping secrets and concealing information." This is necessary "even with the closest people, for deceiving the enemies is not easy." The document encourages recruits to follow the example of the Prophet Muhammad, who "used to keep work secrets from the closest people, even from his wife Aisha." Sayf al-Adl, one of al-Qaida's military commanders, urged terrorists not to divulge anything even to comrades outside of their compartmentalized cells. "Whoever believes in God and the Final Day [the day of divine judgment] should speak well or keep silent," al-Adl wrote, quoting a saying of the Prophet Muhammad. "Commitment to this guidance from the Prophet makes a Muslim eager not to leak information to people outside of his sphere of authority."[35]

The reason for this secrecy is simple—Islamist terrorists are on the lam almost everywhere in the world. Contrary to the impressions of some Westerners, no Islamic state openly supports Islamist terrorism, though factions within some of these governments may clandestinely support terrorism. The government of Saudi Arabia, for example, tried for years to get the Taliban to turn Bin Ladin over for prosecution. Since the terrorist attacks in Riyadh in 1995, and especially since the Riyadh bombings in 2003, the Saudi government has actively suppressed terrorist groups, arresting 3,000 alleged "extremist sympathizers" plus several hundred militants, including all but one of its 26 "most wanted" suspects. The sympathizers have been encouraged to participate in prison counseling programs led by pro-regime religious scholars who teach nonrevolutionary Islamic tenets.[36]

Would-be terrorists run a real risk of being arrested and—in many places—tortured, except in scattered, remote regions where states have limited control, such as parts of northwestern Pakistan. These regions are not simple to reach, and the routes and way stations are under heavy surveillance by local and global security services, as well as spy satellites. The Internet is the only safe haven, and even there terrorists must constantly seek new methods to avoid detection. The terrorist version of Wikipedia, *The Encyclopedia of Preparation,* is constantly being moved from one file-sharing website to another as its hosts are shut down or infiltrated by government agents. It took me weeks of clicking around radical Islamist chat rooms and bulletin boards before I found a live Web address for an index to the encyclopedia, which linked me to a series of files on Yahoo's "briefcase" webspace, where I got an error message saying that I didn't have access to these files. It seems reasonable to assume that Yahoo is under U.S. government orders to monitor the users who do have access to these files. Terrorists seem to assume the same thing. "I want to go to jihad against the Zionists and the Crusaders, but how?" somebody wrote on a militant discussion board called al-Firdaws (Paradise) in 2006. About 1 percent of the postings on the site were along similar lines. Don't ask such questions, others responded, this space is not safe. The discussion thread was closed by administrators the next day. Terrorists still manage to upload tracts and videos to the Web, logging in from Internet cafés using anonymous accounts, but they do not feel immune.[37]

As a result, it is hard for most potential terrorists to find a real comrade in arms. The record for the longest trek to find fellow Islamist terrorists may belong to a group of four Muslims from Portland, Oregon, who decided in October 2001 to go help the Taliban defend against the U.S.-led invasion of Afghanistan. They took a roundabout route to the region, flying to Hong Kong and then traveling all the way across China to Kashgar, where they were unable to cross the border to Pakistan. They then returned to Beijing to get Pakistani visas. That failed, too. Running out of money, all but one member of the group gave up and headed back to Oregon, where they were arrested and convicted for conspiracy to levy war against the United States. The final member of the group, Habis Abdulla al-Saoub, stayed on and finally managed to join up with a terrorist group in Pakistan, where he was killed in 2003 during a shoot-out with the military.[38]

Occasionally, though, Muslims don't have to go looking for terrorists, since the terrorists come looking for them. In stateless territories where government presence is limited, militants visit neighborhoods and impose a kind of protection racket—you let us hide out here, and we won't kill you. These were the rough arrangements made in al-Anbar province in Iraq, the southern and eastern regions of Afghanistan, Pashtun villages in northwestern Pakistan, and distant Muslim-majority provinces in southern Thailand and the southern Philippines—places where the government was in no position to protect the locals in any meaningful way, aside from periodic and short-lived invasions that frequently killed more noncombatants than terrorists. Locals are caught in the middle. Islamist terrorists in the predominantly Muslim Pattani region of Thailand, for example, attacked two teenagers on their way home from school in January 2004, apparently with the intention of intimidating one of the boys' fathers, who was chief of a nearby village. The boys escaped on a motorbike, one with a machete still stuck in his back. The chief told investigators from Human Rights Watch that he knew who attacked his son but couldn't do anything about it. "After the attack, my villagers look down on me. They said I could not protect my own son, then how could I be able to protect them? Some of them even said that it might be practical to give support to the militants to ensure their safety. Soldiers and police patrols come and go. But, they will not be here when the militants attack. That is the survival logic among villagers here."[39]

In between these extremes—the terrorists next door or halfway around the world—are Muslim communities where terrorist wannabes might know somebody who *might* be able to put them in touch with a recruiter. A computer database captured by the U.S. military near Sinjar in western Iraq in 2007 documented just how local these networks could be. The database included names, city of origin, birth date, occupation, and other information for 563 foreign fighters who had been infiltrated into Iraq over the previous year. Jihad against the "Crusaders" occupying Iraq was a major rallying cry among Islamist terrorists ever since the United States and its allies invaded the country in 2003. Religious scholars who denounced terrorism elsewhere argued that violence against occupation was legitimate in Iraq, though there was less agreement about the legitimacy of targeting foreign civilians than about targeting foreign soldiers. (By many Western definitions, as well, targeting soldiers does not count as terrorism but rather as warfare or insurgency.) The shaykh of al-Azhar, Muhammad Tantawi—an establishment figure, not a revolutionary by any means—held a press conference to say that defending Iraq was a religious obligation and encouraged volunteers to travel to Iraq to assist the resistance that he labeled jihad. "Go in peace," he said. "I wish you the best." Relatively few Muslims actually went to Iraq—several thousand, according to the U.S. military and the Sunni insurgents themselves, so few that Bin Ladin complained about the failure of Muslims to join the insurgency. "Where are the soldiers of the Levant and the reinforcements of Yemen? Where are the knights of the Quiver [Egypt] and the lions of the Hijaz and al-Yamamah [regions of Arabia]? Come and aid your brothers in Mesopotamia [Iraq] and relieve them by coordinating with them by way of dependable guides."[40]

Foreign fighters in Iraq did not draw equally from all Muslim-majority societies. If the Sinjar records were representative, disproportionate numbers came to Iraq from a handful of cities in North Africa and Arabia. One of these was Darna, a small Mediterranean town in eastern Libya that supplied one-tenth of the Sinjar recruits—more than 50 in all. *Newsweek* magazine sent reporter Kevin Peraino to Darna "to try to figure out why it was contributing such a large portion of its young men"—almost 1 percent, by my reading of Libyan population statistics—"to fight the Americans in Iraq." Some of the families that Peraino contacted knew that their young men were becoming "too religious," as one resident described a brother who had gone to Iraq. Some knew that the men intended to leave and tried to stop them by blocking their emigration papers. The men slipped out of the country through connections that they did not share with their closest relatives. The brother of one man who died in Iraq told the reporter: "If I was planning to go, I wouldn't tell anybody." Foreign insurgents captured by the U.S. military in Iraq told interrogators the same thing: "Most were reluctant to tell their families for fear of disapproval." Al-Qaida in the Arabian Peninsula lamented in its online magazine that "the mujahidin have become strangers among their families, relatives, and friends." In northwest Pakistan, where the Taliban began to recruit Pashtun suicide bombers in the early 2000s, families would sometimes travel to the training camps to retrieve their sons.[41]

In a poor neighborhood of Tetouan, in northern Morocco, one group of friends plotted train bombings in Madrid in 2004, killing 191 people, and another group of friends left to engage in jihad in Iraq after making contact with recruiters through an imam at an unlicensed local mosque. One of the men implicated in the train bombings, who blew himself up as police surrounded his apartment to arrest him, left a scolding message to his family: "You have only to cry for yourselves and repent for the opportunity you have lost, since none of you has had the merit of encouraging me to join the road of jihad. Furthermore, you have opposed my thoughts and my wishes.... I have already told you this repeatedly. Nevertheless, [my arguments] were cries in the desert, or like ashes in the wind, all was in vain." Other radicals, by contrast, felt warmer feelings and a sense of responsibility toward their families. The relatives of men who engage in terrorism lose a source of income as well as a loved one and are frequently placed under surveillance, and recruits may feel guilty in advance that this will happen. In Tetouan, *New York Times* reporter Andrea Elliott interviewed many of the families and friends of the young men who had gone off to fight. Some of the young men she interviewed were themselves contemplating jihad. One of them said he would like to go fight in Iraq but that he couldn't. "If I go, who will support my family?" Even some recruits who go off for terrorist training may come to feel the pull of family responsibilities. One young man at a jihadi training camp in Afghanistan in 2000 voiced such concerns: "[W]hat is your advice... [to] an individual who says, 'I [will] train in this camp on [a] few courses then return home to my mother, father, wife and children, because they are not happy or satisfied with what I am doing, and I have duty towards them too?'" This question and others were summarized in notebooks captured by U.S. troops in Afghanistan in late 2001 and translated by the Combating Terrorism Center at the U.S. Military Academy. "Which has priority, jihad against the infidels or paying the debts first?" another recruit asked. "What is the ruling on fighting on the side of Taliban if the parents are against jihad?" "I migrated here to join the freedom fighters to defend the word of God and the Muslim nation, but I always had to worry about how to take care of myself financially because I have no income. Do you have a solution for this problem?" "What is the period of time a married man is permitted to stay away from his wife when he is in the preparation phase or the front line, whether individual or collective duty?"[42]

Islamist terrorists try to pry recruits loose from their families, in part by arguing that parental permission is not required for enlistment in the revolutionary cause. They have to counter the standard judgment on this topic, which was summarized in a fatwa from IslamOnline.net, one of many Internet sites where Muslims can request fatwas on any subject. (Fatwas are not just death sentences, as Western popular culture would have it—they are scholarly responses to questions of any sort from Muslims.) This fatwa quoted the Prophet Muhammad's response when a companion asked about the best deeds in life: "The Prophet replied, 'Performing prayer on time.' Ibn Mas'ud asked, 'Then what?' The Prophet said: 'Obeying one's parents.' Ibn Mas'ud said, 'Then what?' The Prophet said, 'Jihad.'" Citing a statement from al-Azhar, the fatwa concludes, "Obeying parents is an individual obligation (*fard ayn*), while jihad (fighting in the cause of Allah) is a collective obligation (*fard kifayah*). So, the former takes precedence over the latter. Hence, one is not allowed to participate in jihad without seeking the consent of one's parents. Consequently, parents can prevent their son from fighting, if they consider it too dangerous." Islamist terrorists argue that present circumstances have made jihad an individual obligation, so parental permission is not required.[43]

At the same time, terrorists don't take just any volunteer who expresses a desire to join up. They are paranoid—and justifiably so—about inadvertently admitting agents from security services that are eager to infiltrate their movements. "Unfortunately, the goal of every intelligence agency in the world…is to try to catch believing youths," warned a book of instructions for terrorist recruitment, which advised militants not to divulge sensitive information on Internet bulletin boards. Sayf al-Adl's instructions for recruitment, published in an online magazine of al-Qaida in the Arabian Peninsula, urged terrorists to find out everything they can about potential recruits—their educational background, their political beliefs, their piety and way of life, and so on—so as to weed out potential security risks. It's not just spies that he worried about but also recruits whose personal weaknesses might be exploited in the future by security services. "How do you become a member of al-Qaida?" asked a would-be terrorist with the bulletin-board handle Wali al-Haqq in early 2008. This time the question received an answer: You can't, at least not directly. "Either you join organizations of battalions of mujahidin, any Salafi jihadi group that you can reach, or you go in the same path and practice as them"—that is, start your own terrorist organization. If you are able to accomplish this, "we congratulate you on having become one of the mujahidin, answering the call of God." As counterterrorism specialist William McCants has noted, this matches other hints about al-Qaida recruitment: if you have an Islamist terrorist track record, they will find you. You don't find them.[44]

Somebody has to vouch for the recruits' trustworthiness, and as a result recruitment generally takes place on a small scale through personal contacts. Terrorism expert Marc Sageman has popularized the "bunch of guys" theory of terrorism, which he credits to Canadian police who were monitoring a small group of young Muslims as they egged each other on toward radicalization, led by several friends who had been to militant training camps in Afghanistan. People don't generally join terrorist organizations one by one; they join it by hanging out with buddies who are already involved. The same was true of the "Lackawanna Six"— young Yemeni-American men in Lackawanna, New York, who traveled to Afghanistan in the summer of 2001 to attend al-Qaida training camps. All but one of them quit and came home early, much to the disappointment of Kamal Derwish, their American-born, Saudi-raised recruiter. As described in detail by journalist Dina Temple-Raston, these young men spent months of evenings together in an apartment in Lackawanna—Derwish's radicalism was not welcome at the local mosque—eating pizza, debating their religious duties, and becoming more and more fervent in their convictions, until Derwish finally convinced them to go as a group to Afghanistan. Taheri-Azar in North Carolina, isolated and antisocial, never had a chance to join al-Qaida, and not just because his background is Shia. He wasn't part of a social circle that might have connected him, ultimately, to a terrorist organization.[45]

Under such circumstances, direct action is carried out by tiny units, meeting in secret, unable to amass large numbers of recruits or weapons for fear of attracting the attention of the authorities. Successful guerrillas—and territorial movements such as Hamas, Fatah, and Hizbullah—may swim in a sea of popular protection, according to the dictum popularized by Mao Zedong, but Islamist terrorists swim in a sea of possible informers. Murat, on the ferry in Istanbul, would have no trouble ratting out a terrorist to the Turkish police. In his view, anybody threatening violence in the name of Islam must be acting under the sway of imperialism, whether they realized it or not, and they deserved to be imprisoned. Zuhra, headscarfed on a university campus in Islamabad, would have no trouble turning in a terrorist to the authorities. For her, anybody threatening violence in the name of Islam couldn't possibly understand Islam, and they deserved to be imprisoned. Yasmin, in a chic café in Cairo, would have no trouble with it either. She had a moment of excitement over the terrorist attacks of 9/11, but she had no desire for Islamists to cramp her lifestyle. These young Muslims, and the millions more like them, are the terrorists' biggest challenge.[46]

CHAPTER 3

❧

Thoroughly Modern Mujahidin

On consecutive evenings in June 2004, two Islamist terrorists were killed, 1,600 miles apart: Nek Muhammad, leader of a Taliban group in Pakistan, and Abdulaziz al-Muqrin, leader of an al-Qaida affiliate in Saudi Arabia. Both men shared the same goal—a violent revolution that would establish a strict Islamic state—but in important ways, they could not have been more different. Al-Muqrin, age 31, grew up and died in a large city, was educated in state schools, and traveled widely, participating in radical Islamic movements in Afghanistan, Algeria, Spain, Bosnia, and Somalia, as well as his home country of Saudi Arabia. He wrote articles for a clandestine online journal that aimed to bring paramilitary training and tactics to Islamist terrorists everywhere. Muhammad, age 27, grew up and died in a remote town, was educated in religious seminaries—though he also had a secular high school degree—and never traveled far from his tribal homeland near the border of Pakistan and Afghanistan.

These differences symbolize a great divide among Islamist terrorists: the globalists versus the localists. Globalists are generally well educated, often with scientific training, speak one or more European languages, and pursue a vision of a pan-Islamic government centered in Arabia. Most localists, by contrast, have little education, and more often from Islamic seminaries than from secular schools. They tend to speak only their native tongue, plus a little classical Arabic, and their vision of an Islamic state is limited to a single territory. Al-Qaida is global. The Taliban are local.

As the United States wages war on terrorism, media coverage has frequently painted Islamists as medieval, reactionary, and eager to send the Islamic world back to the seventh century, when Islam was founded. In one sense this is accurate: Islamists and almost all Muslims consider the first years of Islam to have been especially virtuous and wish to model their behavior after the Prophet Muhammad and his early followers, much as Christians draw on the example of Jesus. (However, the analogy ought not be pushed too far: Muslims consider Muhammad to be a mortal who was divinely selected, not the son of God.) But this image can be misleading. Many Islamist terrorists graduated from modern schools, share modern values such as social equality (at least among Muslim men), and organize themselves along modern lines, using modern technologies, including the latest methods of warfare. Like Islamic liberalism, which is discussed in the next chapter, Islamist terrorists seek to modernize society and politics, recasting tradition in modern molds.

What do I mean by "modern"? The term came into vogue in the seventeenth century, as European intellectuals debated whether their contemporaries had exceeded the accomplishments of ancient Greece and Rome. This debate, which came to be known as "the quarrel between the ancients and the moderns," became moot in the following century, as partisans of the ancients disappeared. The moderns came to see their own accomplishments as unprecedented in world history—their science and technology, their imperialist expansion, and even, to a lesser extent, their arts and culture. The concept of the "modern" was originally a form of self-congratulation, and it was used to describe any aspect of European society that

European intellectuals were particularly proud of. By the nineteenth century, however, the term was extended to include negative aspects of European society as well—the economic and public health crises triggered by industrialization, for example. At the same time, intellectuals in other regions began to question whether modernity was a monopoly of Western Europe and its settler colonies. Russian and Japanese thinkers were among the pioneers in proposing that alternative modernities were possible and desirable, and that "modern" meant something distinct from "Western European." Today this approach is widely accepted: a society may be modern without necessarily mimicking Europeans. But there is still no consensus about the distinct meaning of "modern." For present purposes, I treat modernity as consisting of two contradictory trends that have accelerated around the world over the past several centuries: a trend toward ever-more-efficient technologies of control and a trend toward ever-more-egalitarian ideologies of liberation. The spread of secular public schools, for example, embodies both state control, reaching into the lives of children, and emancipation via mass literacy and opportunities for upward mobility. Both of these trends are visible in the case of global Islamist terrorists.

Let's start with Bin Ladin himself. Though he issued fatwas (religious judgments) as though he were a seminary-educated Islamic scholar, his training was in secular fields and his business was civil engineering before he made revolution his full-time job. Many other Islamist leaders also have university rather than seminary backgrounds, most famously Hasan al-Banna of Egypt, a schoolteacher who founded the Muslim Brotherhood, the first mass Islamist group, in the 1920s. Sayyid Qutb, perhaps the most influential Islamist author of the past half-century, was also trained as a schoolteacher, not a religious scholar. Abd al-Salam Faraj, ideologue of the revolutionary group that assassinated Egyptian president Anwar Sadat, was trained as an engineer. Faraj's colleague Ayman Zawahiri, who merged a group of Egyptian terrorists into al-Qaida, has a medical education. Abu Musab al-Zarqawi, who allied a group of insurgents in Iraq with al-Qaida, studied biotechnology. These leaders studied Islamic texts intensively but lacked the formal religious credentials that would qualify them as *ulama*, or traditional Islamic scholars.[1]

These "new religious intellectuals," as some scholars have called them, have competed with *ulama* for more than a century for the right to define Islam. Jamal al-Din al-Afghani, perhaps the most famous Islamic thinker of the nineteenth century, had a limited seminary background, but this didn't prevent him from speaking out on religious issues. He even argued that the lack of credentials might be an advantage, since traditional Islamic scholarship had become "a very narrow wick on top of which is a very small flame that neither lights its surroundings nor gives light to others." Numerous Muslim intellectuals of that era railed against seminarians for being obscurantist and politically inactive, a tradition that continues today among global terrorists. Bin Ladin, for example, lambasted the *ulama* of Saudi Arabia for playing "the most ominous of roles. Regardless of whether they did so intentionally or unintentionally, the harm that resulted from their efforts is no different from the role of the most ardent enemies of the nation." Bin Ladin and many other Islamist terrorists refer to traditional scholars derisively as "the rulers' *ulama*." The seminaries are in the pocket of oppressive governments, according to this view, too timid to speak boldly and preoccupied with doctrinal minutiae rather than the pressing issues of the day. The disparagement of seminary scholars is so widespread that one of Bin Ladin's associates, Muhammad Khalil al-Hakayma—himself a social worker by training, not a seminary scholar—worried that it might actually undermine Islamic faith. At the same time, al-Hakayma wrote that it was fine to label some Islamic experts as "traitors and hypocrites"—militants should continue to disparage such scholars, in his view. Even Islamist leaders with traditional seminary educations—such as Abu'l-Ala Maudoodi, who studied at Deobandi madrasas in India; Ruhollah Khomeini, who studied at the Qum seminaries in Iran; and Umar Abd al-Rahman, who studied at al-Azhar in Egypt—frequently criticized their alma maters for their lack of revolutionary zeal. Seminaries were considered so backward, in Islamist eyes, that for decades Maudoodi hid the fact that he had a seminary degree, according to a biography by political scientist Vali Nasr.[2]

It is not just leaders who emerge from secular universities. The Islamist rank and file also draws heavily on this pool. Of course, there are plenty of poorly educated people in Islamist terrorist organizations, but these movements are composed disproportionately of people who have a college education, in countries where college education is relatively rare. The classic study on this subject was performed in the late 1970s by Egyptian sociologist Saad Eddin Ibrahim. Of the 34 imprisoned Islamist activists he interviewed, 29 had attended university. In a follow-up study in the 1990s, Ibrahim found Islamist militancy had shifted to a poorer, less-educated demographic—but globally, a review of 25 statistical studies of the educational backgrounds of Islamist activists found that in all but three cases, activists were more likely than their peers to have advanced schooling. This is no coincidence—globalists have long sought highly educated recruits. In his 1996 declaration of war against the United States, for example, Bin Ladin identified university students and graduates as prime targets for mobilization. The hijackers of September 11, 2001, included a city planner, a physical education instructor, a business student, a teacher, and two engineers; even the Saudi "muscle" among them were largely middle-class youths educated in state-run high schools. Only 2 of the 19 hijackers had studied at a madrasa.[3]

Some Western observers have inverted these ratios. Donald Rumsfeld, President George W. Bush's secretary of defense, seemed to consider madrasas, not universities, the primary breeding grounds for terrorists. In a memo from 2003 that was leaked the following year, Rumsfeld worried, "Are we capturing, killing or deterring and dissuading more terrorists every day than the madrassas and the radical clerics are recruiting, training and deploying against us?...How do we stop those who are financing the radical madrassa schools?...Should we create a private foundation to entice radical madrassas to a more moderate course?...Is our current situation such that 'the harder we work, the behinder we get'?" Thomas Friedman, the influential *New York Times* columnist, has returned repeatedly to this same theme: "We finance the madrassas by driving big cars and sending the money to Saudi Arabia, which uses it to build the madrassas that are central to Al Qaeda's global supply chain."[4]

These concerns are partly correct—there are dozens of radical madrasas producing cadres for armed movements such as the Taliban in Afghanistan and Pakistan and the Jemaah Islamiya in Indonesia. However, these madrasas educate a tiny proportion of the world's young Muslims. The rise of Islamist movements in the twentieth century was closely associated with the marginalization of seminary educational systems. Beginning in Ottoman Turkey and Egypt in the early nineteenth century, and ending in the mid-twentieth century with the kingdoms of Arabia, Muslim and colonial rulers founded their own schools to operate in competition with the seminaries. At first these were small elite schools, designed to produce government officials. In the past two generations, however, state-run school systems have expanded to include significantly larger sectors of the population. In 22 Muslim-majority countries included in a Harvard dataset, 70 percent of adults had no formal education in 1960; by 1990, this figure had been reduced to 44 percent. In 1960, only four of these countries had more than 1 percent of the adult population with some higher education; in 1990, only four of these countries had less than 1 percent with some higher education. Seminaries have also grown in some countries; but even where seminary-trained *ulama* control the state, as in the Islamic Republic of Iran, these schools remain marginal to the nation's educational system. In Pakistan, madrasas educate less than 1 percent of all students in the country. In Indonesia, the madrasa and pesantren seminary systems encompass a larger portion, estimated at more than one-fifth of all students. In both cases, the huge majority of students and graduates of these schools have nothing to do with terrorism. If madrasas were the main source of Islamist violence, there would be relatively little to worry about.[5]

Reality is more complex. The modernizing efforts that the United States and its allies support so fervently are generating the most dangerous terrorists. The U.S. Agency for International Development and other assistance programs were founded in the belief that improved education, rising incomes, and other forms of modernization would reduce social and political unrest among people whose "poverty is a handicap and a threat both to them and to more prosperous areas," in the words of President Harry Truman, who inaugurated the U.S. foreign aid program after World War II. These expectations have been borne out in many Muslim communities, where secularly educated middle-class youths have launched liberal, pro-democracy movements (see chapter 4). At the same time, these schools have also produced violently illiberal countermovements as well. This has been the case worldwide, not just in Muslim societies. Hindutva communalists, for example, have mobilized a large segment of the middle class in India and the Indian diaspora. For decades, communist movements in many countries focused their recruitment efforts more toward college campuses than toward factories and farms. Fortunately, Islamist terrorists have not been nearly as successful in the competition for college campuses as communist revolutionaries once were. They have taken over even fewer governments.[6]

With the rise of secular education, particularly higher education, more laypeople than ever before now read religious texts for themselves, not relying on seminary-trained experts for their understanding of sacred sources. Those with access to personal computers can now search and sort these sources in minutes, tasks that used to require years of memorization and training. Islamic websites warn autodidacts against trying to study these texts without proper guidance. The Muslim Student Association at the University of Southern California, which hosts a widely used database of Quranic verses and hadith reports, prefaces its search engine with a "warning (especially for Muslims)" that "this database is merely a tool, and not a substitute for learning, much less scholarship in Islam....We would strongly encourage those who want to learn about Islam to purchase a hardcopy of the Quran but with the following conditions: Get one with commentary (tafseer). Make sure the tafseer is scholarly (e.g. references to reasons behind a verse, references to hadith and sunnah, etc.)." Interestingly, the website recommends a commentary by Abu'l-Ala Maudoodi, who hid his scholarly credentials. Despite such warnings, laypeople have generated a profusion of do-it-yourself theology and jurisprudence. Any college grad in a cave can claim to speak for Islam.[7]

The result is a tremendous diversity of Islamic opinion, and a corresponding diversity of Islamic authorities. There is no universally recognized arbiter to resolve Islamic debates. For most of Islamic history, a symbolic arbiter existed: the caliph, or successor (*khalifa*) to the Prophet Muhammad. No caliph was ever powerful enough to impose interpretive uniformity on all Muslims, though some were more inclined than others to try. But since the Turkish Republic abolished the Ottoman caliphate in 1924, even this symbol of authority is gone. Several monarchs were proposed as possible successors to the last Ottoman caliph, but there was no process for selecting a candidate—since the 600s, caliphs had claimed the title by conquering the previous caliph, inheriting the position, or simply declaring themselves to be caliph. None of the candidates for the caliphate in the 1920s—the kings of the Hijaz, Najd, Egypt, and others—took these steps, and campaigns on their behalf were ultimately dropped. Today each Islamic country has a separate religious hierarchy, or even multiple hierarchies, and none is bound to acknowledge the leadership of any other.

There is a time-honored precedent for this diversity of religious authorities in Islam. In the first generations after Muhammad's death, faced with the fallibility of human efforts to interpret revelation, leading Muslim scholars agreed to disagree. Not all approaches were tolerated, but a limited form of pluralism became institutionalized in the ninth century through four main schools of Islamic law, which most seminaries in the Islamic world have recognized and taught alongside one another for centuries. In the 1950s, the rector of al-Azhar even agreed to recognize and teach Shiism as a fifth legal school. Disagreement and debate among Muslim scholars is thus expected and accepted, even as the boundaries of toleration have on occasion been enforced with expulsion or death. Many Muslims are uncomfortable with this legacy. In a survey of 12 Muslim communities around the world, most respondents agreed that "there is only one true interpretation of the teachings of Islam." (The alternative offered on the survey was: "Islam should tolerate diverse interpretations of its teachings.")[8]

To Islamist militants, this diversity of authorities is a disaster. They yearn for the rule of a single Islamic authority. In a videotape released in October 2001, Bin Ladin called the end of the Ottoman caliphate the starting point of 80 years of "humiliation and contempt." Bin Ladin hardly cared for Ottoman religious authority—he and other Arab Islamists rarely cite Turkish religious scholarship. What Bin Ladin appreciated about the Ottoman caliphate is its political authority, the last great attempt to unify Muslims in a single state that could stand up to Western encroachment. The West—Britain, specifically, according to Ayman Zawahiri—was so intent on undermining the Ottoman bulwark that it "moved Abd al-Aziz al-Saud [the founder of Saudi Arabia] and al-Husayn ibn Ali [the ruler of Mecca] to stab the Ottoman state in its back." According to globalists, the emergence of multiple states in the Middle East—Saudi Arabia among them—heralded an era of Muslim weakness and disarray. This is not a fringe opinion. In a survey of four Muslim-majority countries in 2007, most respondents said they sympathized with al-Qaida's goal to "unify all Islamic countries into a single Islamic state or caliphate."[9]

But if globalists are nostalgic for the caliphate, they do not wish to restore the Ottoman, or any other, dynasty. They are republicans. Bin Ladin and his followers swore loyalty to Mulla Muhammad Umar of the Taliban and referred to him as the "commander of the faithful," a title historically bestowed on the caliphs, but nothing in their language suggests that the title can be inherited. In an interview with an Arab journalist, Bin Ladin told a story about an ancient Arab king who killed a commoner. The victim's brother killed the king in retaliation, and "the people were astonished, and said, 'You are able to kill a king just because of your brother?'" Bin Ladin proposed that a more appropriate question would be, "So who permitted the rule of that king?" The king's life and the commoner's life "are both equal souls," Bin Ladin concluded. Leadership of the Islamic state, in the view of Islamist revolutionaries, is something to be achieved by piety and strength, not by birth, in keeping with their vision of the first four "rightly guided caliphs" who succeeded Muhammad in the seventh century.[10]

This is one of many ways that Islamist revolutionaries have reconstructed tradition to match modern sensibilities. Much as they wish to restore the sacred practices of the first Muslims, they downplay early Islamic practices that are at odds with their modern values. One such practice was the dominance of the Quraysh tribe of Mecca over later converts to Islam. It was no accident that all of the first four caliphs were Qurayshis—they were selected in part because of the Qurayshis' privileged position in the early Muslim community, in addition to their individual merit. Today, by contrast, Islamists no longer give precedence to Qurayshis, just as they reject slavery. Islamists do not want to restore every aspect of early Islam.

Instead, Islamists today emphasize many modern values that Muhammad never considered. In place of tribal hierarchies, Islamists emphasize social equality, at least among male Muslims. In place of personalistic regimes, Islamists insist on codified law. Many Islamists also speak the language of individual rights, economic development, and national self-determination. The revolutionaries are hostile toward the West, but their manifestos and political platforms share significant planks with Western modernity. These modern values set Islamists apart from the medieval precursors they identify themselves with, such as Ibn Taymiyya in the fourteenth century and Muhammad Ibn Abd al-Wahhab and Shah Wali-Allah in the eighteenth century. None of these figures suggested that kings and commoners were equal souls.[11]

These modern values do not mean that Islamist states look just like Western states. Islamists are openly hostile to certain elements of modernity in its Western forms, such as gender-neutral laws and the separation of church and state, which they see as signs of the West's moral decadence. Moreover, certain high-profile Islamist goals such as corporal punishment, legalized polygyny, automatic male custody in divorce, restrictive garb for women, bans on heresy and apostasy, and judicial authority keyed to sacred texts are unpalatable to modern Western sensibilities. Yet even these demands are presented in a modern way—not as the continuity of tradition, since these traditions have been abandoned in most Muslim societies, but rather in the modern idiom of rediscovering authenticity. Fundamentalist movements seeking to purify and recover lost traditions emerged in many urban, modern-educated, secularized communities during the twentieth century, not just among Muslims but also among Christians, Jews, Hindus, and others.[12]

The goal of Islamism is to "Islamicize modernity," in the phase of Moroccan Islamist leader Abdessalam Yassine—to forge an alternative modernity that combines basic elements of modernity with selected elements of Islamic heritage. The Islamic Republic of Iran, for example, has tried to forge its own path since it replaced the Pahlavi monarchy in 1979. Yet within its first year it copied global norms by writing a new constitution, ratifying it through a referendum with full adult suffrage, holding parliamentary and presidential elections, establishing a cabinet system, and occupying itself with myriad other tasks that the modern world expects of a state, from infrastructure expansion to narcotics interdiction. The 1986 Iranian census, conducted by the Islamic Republic, was scarcely different from the 1976 census, conducted by the monarchy. Similarly, in Pakistan and the Sudan, where Islamic laws were introduced in the 1980s, there were changes, but there were also massive continuities. The modern state remained.[13]

Ironically, the West, which generally considers itself the overturner of tradition, now supports traditional elites in the Islamic world. The British and French installed monarchies in much of the Middle East after World War I. More recently, Western military might forced a republic to disgorge a monarchy—albeit a liberalized one—when Kuwait was liberated from Iraq in 1991. Since that time, U.S. troops have been stationed in Saudi Arabia to defend the country's absolute monarchy. Bin Ladin and other revolutionary Islamists have made repeated use of the irony: America, supposed proponent of democracy and human rights, clings to a regime that detests these modern concepts.

Global terrorists draw on Western models in practice, as well as in ideology. Al-Qaida and similar groups operate like transnational corporations, with affiliates and franchises, strategic partners, commodity chains, global financing, and other features associated with contemporary global capital. Documents discovered in Afghan training camps after al-Qaida's departure show a bureaucratic organization with administrative lines of authority and a fussy insistence on budgeting. "Why did you buy a new fax for $470? Where are the two old faxes?" an al-Qaida bookkeeper in Afghanistan wrote to an affiliate in Yemen in 1999. "General expenses you mentioned amounted to $235. Can you explain what you mean?" In a return e-mail, the Yemeni resigned in disgust. The globalists use the latest high-tech skills—not just airplane piloting and transponder deactivation, as the world learned tragically on September 11, 2001, but also every new communications technology that comes along, from satellite phones in the 1990s to Internet telephone calls. Terrorist use of the Internet is well known, and online discussion boards frequently offer tips on how to cover one's electronic tracks. For example, according to journalist accounts, some terrorist organizations developed a method for sending e-mail without having it "sniffed" by government software that monitors e-mail traffic through the major Internet hubs. They create an anonymous e-mail account and save messages in the "drafts" folder. Then they alert the recipient that the message is ready, perhaps through an innocuous e-mail message using a different account, and the recipient logs into the shared account to read the message in the drafts folder.[14]

Al-Qaida and other terrorists frequently draw on non-Islamic precedents for strategic and tactical lessons. They even praise the effectiveness of certain Israeli actions, despite al-Qaida's hostility toward Zionism. In a training manual captured and translated by the British government, one short section entitled "Ability to Observe and Analyze" consisted entirely of an example from the Israeli intelligence agency, Mossad. According to the manual, a group of Palestinians took a potato-peddler's cart and modified it with extra chimney tubes to launch missiles at an Israeli airplane. Mossad officers searched the airport looking for terrorists. "One officer passed the potato cart twice without noticing anything. On his third time, he noticed three chimneys, but only one of them was working with smoke coming out of it." The hero of the lesson was the observant Israeli officer, not the Palestinian militants.[15]

Western bias tends to lump Khomeini's Iran and the Taliban's Afghanistan in the same category, and indeed both movements came to power with the goal of building an Islamic state. But one movement created a modern state and the other did not. The Islamic Republic of Iran adopted a constitution, a full array of government ministries, and major public works projects, while the Taliban leadership hardly bothered to staff the government offices in Kabul. The Taliban announced that they had suspended the country's legal code and purged the constitution of all secular terms but did not publish the new documents until 2007, several years after they had been ousted from power. Perhaps the most vivid distinction involves gender. Soon after taking power, the Taliban prohibited women from wearing "Iranian" garb—long-sleeved cloak and hair covering, without face covering. While the Taliban barred girls from attending school, the Islamic Republic of Iran more than doubled girls' education from prerevolutionary levels. The Taliban barred women from working at most jobs, while Iranian women entered the labor force in unprecedented numbers as television anchors, parliamentary deputies, government typists, and sales clerks, dressed in headscarves and long coats. Iranian leaders were as outspoken as Western feminists in condemning Taliban policies on gender and other subjects, and considered the Taliban to be giving Islam a bad name: "The world does not accept what the Taliban are doing in the name of Islam," Iran's leader, Ali Khamenei, said soon after the Taliban took Kabul. "How is this going to introduce Islam in the outside world?" said Ahmad Jannati, a hard-line cleric in Iran. "What violence and narrow-mindedness in the name of Islam!"[16]

Unlike al-Qaida, most of the Taliban's recruits had little or no education, and what schooling they did have came from seminaries. In their fathers' generation, young Afghans pursuing a religious education would have stayed in their own country, which had developed a system of seminaries to train scholars for government service. But the state school system was basically nonexistent after more than a decade of war, so the foot soldiers of the Taliban were drawn largely from the student body of refugee seminaries in Pakistan—hence the name "Taliban," which means "seminary students," from an original meaning of "seekers." (The singular is "talib," so references to a single "American Taliban" are grammatically incorrect.) This force was created in large part by the Pakistani intelligence ministry, which is staffed at its higher ranks by well-educated Muslims, and it made an alliance with al-Qaida, which also appears to draw on the highly educated. But these connections should not obscure the fact that the Taliban had an entirely different social base. Would-be militants who showed up in Afghanistan to join the jihad "had to take a complex entrance exam," a former member of al-Qaida told U.S. officials. "It involved what sounded like an IQ test. Those who scored high, like [the informant], were sent to bin Laden's intelligence training program. Those who scored lowest were sent to fight against the Northern Alliance on the front lines."[17]

The groups' social bases are associated with distinct religious positions as well. Both share a distaste for Westernized secularism and wish to implement sharia provisions, which they interpret in similar ways. But there are significant variations. The Taliban follow the Hanafi school of Sunni Islam, while al-Qaida's Saudi founders follow the Hanbali school—a distinction that troubles some of the Taliban's Arab supporters. "When the Taliban came to power, they held a narrow-minded, strict interpretation of the Hanafi school of thought, as is predominant in Afghanistan," a militant website explained. "As time went on, and the influx of Foreign Mujahideen from different countries who supported and helped the Taliban increased, the Taliban leadership became more relaxed and accommodating in their attitude." The website concluded condescendingly, "One must build up a trust with an isolated people, before teaching them something that they do not know. This trust takes time, effort and sacrifice."[18]

It was more difficult to overcome differing religious perspectives on objects and sites associated with saintly ancestors revered by the Taliban. To gain legitimacy as he was taking over Afghanistan, Taliban leader Mulla Muhammad Umar literally wrapped himself in the cloak of the Prophet Muhammad, a cherished relic stored for two centuries at a shrine in Qandahar. He ordered the custodian to unlock the sanctuary, then stood on the roof of a nearby mosque and placed his hands in the cloth as a crowd of supporters chanted "Commander of the Faithful," a title associated with the first caliphs to succeed the Prophet Muhammad. In early 2001, the Taliban declared that all statues and non-Islamic shrines were to be destroyed—the most famous of them being the giant Buddha figures in Bamyan—but Islamic shrines were spared.[19]

Globalists, on the other hand, disdain relics as verging on idol worship. Even as they allied themselves with the Taliban, they complained bitterly about their hosts' religious practices, which they considered un-Islamic. This has been a concern ever since Arabs came to Afghanistan to help fight against the Soviet Union in the 1980s. "Do we fight alongside Muslims that are below acceptable levels of Islamic education?" Abdullah Azzam, the most prominent leader of the Arab Afghans, asked rhetorically. Afghans "are a people who adamantly follow their Hanafi *madhhab* [school of jurisprudence] and some of them wear talismans," which many Islamists consider to be forbidden idols. Nonetheless,

Azzam defended the Afghans: "Show me a Muslim people on the earth who do not have similar problems. Shall we leave the *kuffar* [non-Muslims] in every Muslim land because these problems are present?" Similar concerns arose in al-Qaida training camps a decade later. Various "indications of polytheism"—especially a saintly tomb in the mosque in front of Mulla Umar's office—are "puzzling me and making me uneasy towards jihad on the side of Taliban," a recruit at an al-Qaida training camp admitted. An unnamed al-Qaida official rebutted these concerns in a memorandum that was later captured and translated by the U.S. military: "Yes, there are cases where the blessing of the graves has been sought or the latter have [been] built upon. While these are violations of Islamic law and heresies, they do not reach the level of atheism, which would be grounds for losing the [Islamic] faith." The memorandum concludes with an uncharacteristic appeal not to cast aspersions on fellow Muslims' faith without solid proof—though this is precisely what al-Qaida does to its enemies.[20]

The Taliban and al-Qaida also differ about representations of the human form. The Taliban object to human images as idolatry. Mulla Umar has never allowed himself to be photographed. Bin Ladin, by contrast, held press conferences and distributed videotapes of himself to the world's media. During the Taliban rule of Afghanistan, this difference was a major source of friction between the two men and the movements that they led. Within a year of moving back to Afghanistan in the mid-1990s at the invitation of the Taliban, Bin Ladin asked Mulla Umar for permission to meet with foreign journalists. "A number of international media agencies have corresponded with us requesting an interview," Bin Ladin wrote. "We view this as a good opportunity to make Muslims aware of what is going on in the land of the two Sacred Precincts [that is, Saudi Arabia] as well as of what is happening here in Afghanistan to strengthen the religion and apply sharia. As you know, in this era media war is one of the most powerful means [of combat]. In fact, it may constitute as much as 90 percent of the total preparation for battle." Umar's response must have been encouraging enough, because Bin Ladin began to grant audiences to television and print journalists over the following months, frequently arriving for the interview in a convoy of vehicles, surrounded by armed bodyguards who fired their automatic weapons in the air for dramatic effect.[21]

In early 1998, less than two years after becoming the guest of the Taliban, Bin Ladin enraged his hosts by holding a press conference at which he and several leaders of like-minded groups declared war on the United States. Umar was furious. According to the Pakistani journalist Rahimullah Yusufzai, Umar called to say that "there could be only one ruler in Afghanistan, either him or bin Laden." He even shut down several of the foreign fighters' training camps in Afghanistan. Some of Bin Ladin's Arab followers worried about the fallout. Two senior strategists wrote to Bin Ladin to complain that the Afghans' "discontent with the Arabs has become clear." This latest turn of events "jeopardizes the Arabs and the Arab presence today in all of Afghanistan, for no good reason." We have even heard "Abu Abdullah's [Bin Ladin] saying that he wouldn't listen to the Leader of the Faithful [Mulla Umar] when he asked him to stop giving interviews. . . . I think our brother has caught the disease of screens, flashes, fans, and applause." Bin Ladin apologized and lay low for a time, but by 2000 he was plotting new media strategies, according to the minutes of a meeting with an Arab colleague, Abu Hudhayfa. The basic problem, they agreed, was a failure to publicize and claim credit for the group's terrorist attacks, which would rally like-minded followers in Arabia and elsewhere. "How nice it would be if in the future the executor of an operation is videotaped while he is giving an inciting speech to the nation and then his speech is published after the operation is carried out successfully similar to what Hamas is doing," wrote Abu Hudhayfa. In fact, al-Qaida had already taped two of the pilots of the 9/11 attacks reading their will and joking in front of the cameras, though the video was not released until five years after their deaths. Mulla Umar shut down some of the foreign fighters' camps again for two weeks in the summer of 2000.[22]

The Taliban's and al-Qaida's distinct religious positions were associated with differing political goals. The Taliban were primarily interested in ruling a single territory: Afghanistan. They had no aspirations to export their revolution to other lands; that was al-Qaida's obsession. So while the globalists picked fights with new enemies in order to widen the conflict, localists wanted to narrow the conflict and keep the goals local. Khalid Sheikh Mohammed, the main organizer of the 9/11 attacks, reportedly told his American captors that many senior Taliban leaders "rejected what they [al-Qaida militants] were doing.... Never in their life at all, before America invade[d] them, [did] they intend to do anything against America. They [had] never been with al-Qaida." The tension between local and global goals was evident even to recruits in al-Qaida's training camps, one of whom asked Bin Ladin in 2000, "Has al-Qaida under your command pledged allegiance to the Islamic emirate in Afghanistan? If so, how do you call for fighting the United States [since] it is well-known that the Taliban will not hear of it for reasons concerning the security and stability of Afghanistan?"[23]

"The Taliban have wasted four years of my life," Bin Ladin complained to a delegation of Taliban officials who met with him to curb his global violence. One member of the delegation described the meeting in his memoirs. "They have set up barriers and obstacles to the path of jihad, which is a duty upon us under present conditions. I have sworn allegiance to the Leader of the Faithful"— Taliban chief Mulla Muhammad Umar—"and he is our leader, but when a follower lines up [for prayer] behind a leader, the leader cannot tell him, 'Don't line up behind me.'" A Taliban official retorted, "When somebody lines up behind a leader, does he have the right to go against the orders of the leader?" "No," Bin Ladin admitted. He thought for a moment, then rephrased his objection. "The follower does have some claims upon the leader. For instance, if the leader stands up instead of completing his prayers, the follower should say, 'God is great!' and point out his mistake." The Taliban official laughed. "Oh shaykh, at the very least, give us time to get to the end. We are still at the beginning of our prayers! We are already dealing with hundreds of difficulties, both internal difficulties and the difficulties of foreign pressure. At least, don't make more difficulties for us." Bin Ladin looked around to make sure they were not being overheard. He whispered, "Very well. I will solve your internal difficulties." This cryptic comment may have foretold al-Qaida's assassination of Ahmad Shah Massoud, the leading Afghan opponent of the Taliban, on September 9, 2001. But al-Qaida did not drop its global plans, despite the objections of the Taliban. Rumors were rife in Afghanistan in early 2001 that the Arab visitors were planning an attack on the United States. According to some versions of the account, al-Qaida had amassed 3,000 kilograms of explosives for the attack. "The guests are destroying the guesthouse," the Taliban's foreign minister told an aide in July 2001. He sent a messenger to warn American and United Nations officials. Unfortunately for the United States and for the Taliban, he had no precise information to relay.[24]

Despite their differences, the Taliban and al-Qaida huddled closer after United States retaliations—the missiles that President Clinton launched at al-Qaida's camps in 1998 in response to the Kenya and Tanzania embassy bombings, and the army that President Bush sent in 2001 in response to 9/11. Under attack, the Taliban dug in their heels and refused to give up their foreign "guests." In the late 1990s, the Taliban were not moved by a United Nations Security Council resolution calling on all governments to freeze the Taliban's assets until they turned over Bin Ladin. Mulla Umar had personally rebuffed a high-level delegation from Saudi

Arabia and Pakistan, the Taliban's main international sponsors, seeking Bin Ladin's extradition. After 9/11, the Taliban prepared for battle rather than abandon al-Qaida. As a result, both groups were chased into hiding in even-more-remote areas of Afghanistan and Pakistan. The Taliban had their own methods of brutal violence, but in the years after the United States ousted them they started to use suicide attacks and improvised explosive devices (IEDs), al-Qaida signature tactics, which had not been seen much in Afghanistan since the CIA and the Pakistani intelligence service trained the mujahidin in terrorist tactics in the 1980s. Several years after adopting al-Qaida tactics, one Taliban commander bragged, "I think we are better at making IEDs now than the Arabs who first taught us."[25]

Still, the Taliban leadership remained dubious of al-Qaida's global aspirations and killing of civilians. In late 2006, Mulla Umar issued a pronouncement urging his followers to redouble their efforts, while cautioning them against indiscriminate attacks: "Avoid operations that cause death and injury to innocent people.... We are obliged to target only our enemy." Several days later, in his first exchange with journalists since he went into hiding, he expressed his sympathies with Bin Ladin and associates but noted that "they have set jihad as their goal, whereas we have set the expulsion of American troops from Afghanistan as our target." In 2009, Mulla Umar reemphasized this position in a statement offering "good and positive relations with all neighbors"—including Pakistan, China, and other countries that al-Qaida and its affiliates have targeted. Another commander announced that the Afghan Taliban wouldn't cooperate with the Pakistani Taliban, who are attempting to overthrow the government of Pakistan. "There will not be any support from us," he told a reporter. We "don't have any interest in fighting against other countries."[26]

It may not be a coincidence that Taliban commanders who adopted al-Qaida's methods and goals have not fared well in recent years. The man most responsible for importing al-Qaida's approach into Taliban operations was Mulla Dadullah, a vicious commander who gave numerous television interviews with al-Jazeera, al-Sahab Media Center (al-Qaida's video production unit), and other outlets. Dadullah's group also produced its own promotional videos showing him and his followers beheading captives, a tactic adopted from global terrorists in Pakistan and Iraq. In 2007, Dadullah granted television interviews boasting of sending suicide attackers to the United States and other countries. Several days after his final interview, he was dead, killed by British and Afghan soldiers under circumstances suggesting the Taliban may have leaked his location. Dadullah's successor, his brother Mansur Dadullah, was fired by Mulla Umar for disobeying unspecified orders and carrying out "acts that are not compatible with the aims of the Islamic Emirate." This rebuke may have been spurred by the outdoor press conference that Mansur gave in June 2007 to show off 200 supposed suicide bombers heading for the United States and Europe. The same month, he gave a television interview allying himself with al-Qaida's transnational vision rather than Umar's local vision: "Jihad must not be restricted to Afghanistan or Iraq. Ours is a global struggle, and I have promised Allah that I will spread it across the world until the end of my days." (Mansur was also rumored to have been fired for engaging in negotiations with the British.) In early 2008, lacking Taliban protection, Mansur Dadullah was captured by Pakistani troops near the border with Afghanistan. (The Taliban still thought him worth a prisoner swap in mid-2008.)[27]

As the Taliban have regained territory in Afghanistan, tensions with al-Qaida have resurfaced. Once again, the Taliban's interest in avoiding excuses for foreign intervention in the country occasionally clashes with al-Qaida's global aspirations, which increase the risk of foreign intervention. Maulvi Mohammad Haqqani, the son of a major commander allied with the Taliban and a significant pro-Taliban figure in his own right, spelled out this logic in an interview with journalist Sami Yousafzai: "Now that we control large amounts of territory, we should have a strict code of conduct for any foreigners working with us. We can no longer allow these camels to roam freely without bridles and control." The Taliban want foreign fighters to help them retake Afghanistan, but they may be hoping to avoid getting stuck with a large number of foreign fighters in the country, as happened in the 1990s. This could explain why there has been no migration of al-Qaida training camps from Pakistan into Taliban-controlled areas of Afghanistan.[28]

Yahya Ayyash did not fit into either of the two main categories of Islamist revolutionaries, localists or globalists. Like al-Qaida and other globalists, he was well educated—a science whiz who studied electrical engineering in college and then used these skills to devise explosive devices for suicide bombings and other acts of revolutionary violence. His comrades called him "the engineer." But instead of joining the international movement, he stayed close to home and fought exclusively for an Islamist revolution in his own land, as the Taliban did. Ayyash was born in Rafat, a Palestinian town in the Quds region of Jordan. When he was one year old, Israel occupied Rafat and the rest of the West Bank. But as international boundaries shifted around his hometown, Ayyash's Palestinian identity remained the same. Beginning in his teen years, Ayyash helped to establish cells for the Islamic Resistance Movement, known by its Arabic acronym Hamas, a revolutionary organization that aims to create an Islamic Palestinian state, not just in Gaza and the West Bank but also in the areas that comprise the state of Israel. Soon after he graduated from Bir Zeit University in the early 1990s, Ayyash went underground. After three years on the run, making bombs and training bomb-makers, he was assassinated by a bomb that Israeli security forces had rigged inside a cell phone.[29]

Ayyash's choice of Palestine as his field of battle followed the advice of Abdullah Azzam, the leading recruiter of foreign fighters in Afghanistan. Azzam, who was born in Palestine during the British colonial period, argued in his most widely distributed pamphlet, *The Defense of Muslim Lands*, that the two most important sites for Islamist activism are Afghanistan and Palestine. For most Muslims, he wrote, Afghanistan comes first—"not because Afghanistan is more important than Palestine, not at all, Palestine is the foremost Islamic problem. It is the heart of the Islamic world, and it is a blessed land, but there are some reasons which make Afghanistan the starting point." These reasons included the Islamic leadership of the Afghan movement, as opposed to Palestine, where "leadership has been appropriated by a variety of people, including sincere Muslims, communists, nationalists and modernist Muslims. Together they have hoisted the banner of a secular state." Azzam also noted Afghanistan's long and unprotected borders. In Palestine, "the borders are closed, their hands are bound, the eyes of the authorities spy from all sides for anyone who attempts to infiltrate its borders to kill the Jews." Nonetheless, any Arab who is able to make it to Palestine "must start there. And, if he is not capable, then he must set out for Afghanistan."[30]

A few Palestinians have joined the globalists. In the 1950s, the Islamic Liberation Party (Hizb ut-Tahrir al-Islami), a global movement to establish a transnational Islamic state, was founded by Taqiuddin al-Nabhani, an Islamic scholar from Jerusalem. In the 1980s, Azzam's call to arms in Afghanistan attracted a small community of "Palestinian Afghans," and more recently several Palestinians have been associated with al-Qaida, including Abu Qatada, who has been charged with recruiting Islamist terrorists in Europe, and Abu Zubayda, an alleged commander who is currently held by the U.S. military at Guantánamo Bay. More Palestinians than any other Muslim nationality say that they have confidence in

Bin Ladin to "do the right thing regarding world affairs," according to surveys conducted by the Pew Global Attitudes Project.[31]

But Palestinian globalists have been far rarer than these survey results would imply. In the 1990s, Syrian globalists were numerous enough that they established their own training camp in Afghanistan. Libyans had their own camp. Egyptians had their own camp. Palestinians did not. There were few Palestinians among the alleged militants captured by the United States and its allies in Afghanistan and Pakistan—only 5 out of more than 750 detainees at Guantánamo Bay have been Palestinian. There have not been many Palestinian insurgents in Iraq, either. Out of several hundred foreign fighters in Iraq eulogized on militant Islamist websites in early 2004, only a handful came from Palestine; of 595 foreign fighters listed in a database discovered by the U.S. military on a computer in Sinjar, Iraq, in 2007, none was Palestinian.[32]

Hamas and al-Qaida are like twins separated at birth. Both were inspired by Palestinian religious scholars who were originally affiliated with the Muslim Brotherhood: Azzam and Ahmad Yasin. Both turned to militancy after establishing their reputation through social-welfare activities: Azzam's Services Bureau (Maktab al-Khidmat) in Peshawar, which supported foreign volunteers in the Afghan war, and Yasin's Islamic Society (al-Mujama al-Islami) in Gaza, which supported Palestinian activists and needy families. When both movements began their revolutionary activities in the 1980s, they adopted the same novel position that armed jihad was an individual duty for each Muslim. In addition, they both adopted modern methods of insurgency, such as technologically advanced explosives and media-savvy outreach. In the early 1990s, Hamas pioneered the use of video testaments, recordings of the final statements of suicide bombers, a tactic intended to cement the commitment of the operative and serve as inspiration to others. Al-Qaida started to copy the tactic several years later. Both Hamas and al-Qaida draw primarily on educated cadres—more than half of Hamas's members have some higher education, as compared with less than 10 percent of other Palestinians. Both Hamas and al-Qaida scorned the Taliban's traditionalism—Yasin, the founder of Hamas, condemned the Taliban's understanding of Islam as "completely wrong and misleading.... How dare they ban women from contributing in our lives by preventing them from working and teaching?... Their ways can only harm the Islamic religion."[33]

Despite these parallels between Hamas and al-Qaida, the two movements are more competitors than collaborators. Hamas never aligned itself as a branch of the global al-Qaida franchise the way that some other groups did (for example, the Egyptian Islamic Jihad, the Salafist Group for Preaching and Combat in Algeria, Noordin Top's faction within Jemaah Islamiya in Southeast Asia, and Abu Musab al-Zarqawi's insurgent faction in Iraq). Hamas did not share personnel or operations with al-Qaida the way that the Islamic Group in Southeast Asia and various Pakistani militant groups did. Instead, the two movements distrust each other. Asked in 1999 about collaboration with al-Qaida and other globalists, Yasin answered diplomatically, "We are not prepared to seek an alliance with those movements.... We have no intention of intervening in the affairs of other countries of the world." Days after September 11, 2001, Yasin signed a strongly worded statement of condemnation, along with dozens of other revolutionary Islamist leaders (see chapter 2). In an interview in 2006, a Hamas militant ridiculed the possibility of alliance with al-Qaida and dismissed al-Qaida as murderers of civilians. (Hamas's position is that Israelis are not civilians.) "How can you say Hamas and al-Qaeda in the same statement? There is no comparison," the militant said heatedly.[34]

Hamas's name does not refer to Palestine—it means "zeal" in Arabic and is a modified acronym for the Islamic Resistance Movement—and its charter, written in 1988, defines the organization as a branch of the global Islamic movement. However, the charter privileges local goals: "The problem of the liberation of Palestine relates to three circles: the Palestinian, the Arab and the Islamic. Each one of these circles has a role to play in the struggle against Zionism and it has duties to fulfill." According to the charter, Palestine is the most sacred Islamic location under occupation by non-Muslims, and therefore "the liberation of that land is an individual duty binding on all Muslims everywhere." Al-Qaida statements, by contrast, consider the most sacred sites under occupation to be Mecca and Medina, as a result of the foreign troops that Saudi Arabia has hosted since 1990. (The government of Saudi Arabia, sensitive to this line of criticism, bused religious scholars around the two cities to prove that foreign troops were nowhere nearby.)[35]

Hamas is up-front about its nationalism. Article 12 of its charter states, "Hamas regards nationalism as part and parcel of the religious faith. Nothing is loftier or deeper in nationalism than waging jihad against the enemy and confronting him when he sets foot on the land of the Muslims. And this becomes an individual duty binding on every Muslim man and woman; a woman must go out and fight the enemy even without her husband's authorization, and a slave without his master's permission." Globalists, on the other hand, consider nationalism as a distraction at best, and at worst an un-Islamic identity. Azzam, for example, denounced nationalism as a relic of colonialism: "Unfortunately, when we think about Islam we think nationalistically. We fail to let our vision pass beyond geographic borders that have been drawn up for us by the *kuffar* [unbelievers]." Zawahiri recently lectured Muslims on the need "to highlight the concept of Islamic brotherhood and disown all partisanship, loyalties, and animosities based on nationalism."[36]

The Islamist revolutionaries' debate over nationalism eerily mirrors Western social-scientific debates on the same subject. For generations, social scientists considered nationalism to be the natural outgrowth of a community's ancient history, with as much of a distinct identity as an individual. Ernest Renan, an influential nineteenth-century scholar of nationalism, formulated a canonical version of this perspective. "The nation, like the individual, is the culmination of a long past of endeavours, sacrifice, and devotion," Renan wrote in a famous essay on the idea of the nation. "Of all cults, that of the ancestors is the most legitimate, for the ancestors have made us what we are." This view of the nation as an organic, long-lasting entity has come under challenge, however, as attention came to focus on the artificiality of modern national identities. According to this newer view, nationalist movements may claim the mantle of ancient ancestors, but these inheritances are recent inventions promoted by states and would-be states in order to create the appearance of authenticity and a spirit of national identity. Take France, for example. We tend to think of France as an old nation, since its borders have been more or less stable for centuries. But it was only in the nineteenth century that the French state sought to create a national identity. At that time, many residents of France did not speak French—they spoke mutually incomprehensible regional languages. They considered their *pays* (country) to mean their region, not France. To undermine these regional identities, the French state invented a shared genealogy by promoting the Gauls as supposed ancestors of the French, despite the fact that Gaul was itself an administrative entity created by foreign occupiers, the Romans, out of multiple political units that spoke multiple languages and practiced multiple customs. Gallic identity and French identity are modern creations.[37]

Similarly, Hamas's invocation of Palestine as a future state, with borders from the Jordan River to the Mediterranean Sea, mirrors secular nationalisms in claiming legitimacy through historical precedent. Al-Qaida's leaders—like Israeli and Western critics of Palestinian nationalism—point out that these boundaries were created by Europeans less than a century ago. Modern Palestine, the territory that Hamas aspires to rule, is based in large part on the boundaries drawn in 1916 by diplomats Mark Sykes of Great Britain and François Georges Picot of France, who negotiated an accord that divided the Levant into spheres of influence and out-right control. British forces implemented a modified version of these borders at the end of World War I, when they conquered the region from the Ottomans, despite the protests of many leading Palestinians, who debated among themselves whether Palestine should be a separate entity or annexed to Syria. Prior to World War I, the land that is now Israel and Palestine lay in three distinct administrative units, one in the south (part of the Hijaz region of Arabia), one in the middle (extending east into present-day Jordan) and one in the north (part of Beirut province in modern-day Lebanon). Palestinian identity has ancient precedents—centuries earlier, it had been an Ottoman province of its own, with similar boundaries as today, and Palestine was long considered by its residents to be a land with a distinct identity. Nevertheless, the emergence of a Palestinian national independence movement only dates from World War I and the Europeans' creation of separate countries and mandates in the Levant.[38]

Palestinian nationalism mirrored nationalist movements in other Muslim societies, which emerged in the second half of the nineteenth century (the same period as Zionist nationalism emerged). In all of these lands—as in most parts of the world—nationalist movements worked to link the borders that they aspired to control with ancient peoples and heritages: Egyptian national-ists claimed the mantle of the pharaohs, Iranian nationalists the Achaemenids, Israeli nationalists the ancient Jewish kingdoms, Lebanese nationalists the Phoenicians, Turkish nationalists the Hittites, and so on. These movements used archaeology, eth-nology, historiography, literature, museums, monuments, school-books, and other public representations of the national narrative to stress continuity from olden times through the present.[39]

Palestinian national liberation is something of a sacred cow for many Muslim leaders, but not for al-Qaida. Ayman Zawahiri, Bin Ladin's second-in-command, promised that globalists "will neither recognize the borders of Sykes-Picot nor the rulers whom colonialism put in place." Zawahiri also criticized Hamas's participation in parliamentary elections in 2006 and its consent to the Mecca Accord of 2007, recognizing the Palestinian constitution and the de facto borders of the Palestinian Authority. By 2008, Zawahiri sounded downright defensive in his response to questions submitted to an al-Qaida website. Only 5 percent of the 1,888 questions addressed Hamas and Palestine, but Zawahiri devoted most of his response to the subject. "Why do you intentionally direct sharply worded advice to Hamas through audio recordings?" one entry asked. "Why have you—to this day—not carried out any strike in Israel?" "Hamas is known for its Islamic slogans like 'Islam is the solution' and 'Allah is our objective and the Quran is our constitution.' So could you clarify what you mean by Hamas abandoning the right of the sharia to rule?" Zawahiri's response: "Why does the questioner focus on how al-Qaida in particular must strike in Israel, while he didn't request—for example—the jihadist organizations in Palestine to come to the aid of their brothers in Chechnya, Afghanistan, and Iraq?...I took a gradual approach with Hamas, from support to repeated advice to warning to general criticism, but when they signed the Makkah accord, frank criticism was a must. I took a gradual approach with them, but they didn't heed the opinion of their brothers and continued in what they had plunged into, from their entering the elections in compliance with the secular constitutions to their abandonment of their brothers in Chechnya and finishing up with their abandonment of four-fifths of Palestine in Makkah [that is, recognizing the borders of the Palestinian Authority in the Mecca Accord]." If Hamas's leadership persisted on this path, Zawahiri warned, its military wing should overthrow them. "Let loyalty to

Allah and His Messenger come before loyalty to the organization." Other globalists are less circumspect. The leader of al-Qaida in Iraq denounced Hamas as "traitors" in early 2008, and militant Islamist bulletin boards were full of similar deprecations. "May those despicable *ikhwani* [Muslim Brotherhood] apostate apes suffer destruction soon and be punished for their crimes," one posting read. "Hamas is after Israel the worst thing that could have happened to the Palestinians."[40]

In 2005, small groups began to emerge in Palestine that seemed to support al-Qaida's global vision rather than Hamas's territorial one. The most active of these groups, the Army of Islam, announced that it was not fighting for "a piece of land," but rather for a transnational Islamic caliphate. When Hamas entered the Palestinian government through a power-sharing agreement with the Palestine Liberation Organization in 2007, the Army of Islam sought to widen the Israeli-Palestinian conflict by kidnapping a British journalist. Hamas arrested several members of the group in an effort to release the hostage, and has been in a low-level conflict with the Gaza globalists ever since. During one crackdown in May 2008, Hamas forces ransacked a mosque where the globalists congregated. "Hamas represents an American style of Islam. They have tried to curry favor," one militant told a reporter. After another crackdown in September 2008, the Army of Islam issued two statements denouncing Hamas for killing innocents and true revolutionaries in its dictatorial attempt to impose "the law of the infidels."[41]

Globalists have engaged in similar competition with localists in Lebanon. Here the rivalry coincides with efforts to play up sectarian differences, since the main group of local Islamists, Hizbullah (the Party of God), is Shia and the globalists are Sunni. They have cooperated in the past. In the 1990s, al-Qaida militants appear to have requested and received Hizbullah training in car-bomb techniques, which they put to use in bloody attacks on U.S. embassies in Kenya and Tanzania in 1998. Over the past decade, however, the groups have largely been at odds, especially since al-Qaida's Sunni allies in Iraq responded to the U.S. occupation with grotesque sectarian violence against Iraqi Shia. In the summer of 2006, when Hizbullah fought a war with Israel and briefly rocketed to popularity among Sunni Muslims around the world, globalists debated whether to put aside their sectarian differences and state their support. Zawahiri issued a carefully worded statement that sympathized with "our brothers in Gaza and Lebanon" but never got around to congratulating or even mentioning Hamas or Hizbullah. Instead, he took the opportunity to repeat his opposition to national liberation movements and to "cease-fire, the Sykes-Picot Treaty agreements, patriotism, or disputed borders." The true battle, he insisted, is global: "jihad for the cause of God until the entire religion is for him only. Jihad seeks the liberation of Palestine, the entire country of Palestine and to liberate every land that used to be a territory of Islam, from Spain to Iraq. The entire world is an open field for us, so just like they attack us everywhere we will attack them everywhere, and just like they united to fight us, our *umma* [Muslim community], we will unite to fight them." More recently, as noted in chapter 2, Zawahiri blamed Hizbullah's television station, al-Manar, for conspiracy theories that denied al-Qaida's responsibility for the attacks of September 11.[42]

In the late 1980s, globalists established themselves in Ayn al-Hilwa, a Palestinian refugee camp in Lebanon, partnering with Abdullah Azzam's Pakistani operations in competition with various other Lebanese and Palestinian movements, which they accused of focusing too narrowly on territorial goals. In recent years, a new crop of veterans from the Iraqi insurgency has arrived in Lebanon, including several militants who have apparently tried to assassinate Hizbullah leaders. The most prominent organization of Lebanese globalists was a group called Victory of Islam, based in the Nahr al-Barid refugee camp and led by Shakir al-Absi, a college-educated Palestinian who had switched from secular leftist militancy to global Islamism after the Oslo peace accords. Thought to consist of a couple of hundred militants, Victory of Islam clashed with the Lebanese armed forces in May 2007 and was ultimately routed in a four-month military campaign that flattened much of the camp. Al-Absi apparently survived the assault and issued an audiotape the following year calling Lebanese Sunnis "traitors" in cahoots with the United States, the Palestinian Authority, Hizbullah, and Iran—an unlikely set of collaborators whose only common characteristic is their ill will toward Sunni Islamist militants. Al-Absi pledged to send suicide bombers to Lebanon and other countries to attack "God's enemies wherever they are." He and his remaining followers may have been behind an attack on a military bus in northern Lebanon that killed five soldiers in September 2008, as well as several other recent acts of violence.[43]

Global and local terrorist organizations are engaged in similar competitions in many countries. Some of the localists are neo-traditional, like the Taliban, and some are more modern, like Hizbullah, which developed the use of car bombs, and Hamas, which developed video testaments—two techniques that globalists later imitated. The modern movements compete for recruits among relatively well-educated youths, while the neo-traditionalists draw from a pool of recruits that is less educated and less cosmopolitan. These categories are not hard and fast. Nonetheless, they are real enough to remind us that Islamist terrorists are not all alike. Tensions between globalists and localists, modern-oriented movements and neo-traditional movements, form potential fissures that continually concern the terrorists, and that their opponents should work to exploit.

CHAPTER 4

༄

Liberal Islam versus Revolutionary Islamism

"Why do you suppose there are so few Muslim terrorists?" I asked a middle-aged Muslim businessman in Toronto, Canada. Hasan repeated the question to make sure that he had heard right. "Clever," he said. "Usually people ask the opposite." For years he had worked to help integrate local Muslim communities with the rest of Canadian society, participating in interfaith initiatives and getting involved in local politics. Well-meaning non-Muslims often confided their concerns to him: Why are so many Muslims angry with us? they would ask. Hasan had developed a pat set of responses: Colonialism. Islamophobia. Western support for Muslim dictators. Poverty and inequality. He would describe the efforts that he and other Muslims in Canada, and elsewhere, were making to counteract extremism. Hasan knew that I was familiar with all this. But he wasn't going to let me off the hook. "What do you mean by 'so few'? Do you expect Muslims to be terrorists? I don't know any Muslim terrorists. I don't know anybody who knows any Muslim terrorists. We are law-abiding people. We are not violent people. What will it take for everybody to realize that?"

It did not help that 18 young Canadian Muslims had been arrested in Toronto a few months earlier on charges of conspiracy to commit acts of terrorist violence, including the purchase of several tons of fertilizer to be used for explosives. "Canada is not immune to the threat of terrorism," the assistant commissioner of the Royal Canadian Mounted Police told a press conference, announcing the arrests. "This group posed a real and serious threat. It had the capacity and intent to carry out these attacks." News later emerged that the group had no access to real fertilizer. Its training camp was so lax that the group frequently ate at a nearby fast-food franchise in their camouflage fatigues, and one of the group's main organizers was a police informant. Nevertheless, despite the incompetence of the plot, it appears that some of the young people involved were willing to associate themselves with leaders who pledged violence to bring down "Rome" and told their followers that "we're not officially part of al-Qaeda, but we share their principles and methods."[1]

The response of Canada's Muslim organizations was to denounce violence. "Thank God these men were stopped before they could carry out their alleged plot," the Muslim Canadian Congress wrote in a press release. After a conviction was announced, the organization issued another press release to congratulate the judge, suggesting that a not-guilty verdict "would have been a huge victory for the world-wide jihadi movement." The Muslim Association of Canada called the arrests "welcome news" and reiterated its "firm belief that terrorism has no place in our world. Islam does not condone the use of violence against civilians. This position is widely shared by Muslim communities across Canada and the world. If indeed the allegations prove true, we must all redouble our efforts to ensure that our communities are free from such ideologies." A survey of 500 Canadian Muslims several months after the arrests found 73 percent of respondents calling the planned attacks "not at all justified" and 82 percent expressing no sympathy for violent plotters. Seventy-three percent of respondents described them-selves as "very proud" to be called Canadians.[2]

Similar responses emerge in the United States when Muslims are associated with terrorist plots: outrage, condemnation, and earnest pleas asking non-Muslims not to associate Islam with vio-lence. Many Americans ask why Muslims haven't denounced violence—*New York Times* columnist Thomas L. Friedman, for example, wrote in 2005 that "the Muslim village has been derelict in condemning the madness of jihadist attacks." Friedman appar-ently never got the memo from the Saudi Arabian government containing dozens of public statements by Saudi religious and political leaders denouncing violence against civilians (there really was such a memo, posted online by the Saudi embassy in Washington in 2004 as part of an effort to improve the kingdom's public relations in America). Friedman never saw the statements in Arabic and other languages by virtually every major Muslim religious leader in the world, condemning the attacks of September 11. He missed the unanimous and frequent statements by American Muslim organizations every time that a Muslim-American is arrested on suspicion of terrorism.[3]

Only a handful of tiny organizations in the United States pub-licly support violence—abroad, not in the United States. All of these groups are disgusted with their fellow Muslims, and espe-cially their religious leaders, for their lack of revolutionary fervor. Chief among these groups is the Islamic Thinkers Society, based in New York City. This group, which aims to establish a global caliphate, urges Muslim-Americans not to vote, on the grounds that democracy is a form of polytheism, and its website includes a banner that superimposes a mushroom cloud over the Israeli flag. The group denounces, by name, virtually every national Islamic organization in America, calling them unworthy because of their opposition to Islamist revolution: "As the events on the War on Terrorism unfold, we see the behavior of so-called Muslim organizations and their spiritually impotent and politically retarded 'leadership' come to life. These Muslim organizations, who never respond nor issue a fatwa and demand an apology when Muslims are being butchered by the Crusaders & Zionists, respond in a lightning fast manner and condemn terrorist acts when their masters at the White House tell them to." The accusation is false—American Muslim organizations almost always demand an apology when Muslims are victimized, to the point that they seem like broken records. In any case, surveys of American Muslims show that a huge majority side with the views of mainstream organizations rather than with the views of the Islamic Thinkers Society.[4]

Around the world, too, most Muslims are far less interested in Islamist revolution than in liberal Islam. By liberal Islam, I mean movements that espouse key ideals of the Western liberal tradition, such as democracy, human rights, social equality, and tolerance—but that approach these ideals through a distinctly Islamic discourse, not just borrowing Western discourses. When I edited an anthology of influential liberal Muslim thinkers a decade ago, some of my friends joked that this was going to be a short book. Fortunately, I didn't need to pad the volume in order to prove them wrong. Almost every Muslim society around the world has generated a significant body of liberal Islamic thought, along with social and political movements aiming to turn these ideas into reality. Not all of these movements call themselves "liberal"—in fact, some of them actively dislike the term, which they associate with the hypocrisy of Western imperialists who claimed to be agents of "liberalism" even as they suppressed their subjects' liberties.[5]

Regardless of what label we apply to them, these liberal Islamic movements have been active for more than a century and have undergone a renaissance over the past two decades. They represent a significant challenge to Islamist terrorists, who loathe them for it.

The pioneers of liberal Islam were Ottoman intellectuals of the mid-nineteenth century who asked why European Christian societies were becoming so much more powerful than Muslim societies and who concluded that the answer lay in Europe's emerging liberalism. Khayr al-Din, an Ottoman official in Tunisia, was among the first to put these ideas in print. He had been educated in traditional Islamic subjects, but he also had a modern military training and was sent on government missions throughout Europe. His treatise on governance, published in Arabic in 1867 and translated into Urdu in 1875 and Turkish in 1879, is a remarkable document. "Liberty is the basis of the great development of knowledge and civilization in the European kingdoms," Khayr al-Din concluded. "The expression 'liberty' is used by Europeans in two senses. One is called 'personal liberty.' This is the individual's complete freedom of action over one's self and property, and the protection of one's person, honor, and wealth. Each is equal before the law to others of the race, so that no individuals need fear encroachment upon their person nor any of their other rights. They would not be prosecuted for anything not provided for in the laws of the land, duly determined before the courts. In general, the laws bind both the rulers and the subjects." But this is not sufficient for a nation to progress without a second form of liberty, "political liberty, which is the demand of the subjects to participate in the politics of the kingdom and to discuss the best course of action." In addition, Khayr al-Din wrote, there was a third form of liberty, "which is called freedom of the press, that is, people cannot be prevented from writing what seems to them to be in the public interest, in books or newspapers which can be read by the public. Or they can present their views to the state or the chambers, even if this includes opposition to the state's policy." This was very liberal stuff for the nineteenth century.[6]

Europe had a head start on the path toward liberalism, Khayr al-Din argued, but nothing prevented Muslims from leapfrogging into the lead, since liberalism was part of the original heritage of Islam. In the view of Khayr al-Din and other liberal Muslims, the institutions associated with Europe's military and industrial power happened to coincide with the original principles of Islam. By adopting these institutions, according to the liberals, Muslims would simultaneously join the "civilized world" and return to the proper practice of Islam. On the subject of democratic governance, for example, did not the Quran require the Prophet Muhammad to "seek counsel" (chapter 3, verse 159)? Muhammad did not need counsel, "since he received inspiration directly from God, and also because of the many perfections which God had placed in him"—so the only reason for such a requirement must have been to set a precedent that would be "incumbent upon later rulers." Muhammad's most illustrious successors obeyed this principle of consultation, according to Khayr al-Din. He quoted the story of Umar, the second caliph, announcing to his followers, "Let him among you who sees any deviation in me set it right." A man stood up and said, "By God, if we saw in you deviation we would rectify it with our swords." Umar praised God in thanks—just as all Muslim rulers should praise God for oversight by their subjects, Khayr al-Din proposed.

Liberal Islam was a radical idea in the Ottoman Empire of the nineteenth century, but Khayr al-Din was himself no radical. He was an appointee of the Ottoman sultan and was sufficiently trusted that he was later promoted to governor of Tunisia and then—briefly—prime minister of the entire empire. He and other liberal Muslims of the nineteenth century believed that liberalism would strengthen their monarchies, not undermine them. Liberal rule was supposed to heighten their subjects' loyalty, promote social solidarity, and unleash economic development, but it never had a chance to try. Khayr al-Din and his liberal colleagues were unable to implement their ideas in any lasting way—the Ottoman monarchy was too jealous of its prerogatives to allow more than fleeting reforms.

However, a network of intellectuals began to espouse similar views, not just in the Ottoman Empire but in many Muslim societies. Liberal Islamic newspapers published in Cairo and Istanbul were read eagerly in Singapore and Malabar and Sarajevo, where they spawned local offshoots. Major liberal Islamic movements emerged in North India, Tatarstan, and elsewhere. The audience for liberal Islam multiplied with the establishment of modern schools, both secular public schools and reformist madrasas that incorporated natural and social sciences. By the first decade of the twentieth century, a new generation of educated young Muslims felt ready to put liberal Islam into practice.

The first movement to do so was in the Russian Empire, where Muslims participated alongside Christians and Jews in the constitutional revolution of 1905, forcing the tsar to hold elections, convene parliament, and recognize his subjects' basic freedoms. "Have Muslims no need for freedom and justice?" one of the many newly established Muslim-owned newspapers asked rhetorically. Certainly they do, the newspaper answered, and that is why Muslims have agitated actively for these ideals. Liberal Muslim leaders from around the Russian Empire convened three times to organize support for the democracy movement and the new parliament, as well as to propose legal and social reforms within the Muslim communities of Russia. "Long live freedom!" the delegates shouted at the end of the third conference.[7]

More constitutional revolutions soon followed in Iran (1906) and the Ottoman Empire (1908), where liberal Muslims again helped to foist constitutions, elections, and press freedoms on reluctant monarchs. Two of the leading Shia scholars of the era blessed the reforms in a famous telegram that equated Islamic rule with liberal rule: "We would like to know if it would be possible to execute Islamic provisions without a constitutional regime!" The shaykh al-Islam in Istanbul, the chief religious authority of the Ottoman Empire, appointed directly by the caliph, also spoke on behalf of constitutionalism. "These matters under discussion are basically in accord with the principles of sharia," he told a crowd on the day that the constitution was announced. "Our king has also accepted this as necessary and society's wish has been realized. For this reason, the establishment of the constitution is definitive, and from now on its removal will in no way be possible."[8]

Many Muslims greeted these new freedoms enthusiastically. In Ottoman Jerusalem, for example, a crowd estimated at 40,000—larger than the permanent population of the city—gathered for a public proclamation by the governor, who described the scene poetically: "The voices of joy in the city of Jerusalem, which has no equal in the world to the contrast of religions, sects, and races in it, were raised to the heavens in a thousand languages and styles. Speeches were given. Hands were shaken. Pleasant tunes were played. In short, the proper things were expressed for the honor of liberty." A Jewish resident of the Jerusalem district concurred: "The news of the re-establishment of the Constitution was realized everywhere with an enthusiastic joy. There are meetings taking place all over the streets, where the charms of freedom are praised. Speakers orate in the public places, and threaten with all the powers of the heavens and the earth those who would make an attempt against the constitution." Copycat constitutionalist movements emerged in the Central Asian kingdoms of Afghanistan, Bukhara, and Khiva.[9]

Liberal Islam had its opponents, of course. It was easily crushed by the emir of Afghanistan and the khans of Bukhara and Khiva, while the shah of Iran and the Ottoman sultan schemed with conservative Islamic movements to regain absolute power. In Iran, Shaykh Fazlullah Nuri, a prominent scholar in Tehran, proclaimed the constitution un-Islamic: "If any Muslim attempts to bring about constitutionalism among us Muslims, such actions undermine the religion and such a person is an apostate." Derviş Vahdeti, the founder of an Islamist movement in the Ottoman Empire, denounced liberal Muslims as atheistic "cucumber people": "To expect religion from those who don't know their religion and have no Islamic training is like extracting oil from a cucumber." Nuri and Vahdeti both led uprisings to abolish the constitution. In Iran and the Ottoman Empire, the Islamists succeeded, for a time. But it was not ultimately the Islamists who defeated liberal Islam in the early twentieth century. Nuri and Vahdeti's uprisings were suppressed and both men were executed. The reactionary monarchs they supported were dethroned in favor of more pliant relatives. Parliament reconvened but was soon undermined definitively by a new form of illiberalism: military dictators. Martial law replaced the brief democratic experiments in both Iran and the Ottoman Empire.[10]

Liberal Islam revived after World War I with the demand for democratic constitutions in the new nations that gained independence from the old imperial order. The Egyptian revolution of 1919, for example, involved millions of Muslims, as well as Coptic Christians and other minorities, who participated in massive demonstrations and months of general strikes, seeking not just independence from Britain but also a democratic constitution. They got both—only to have parliament and elections undermined by the monarchy and the military, as in so many countries around the world at the time, Islamic and otherwise.

Again after World War II, as European colonies around the world won independence, liberal Islamic movements sought democratic institutions and freedoms. In Pakistan, which was invented in the mid-twentieth century as a homeland for South Asian Muslims, liberal movements pressed for a constitution that would both allow majority rule through parliamentary elections and protect the rights of minorities. In the first years of independence, the liberals had the upper hand. At the newly founded United Nations, Pakistan's representative was a vocal proponent of the Universal Declaration of Human Rights. In

Pakistan, the Constituent Assembly, that was convened in order to write a constitution for the country passed an Objectives Resolution committing itself to democracy, freedom, tolerance, and other liberal goals, while preserving the right of Muslims and other communities to practice their religions in their private lives. By the mid-1950s, however, military leaders and Islamist movements had begun to undermine these objectives. The constitution of 1956 incorporated the Objectives Resolution but hedged its commitments with provisions that privileged conservative interpretations of Islam; in 1958, the first of many coups abrogated the constitution, beginning a cycle of military and civilian rule that has dogged Pakistan to this day.

Coups in the 1950s and 1960s cut short democratic interludes in Egypt and Indonesia, as well as Pakistan and other Muslim societies—part of the global wave of dictatorships that consumed so many newly independent countries, Muslim and non-Muslim, during that period. Liberal Islamic movements struggled for the next several decades against secular ideologies such as socialism and nationalism, as well as illiberal Islamism. When liberal Islam burst back onto the scene at the end of the twentieth century, it had evolved into a new, more theologically powerful form.

The earliest forms of liberal Islam proposed that liberal ideals were a divine mandate required by the sacred sources of Islam, if properly understood. This was Khayr al-Din's approach, and it continues to dominate liberal Islamic movements. It is common, today, to see liberal Islamic treatises explaining how the Quranic injunction to "seek counsel" means that democracy is the most appropriate form of government for Muslims. These treatises tend to reinvent the wheel. They rarely cite the century and a half of earlier arguments on the subject, dating back to Khayr al-Din, Turkish liberal Namık Kemal, and Indian liberal Sayyid Ahmad Khan in the 1860s.

However, this is not the only approach to the subject. A second form of liberal Islam emerged in the 1920s, proposing that liberalism is not required by revelation, but rather permitted by revelation. The sacred sources are silent on some issues, not because revelation is incomplete—that would be blasphemous—but rather because God has left these subjects for humans to decide for themselves, in accordance with the needs and values of the age. Ali Abd al-Raziq, an Egyptian pioneer of this second form, made the case that government falls into this category. His famous treatise, *Islam and the Basis of Government* (1925), challenged Muslims to find verses from the Quran or statements of the Prophet Muhammad that indicate what form of government Muslims should adopt. "Look between the two covers of the Quran for open or latent evidence supporting those who think that the Islamic religion has a political character, and then look for evidence, as hard as you can, among the *hadiths* [reports] of the Prophet, peace be upon him—these pure sources of religion which are within your hands, close to you. If you were to look in them for evidence or anything resembling it, you will find no proof, only guesses, and guessing does not replace Truth." Instead, Abd al-Raziq quoted dozens of verses in the Quran stating that Muhammad's primary role was that of a messenger, not a ruler: "We have not appointed you their guardian.... We have not sent you as warden over them.... It is not for you to compel them.... You are only a bearer of warnings.... We have sent you only as a bearer of good tidings and admonisher for all mankind." Abd al-Raziq urged readers "not to confuse the two kinds of governments, and not to conflate the two kinds of trusteeships—the trusteeship of the Messenger, on account of his being a messenger, and the trusteeship of powerful kings." Muhammad's authority stemmed from his prophethood, while the authority of twentieth-century governments stemmed from worldly power. "The former is a religious leadership, the latter a political one—and there is much distance between politics and religion." This distance is precisely what Islamists deny. Abd al-Raziq was fired from the faculty at al-Azhar, the ancient seminary in Cairo, for expressing these views.[11]

Liberal Islam took another interpretive leap in the 1990s. Instead of identifying particular subjects that the sacred sources left open to human devising, this new form of liberal Islam emphasized the inherently human and fallible nature of understanding *all* the sacred sources. The writers and activists who developed this approach were not, at first, aware of each others' work. In Egypt, Hassan Hanafi wrote, "There is no one interpretation of a text, but there are many interpretations given the difference in understanding between various interpreters. An interpretation of a text is essentially pluralistic." Amina Wadud-Muhsin, an American writing in Malaysia at the time, argued that "when one individual reader with a particular world-view and specific prior text [the language and cultural context in which the text is read] asserts that his or her reading is the only possible or permissible one, it prevents readers in different contexts from coming to terms with their own relationship to the text." Abdullahi An-Na'im of the Sudan, writing in the United States, suggested that "there is no such thing as the only possible or valid understanding of the Quran, or conception of Islam, since each is informed by the individual and collective orientation of Muslims." Rusmir Mahmutćehajić of Bosnia concluded, "No institution or group of believers has the exclusive right to 'understand' and 'interpret' a faith and its origins." "Among the freedoms of the individual, the freedom to think and to express opinions are the most valuable," insisted Nurcholish Madjid of Indonesia. "Perhaps it was not entirely small talk when our Prophet said that differences of opinion among his umma [community] were a mercy [from God]."[12]

One of the leading figures in this intellectual movement is Abdolkarim Soroush of Iran, a former revolutionary whose disillusionment with the Islamic Republic made him persona non grata in his homeland. He was fired from his university position, banned from radio and television, and blocked by thugs from giving public lectures, all for suggesting that the ruling interpretation of Islam in Iran was not the only possible interpretation. "Religion is divine, but its interpretation is thoroughly human and this-worldly," Soroush proclaimed. "The text does not stand alone, it does not carry its own meaning on its shoulders, it needs to be situated in a context, it is theory-laden, its interpretation is in flux, and presuppositions are as actively at work here as elsewhere in the field of understanding. Religious texts are no exception. Therefore their interpretation is subject to expansion and contraction according to the assumptions preceding them and/or the questions enquiring them."[13]

Soroush became the guru of the reform movement that sought to liberalize the theocracy in Iran. Muhammad Khatami, the smiling cleric who won the presidency of Iran in a landslide in 1997, was the movement's political leader, but Soroush was the intellectual spark. His essays were copied and discussed all over Iran, even by young religious scholars in the seminaries of Qom. Some of these seminarians pursued similar approaches in their own speeches and writings, earning themselves trials at a Special Clergy Court set up to punish wayward clerics. Abdullah Nuri, an outspoken reformist cleric and an aide to President Khatami, summarized his defense statement in 17 points that are worth reproducing in whole:

1. No fallible human can claim to be the only one in possession of the truth.
2. Religious knowledge is relative, and various and diverse readings of religion are entirely possible.
3. Piety, without reluctance and compulsion, will bring to pass the sublime realization of the essence of religion, that is, faith and religious experience.

4. There is no red line limiting the debate of perspectives and political problems, except that which is expressly specified and designated by the Constitution. No official is immune to criticism and questioning.

5. Iran belongs to all Iranians, and securing citizens' fundamental rights is their divine and legal right. Dialogue among all social forces is imperative and necessary.

6. Within the framework of religious law, [civil] law, and morality, diverse ways of life are imaginable and possible. Nobody can or should, in the name of religious law, impose his way of life on others and consider it definitive.

7. Cultural rights are among the fundamental rights of citizens. Cultured persons have a variety of views and tastes. A univocal monopoly of culture is neither possible nor desirable.

8. Cultural circles are completely independent of politics. Cultured persons and their viewpoints cannot be opposed on the basis of political affiliations and tastes.

9. The legal order of society and the relations between citizens and government are based on the people's right to rule.

10. The establishment of security and stability in society is not possible or practical without the recognition of the rights of the opposition.

11. No single group should consider the country as its own. Efforts should be made to convert even radical oppositionists into legal oppositionists.

12. The standards and criteria for debates over society and politics are the security and interests of the nation, not the security and interests of any particular group.

13. Abrogation of freedom is the sign of a government's weakness, not its strength.

14. The increase and deepening of respectful emotional ties among citizens, and the spread of solidarity and familiarity

between the government and the people, are requisites for the stability and survival of society and government.

15. A spirit of freshness, joy, and liveliness is the secret to the health, survival, and flourishing of society.

16. Flattery and sycophancy will lead to the deterioration of humanitarian values and the destruction of the foundations of the regime. In view of this, propagation and reverence of such things as "critique and protest," which tend to promote the legitimacy and strength of the political regime, are of urgent necessity. Based on this premise, it is the government's duty to banish the sycophants and praise the critics, not vice versa.

17. Detente with all the states and nations of the world, based on national interests and the civilizational dialogue, is essential in all fields.

Nuri was convicted. Yet his defense statement, published as a book just after his conviction, sold out 10,000 copies in a few hours. I was in Tehran that day and couldn't find a copy to buy.[14]

During its heyday, the Iranian reform movement helped encourage liberal Muslim activists around the world, just as the Iranian Revolution had spurred revolutionaries two decades earlier. A network of transnational activism developed around international conferences such as those organized by the Islam 21 group in London, the Center for the Study of Islamic and Democracy in Washington, the Liberal Islam Network in Indonesia, Musawah in Malaysia, the Asian Muslim Action Network in Thailand, as well as a host of academic organizations. In 1990, it is a good guess that few of the leading liberal Islamic thinkers in the world had ever met each other. By 2000, they had probably all met. It is hard to tell for sure who has read what, because there is very little cumulative citation in contemporary Islamic scholarship, but there was an active translation industry at work, so that Soroush could be read in Arabic, Indonesian, Turkish, and other languages of Muslim societies, as well as in English. I am proud to have played a bit part in this process by publishing Soroush's first essay in English.[15]

Western observers sometimes dismiss liberal Muslim thinkers and activists as elite and unpopular Westernizers. "[I]f the radicals have major problems competing with the traditionalists, the liberal Muslims are in the worst situation of all," according to one expert. Two American specialists agreed in a recent debate that liberal movements are still "embryonic" in Arab societies and that "liberal elites are not proving to be successful opinion leaders in their own communities." According to one particularly unsympathetic Western account, the work of Soroush and similar thinkers forms "the nadir of man's attempt to grapple with the divine," an inauthentic vision of Islamic authority that is "cavorting" with American imperialism. Expert pessimism about the potential for Islamic liberalism has a long heritage in the West. In the early twentieth century, for example, an American Orientalist concluded from his pathbreaking study of modern Islamic movements that they were basically futile, and "we need not expect much to result in the way of uplift to Islam."[16]

But what do Muslims think? A quarter-century ago, when the Islamic Republic of Iran was freshly triumphant from its popular overthrow of Shah Mohammad Reza Pahlavi, attitudes may have been different. We don't have systematic survey evidence from that period, but the Iranian model clearly inspired cadres of Muslims around the world, even Sunni Muslims, notwithstanding the Shia specificities of the Iranian revolutionary movement. Islamist activists from Southeast Asia to West Africa visited Iran to express their solidarity and learn from its example, and the writings of Imam Ruhollah Khomeini were translated from Persian into Arabic and other languages. In London, *Crescent International*, the self-described "newsmagazine of the Islamic movement," crowed that the Iranian Revolution foreshadowed a global transformation: "It is quite clear that the two civilizations, that of Islam and the West, are on a collision course. This is a fight only one can win." The following year, Middle East historian Bernard Lewis repeated the theme, which he had been sounding for decades: "This is no less than a clash of civilizations—that perhaps irrational but surely historic [Islamic] reaction of an ancient rival against our Judeo-Christian heritage." Political scientist Samuel Huntington popularized the "clash of civilizations" three years later—not that he advocated conflict the way that *Crescent International* did. For all this clash-talk, there was relatively little clashing. In the 1980s, transnational Islamic terrorism accounted for half as many incidents as transnational leftist terrorism. The most active Islamist revolutionary movement of the period—the Afghan mujahidin—was not directed against the West and its allies, but in *collaboration* with the West against the Soviet occupation of Afghanistan.[17]

By the time that Islamist terrorism began to take off in the 1990s, with vicious cycles of government repression and revolutionary violence in Algeria, Egypt, and several other countries, the Iranian model was widely considered a failure. Even *Crescent International* expressed its disillusionment, though softened with hopeful sympathies:

> [T]he expectations which people had for an Islamic state which was bound to be embryonic and experimental, as well as being subjected to the most venomous hatred and enmity by the west, were not reasonable. Not all officials of the state can be expected to share the qualities of the Imam [Khomeini] himself. Having said that, in terms of nationalism and sectarianism in particular, too many have failed to maintain even minimum standards. However, as long as the understanding and vision of the leadership remains sound and unwavering, Iran will remain the leading edge of the Islamic movement, thanks to the momentum generated by the Imam's unique leadership, and that of [Khomeini's successor,] Ayatullah Sayyid Ali Khamenei.[18]

Other Sunni Islamist revolutionaries were less forgiving. "After the triumph of the Iranian Revolution in the late 1970s, Muslims east and west rejoiced and thought that the dawn of Islam had arisen anew," an anonymous author recalled in a 2008 al-Qaida magazine article. "But alas, the lies, deceit, and deception soon became apparent." Still others simply rejected the Islamic Republic of Iran because it was Shia. In 1994, as al-Qaida began to organize itself, Ayman Zawahiri denounced the government of Iran as "rafidiyya," a common Sunni slur against the Shia that means "rejectionist," or those who refuse to accept legitimate Muslim authorities.[19]

Few Muslims espoused Sunni visions of an Islamic state, either. The image of the Taliban regime in Afghanistan shutting girls' schools and banning the Internet probably offended even more Muslims than had been disillusioned by the Iranian Revolution. Disgust with the Taliban did not translate into support for the U.S. invasion to overthrow them—only 2 to 19 percent of Muslims in nine countries considered the U.S. invasion of Afghanistan morally justifiable, according to a Gallup survey in late 2001 and early 2002. But almost no Muslims wanted Taliban-style rule in their own countries.[20]

At the turn of the millennium, as we begin to get reliable surveys of Muslim attitudes in many countries, Muslims appear to be sympathetic to the idea of Islamic governance in principle, but not in practice. The World Values Survey, the first major cross-national sample to include Muslim-majority countries, asked whether Muslims thought that "good government...should implement only the laws of the sharia." A large percentage agreed, from 44 percent in Bangladesh and 50 percent in Indonesia to 62 percent in Pakistan, 72 percent in Algeria, 79 percent in Jordan, and 80 percent in Egypt. An even broader sample surveyed by the Gallup Organization also found majorities or near-majorities in dozens of Muslim societies favoring the implementation of sharia, though only a handful of countries said sharia should be the sole source of legislation.[21]

These pro-sharia responses may be symbolic gestures of Islamic identity rather than deep-seated political opinions. When the question is posed in a different way, the results come out opposite. A 2007 survey by the Pew Global Attitudes Project asked whether "religion is a matter of personal faith and should be kept separate from government policy." Majorities in 13 out of 14 Muslim societies agreed—only in Jordan were the responses slightly under 50 percent. In any case, these surveys did not ask directly what respondents meant by sharia—whether seminary-trained Islamic scholars would run the judiciary and approve legislation, for example, and if so, who would choose which seminarians would be in charge.[22]

However, we do have direct questions about democracy, and it is clear from the responses that Muslims support majority rule even more widely than they support the ideals of sharia. Numerous surveys over the past decade have documented a large, and largely unmet, demand for democracy among Muslims. For example, the World Values Survey and a variety of subsequent polls have asked respondents whether they agreed or disagreed with the statement, "Democracy may have problems, but it's better than any other form of government." More than three-quarters of Muslims agreed—the same rate as non-Muslims who were asked the same question. This included 71 percent of Saudi citizens, 83 percent of Palestinians, and 85 percent of Afghans. In countries with mixed Muslim and non-Muslim populations, such as Bosnia, Kazakhstan, and Nigeria, the rate of Muslims who supported democracy was equivalent to or higher than the rate of non-Muslims. Even among respondents who supported sharia, a majority agreed that democracy was the best form of government. The Pew Global Attitude Project's survey of eight Muslim-majority countries in 2002 found far more respondents agreeing that "democracy is not just for the West and can work well here" than those who felt that "democracy is a Western way of doing things that would not work here." (Oddly, only in Turkey were these responses equal—the same year that Turks voted a pro-democracy Islamic party into office.) Even among respondents who told Pew that Islam should play a very large role in political life, a majority agreed that democracy would work well in their country.[23]

Compare these views with Islamist revolutionaries' positions on democracy. According to Ayman Zawahiri, "Whoever labels himself as a Muslim democrat or a Muslim who calls for democracy is like saying he is a Jewish Muslim or a Christian Muslim." Democracy, in Zawahiri's view, is "a new religion to allow God-like men to legislate for themselves... versus the religion of God that gave the right of legislation to God and God alone." Abu Yahya al-Libi, another leading figure in al-Qaida, called Muslim participation in elections part of the Crusaders' strategy to undermine Islam. By "strengthening and backing some of the methodologies adopted by Islamic movements far removed from jihad, particularly those with a democratic approach," the West hopes "to isolate the mujahidin inside their societies." Not all Islamist revolutionaries agree with this hostility toward democracy—Hamas, for example, decided to engage in electoral politics as a peaceful route toward sharia and was denounced by al-Qaida and other revolutionary groups as a result. A Syrian revolutionary recently declared that Yusuf al-Qaradawi, one of the most influential Islamic scholars of the present era, is an apostate because he supports democratic elections (and for other reasons as well, such as his fatwa against the attacks of 9/11).[24]

Given a choice between Islamist revolution and democratic elections, Muslims overwhelmingly prefer democracy. Take the example of the country with the most Muslims, Indonesia. A revolutionary movement there called Lashkar Jihad—"Army of Jihad"—has consistently denounced democracy as un-Islamic. "Those who agree with general elections and are active in them have positioned themselves as the enemies of Islam," a leader of the Lashkar Jihad movement in Indonesia wrote in 1999, the same year as Indonesia's first democratic elections in more than a generation. During that generation, virtually all Muslim intellectuals in the country defended the principle of democracy, even Islamic scholars who felt that popular sovereignty ought to respect the sovereignty of God. The sole legal Islamic party of the period, the United Development Party, participated in the partially competitive elections that President Suharto permitted, earning 15 to 29 percent of the vote. Yet its ideological constituency may have been far larger. According to a survey in 2002, 71 percent of Indonesians agreed that "the government must make obligatory the implementation of sharia." Sixty-seven percent agreed that "government based on the Quran and sunna [the precedent of the first Muslims] under the leadership of Islamic authorities such as kiai [a Southeast Asian term for religious leaders] or ulama, is best for a country like ours." At the same time, only 46 percent agreed that "in elections we must choose the candidate who fights for the implementation of sharia." A full 21 percent agreed that "in elections there should only be Islamic parties." So how did Indonesians behave when given free political choices after democratization in 1998? While Lashkar Jihad railed against democracy, most Muslims in Indonesia rushed in the other direction, forming political parties and engaging enthusiastically in the democratic process. Six new self-consciously Islamic parties emerged to run for seats in the Indonesian parliament, along with dozens of other parties. With remarkably high voter turnout, the United Development Party dropped to 11 percent in 1999, then 8 percent in 2004, then 5 percent in 2009, while a new liberal Islamic party committed to toleration and democracy, Abdurrahman Wahid's National Awakening Party, earned 17 percent in 1999. Several hard-line Islamist parties won only 1 to 3 percent of the vote. From the first free parliamentary election in 1999 to the third in 2009, the percentage of votes for Islamic parties of any sort had dropped by more than a quarter.[25]

Election results are similar in other Muslim societies. When Islamic parties run for parliament, they are rarely successful. Not all of these elections are fully free, to be sure, but it is striking that in more than 80 elections in Muslim societies over the past generation, Islamic parties do worse in the freest elections than in less-free elections. Overall, most Islamic parties won less than 15 percent of seats, and only once has an Islamic party won an outright majority of votes: the Islamic Salvation Front in Algeria, which led an opposition coalition against the ruling socialist party in 1991 and swept the first round of parliamentary voting with more than 80 percent of seats. The Algerian government then declared martial law and canceled the election, sparking a gruesome civil war. According to numerous observers, the Islamic Salvation Front won such a large percent of the vote only because its leader, Abbassi Madani, was able to convince Algerians that he was committed to multiparty pluralism. "We are Muslims, but we are not Islam itself," Madani declared. "We do not monopolize religion. Democracy as we understand it means pluralism, choice, and freedom." Voters appear to have believed Madani more than they believed the party's second-ranking leader, Ali Belhadj, who took a much more critical view of democracy even as he participated in a democratic electoral campaign: "The democratic idea is one of a number of pernicious intellectual innovations that has obsessed the consciousness of some people. To the contrary, for us, in Islam, freedom is tied to obedience to the sharia and not to the [man-made] law." In 2002, the World Values Survey found that 88 percent of its sample in Algeria favored democracy, including 86 percent of respondents who said they supported government implementation of sharia.[26]

Elsewhere, too, given a choice, Muslim voters almost always prefer more-democratic Islamic parties to less-democratic ones. In Iran, reformist politicians received more than double the votes of their opponents until the Guardian Council barred most of the reformist members of parliament from running for reelection. In Bangladesh, the Jamaat-e-Islami won six or more times as many votes as the Islamic Unity Front and other more radical Islamist movements. In Turkey, the Justice and Development Party received 13 or more times as many votes as the more staunchly Islamist Felicity Party. In Iraq, the United Iraqi Alliance and other Shia parties outpulled Muqtada Sadr's list of more militant candidates. Almost the only exception is Kuwait, where Salafi movements have won slightly more seats than the more liberal Islamic Constitutional Movement in recent parliamentary elections, though still only a fifth or less of the total number of seats in the Kuwaiti parliament.[27]

In response to voter preferences, Islamic parties have become more liberal over time, sociologist Ijlal Naqvi and I found when we analyzed 48 Islamic party platforms from the past generation. Platforms do not necessarily represent the true positions of these parties, but they are part of the public face that the parties believe will appeal to voters. This public face shifted significantly during the 1990s. Prior to that time, most of the platforms we were able to locate favored the implementation of sharia and made some mention of jihad; half or fewer of the platforms adopted these positions since that time. Platforms are more likely in recent years to mention democracy, the rights of women, and the rights of minorities than in earlier years. Among the dozen Islamic parties for which we located two or more platforms at different points in time, we also detected shifts toward more liberal positions. Half of the parties that originally supported government implementation of sharia, for example, dropped that position in later platforms, and no party added that position. More than half of the parties that originally referred to jihad removed any mention of the subject in later platforms. Other parties added or strengthened their statements in defense of democracy and women's rights. One of the few Islamic parties to shift in the opposite direction was the

Muslim Brotherhood in Egypt, whose later platforms downgraded women's rights.[28]

This single exception is worth exploring. Women's rights have long been used as a litmus test for the liberalism of liberal Islam, and Islamic parties know that their positions on women's rights will be scrutinized more intensely than almost another aspect of their platforms. The Egyptian Muslim Brotherhood did not consider it necessary to mention women's rights at all in its 1987 platform; by 1995, the party had added assurances that women's civil, criminal, and financial status are equal to those of men, and that women have the right to vote and serve in government, with the exception of the caliphate or a similar post, should such a position ever be established. The party's platform in 2000 reiterated these positions but also "clarified"—that is, watered down—its position by defending "the superiority of the husband over the wife" within family matters. The party's 2005 platform began to hedge on women's right to work: they have this right, the party suggested, but only within the limits of "honor and dignity." In 2007, the party drafted a new platform that went further in this direction. The draft argued that a woman cannot serve as president of Egypt because this role would "contradict her nature and her other social and human roles." More generally, the draft warned against "imposing duties" on any woman "that contradict her nature or her role in the family." The liberal wing of the Muslim Brotherhood objected to these and other controversial elements, and the draft was never adopted as a formal platform. These changes were not nearly enough for the revolutionaries, of course. Al-Qaida devoted seven pages to a point-by-point critique of the Muslim Brotherhood's draft platform, all of which boiled down to the basic point that the Brotherhood was still committed to playing by the rules of the Egyptian constitution and was therefore not properly "Islamic."[29]

Yet the Muslim Brotherhood's positions on the role of women may match the attitudes of many Muslims. The Brotherhood distinguishes between equal political and legal rights for women, which it continues to support (with the exception of a female president), and the social and cultural role of women, which it feels should reside primarily in the home. Many Muslims agree. In the World Values Survey, for example, more than two-thirds of Muslims responded that "when jobs are scarce, men should have more right to a job than a woman," while less than a third of non-Muslims agreed. These views are part of a broader chasm on the issue of gender relations. Eighty-nine percent of Muslims said they disapprove of a woman having a child as a single parent, compared with 42 percent of non-Muslims. Two-thirds of Muslims, both male and female, felt that it is important for women to wear *hijab*—modest garb, defined in most Muslim societies as a headscarf and long, loose garments—in public places. But Muslims' conservative opinions on gender roles did not translate into illiberal politics—more than 80 percent of these respondents also said they supported democracy. Similarly, a Gallup poll of 10 Muslim societies found that a majority in each country felt women should be allowed to vote, hold cabinet-level government positions, and work outside the home, though few women listed gender equality as one of the most important issues facing their country. A Pew survey of 17 Muslim publics found majorities in all of them favoring equal education for boys and girls, and majorities in all but one (Muslim respondents in predominantly Christian Ethiopia) saying that women should have the right to decide whether to wear a veil, while significant numbers also felt that workplaces should be at least partially segregated by gender.[30]

At the same time, Islamic women's movements have emerged in virtually every Muslim society to challenge male domination. These movements often oppose the import of Western feminisms, which they see as un-Islamic. The issues that animate these movements are not cultural practices like *hijab*, which so upsets Westerners. These movements see *hijab* as an expression of personal or societal piety, and for some even a sign of women's empowerment to go about modestly in public. Once they are out in public, these movements take on issues such as state repression, domestic abuse, and the right to leadership positions in the government and within Islamist organizations. Islamist women's movements believe that a democratically selected sharia-based state would be better protection than an undemocratically selected secular state in defending women's rights—not necessarily the same set of rights that Western women emphasize, but a challenge nonetheless to patriarchal patterns.[31]

The dual ideals of sharia and democracy seem to be reconciled, for many Muslims, through a combination of political liberalism and cultural conservatism. The complexities of this combination are visible in a Pew survey that asked Muslims in a dozen countries whether "there is only one true interpretation of the teachings of Islam," or whether "Islam should tolerate diverse interpretations of its teachings." The only sample to side with diverse interpretations was Indonesia, at 54 percent. Interestingly, two of the countries with the lowest support for pluralism were Turkey and Uzbekistan, where the state is explicitly secular (even with a liberal Islamist party in office in Turkey) and hostile to Islamic radicalism, where alcohol consumption is public and widespread, and where radicals are decidedly unpopular. The samples in these two countries were among the least likely to say that they supported violence against civilians in defense of Islam. Indeed, across all of the samples, the percentage supporting violence and the percentage who say that democracy can work in their country were virtually the same among respondents who believed in one true interpretation and respondents who didn't. Religious certainty was apparently no barrier to political liberalism. These respondents seemed to be saying that liberal Islam was the only possible Islam. The situation is parallel to the conundrum in the Western political tradition over whether liberalism should be illiberal toward illiberalism.[32]

In each country, the particular configuration of cultural conservatism and political liberalism is constantly under debate. In Kuwait, for example, women got the right to vote in 2005, after several decades of mobilization by women's rights advocates. This followed women's suffrage in several other Arab monarchies— Qatar (1999), Bahrain (2002), and Oman (2003)—and left only one country in the world with an all-male electorate, Saudi Arabia (though elections are not especially meaningful there, in any case). Kuwaiti citizens—who comprise only a minority of the Kuwaiti population, given the large number of immigrants and their descendants, who are denied citizenship—were evenly divided on the issue, and parliament rejected the emir's proposed enfranchisement of women twice before. Perhaps the strangest aspect of this episode is that women themselves were less enthusiastic about the prospect than men, according to surveys in the 1990s, even controlling statistically for levels of religiosity, educational attainment, and other variables. The makeup of parliament was not noticeably changed when women voted for the first time in 2005.[33]

The possibility of culturally conservative yet politically liberal Islamic movements is terribly disturbing to Islamists. Western observers are sometimes pessimistic about the prospects of liberal Islam, but if they underestimate its potential, their Islamist opponents seem to overestimate it. They routinely denounce liberal Islam as an insidious plot and regard it as outside the bounds of the faith. In 2005, the Indonesian Council of Islamic Scholars issued a fatwa declaring, "It is forbidden for the Muslim community to follow the tenets of pluralist, secularist, and liberal religion." Salih al-Fawzan, a senior Islamic scholar in Saudi Arabia, also issued a fatwa on the subject in 2007: "He who says, 'I am a liberal Muslim,' contradicts himself," al-Fawzan wrote. Those who advocate such a position "should repent unto God in order to become truly Muslim."[34]

In one famous case, Islamists were able to "prove" in court that a prominent liberal Islamic scholar in Egypt, Nasr Hamid Abu Zayd, was an apostate. Abu Zayd, a professor at Cairo University, had written several books analyzing the language and interpretations of the Quran. Like Soroush and other liberal Islamic thinkers, Abu Zayd argued that the revelation became subject to human interpretation the moment that it was revealed to humans, and that efforts to claim a single, authoritative interpretation were little more than power plays. A group of Islamist lawyers argued that these positions constituted apostasy, citing critiques of Abu Zayd's work by several Islamist religious scholars. According to one of these critiques, Abu Zayd was an "ignorant" proponent of the Enlightenment "who understand[s] freedom of thought to mean freedom to lead the people to infidelity." According to another, Abu Zayd's work amounted to "cultural AIDS" and "intellectual terrorism." (This critic was himself assailed as an apostate several years later for his own religious writings.) An appeals court accepted these arguments and annulled Abu Zayd's marriage, on the grounds that a Muslim woman cannot be permitted to marry a non-Muslim man. To stay married, Abu Zayd and his wife emigrated to Europe, where they hold prestigious university positions.[35]

Some liberal Muslims may in fact be atheists, as Islamists suspect. Historians have established that several prominent figures of the nineteenth and early twentieth century, such as Malkum Khan of Iran and Abdullah Cevdet of the Ottoman Empire, used an Islamic discourse out of convenience, rather than out of conviction. Still others, such as Fath Ali Akhundzada of Russian Azerbaijan, were openly antireligious. Today, as well, there are nonreligious and even antireligious liberal movements in many

Muslim societies. While conservative and revolutionary Islamists condemn liberal Islam as secret atheists, these secularists condemn liberal Islam as secret Islamists![36]

The revolutionary Islamist critique of liberal Islam goes beyond denunciation to outright threats. An American Muslim fan of Islamist revolution suggested "how to deal with 'liberal' Muslims" on his blog, applying the advice of a medieval treatise: "Know that he is Iblees [the devil] who has appeared in the form of a human, or that Iblees has possessed him. So if you are a coward, then flee away. If not, then throw him down on the ground, kneel down upon his chest, recite upon him Aayat al-Kursee (Soorah al-Baqarah: 255) [a verse from the Quran], and strangle him." (Several months later, the *New York Times* identified the author as Samir Khan, a 21-year-old North Carolinian who later moved to Yemen to engage in jihad.) The Liberal Islam Network in Indonesia, which organizes conferences on progressive themes and publishes essays on these subjects on its website, received death threats.[37]

Some liberal Islamic leaders have been attacked and killed. In June 2009, a young man walked into the Naeemia seminary complex in Lahore, Pakistan, just after midday prayers, armed with explosives. He made his way to the office of the director, an Islamic scholar named Sarfraz Naeemi, who was greeting congregants, and then detonated his bomb, killing Naeemi and several others, including himself. Naeemi was targeted for his outspoken opposition to Islamist revolutionaries. Several weeks earlier, he had participated in two large conventions of Pakistani Islamic scholars. The first of these meetings issued a resolution that "killing of those having dissenting opinion and getting the demands fulfilled on gun-point are manifestly against Islam.... Suicide bombings on the innocent people are manifestly prohibited. Islam does not admit of them, rather it considers them an act of barbarism and terrorism." The second meeting issued a similar resolution that also objected specifically to the revolutionaries' attacks on religious scholars: "The assassination of *ulema* [Islamic scholars] should be stopped and sacred places, including shrines, should be cleared of extremists." Naeemi, speaking at the second convention, denounced the Taliban and their behind-the-scenes supporters in the Pakistani intelligence services, who are widely believed in Pakistan to be using the Taliban and other revolutionary movements as proxy armies in the battle for influence in Afghanistan and Kashmir. Naeemi was hardly the only Islamic scholar attacked by Islamist revolutionaries. The sharia faculty building at the International Islamic University in Islamabad was bombed in October 2009—apparently the professors were not Islamic enough to suit the terrorists. In the northwest region of Pakistan, the Taliban and its allies have killed dozens of Sufi leaders as part of their campaign to rid local communities of all Islamic competitors. Recent liberal Islamic targets outside of Pakistan include Fouad Ali Hossein al-Durri, a Sunni imam in Baghdad, Iraq, and a proponent of intercommunal reconciliation who was killed in September 2008. Being a traditionally trained Islamic scholar offered no immunity from attack.[38]

Naeemi and these other scholars were not "liberal" in all respects. Many of them claimed that traditional social mores are divinely mandated and ought to be revived and strictly enforced. Naeemi was active in an Islamic political party that sought to implement sharia as the law of the land—through electoral politics, not through revolutionary means. Another form of culturally conservative liberalism is being promoted in many Muslim societies by a new breed of religious leaders: televangelists. These include Abdullah Gymnastiar in Indonesia, whose monthly program and megamosque performances promote his commercial brand of spiritual development, and Yaşar Nuri Öztürk in Turkey, whose frequent television commentaries in the 1990s encouraged Muslims to read the Quran for themselves instead of relying on intermediaries, except perhaps for himself. This Protestant-like modernist message matched his

Westernized look, which featured suits or polo shirts and a gym-trim physique. The superstar of Muslim televangelists is Amr Khaled of Egypt, a former accountant whose satellite TV program is watched throughout the Arab world. Khaled combines an easygoing style, including down-home jokes and freshly pressed shirts casually unbuttoned at the collar, with a motivational appeal for self-improvement through religious discipline. This discipline includes elements of traditional morality, such as a defense of full-face veiling for women, but he presents religious duties as a matter of personal piety, not government enforcement. "There is no compulsion in the religion," Amr Khaled says, quoting a verse from the Quran that Islamic liberals often cite. "Everyone is left the choice to believe or not to believe."[39]

Televangelists are stiff competition for the revolutionaries. They court the same well-educated, middle-class audience that the globalists are trying to reach. They use the same sorts of electronic media, including sophisticated webpages and satellite television (though militants only get on the air when they make news, and they probably don't get paid as much). Both televangelists and revolutionaries offer parallel messages of Islamic renewal, calling for Muslims to reject their debauched ways and return to a stylized version of pure, early Islam—without giving up modern ideals such as technological progress, economic development, and human equality. (This modernism distinguishes globalists from localists, as I discussed in chapter 3.) For young Muslims who wish to purge themselves of Western influences, televangelists and revolutionaries present a clear choice: "fundamentalism lite" and "fundamentalism heavy." The heavies are losing. The number of Muslims who join revolutionary groups is a thousand times fewer than the number of Muslims who watch the televangelists' shows, buy their videos and books, and follow their advice to mind their piety and not worry too much about political change.

Muslim televangelists might not seem so liberal to Westerners who are familiar with right-wing Christian televangelists such as Jerry Falwell and Pat Robertson. Both the Christian and Muslim versions rail against the decadence of contemporary society and seek salvation in a demanding interpretation of the sacred sources. Both versions are essentially modern phenomena, even though they cast themselves as beacons of ancient truths. Despite all their similarities, both versions demonize fundamentalists on the other side. (There is no multifaith televangelist association, so far as I know.) But there is an important distinction: many Christian televangelists encourage their followers to engage in politics as an outgrowth of their faith—"This idea of 'religion and politics don't mix' was invented by the devil," Falwell preached—while Muslim televangelists tend to focus on personal faith as a private matter rather than a political matter. Muslim televangelists' interpretation of Islam may not be liberal, but their privatization of faith is. That is what Islamist revolutionaries object to. "It is sad when an ignoramus like Mr. Khaled is treated like a person of knowledge and wisdom," one militant wrote in an online discussion group. "If this man had any fear of Allah he would silence his corrupted tongue and remove himself from the public sphere." Another posting called Khaled a *munafiq*, a hypocrite who pretends to be Muslim. The Quran promises *munafiqs* that they will be cast into the worst depths of hell.[40]

Yet militants' threats were not Amr Khaled's biggest problem. His biggest problem was Egypt's military government, which viewed all popular movements as potential threats to its monopoly on power. Twice in the past decade the government forced him into exile. The second time, in mid-2009, the security forces reportedly objected to a charity of his that competed with an official antipoverty project and blocked him from producing a television program on the subject of Moses, who is considered an important prophet in Islamic tradition. The story of Moses inevitably includes references to the repressive pharaoh, which was politically sensitive in Egypt and elsewhere in the region. Some oppositionists have taken the analogy to extremes. The Islamist revolutionary who assassinated Egyptian president Anwar Sadat in 1981 shouted, "I have killed pharaoh!"[41]

The Egyptian government—like other militarized regimes and monarchies in the region—treated both revolutionaries and liberals, both secular and Islamic, with the same heavy hand. Oppositionists of all stripes were placed under constant surveillance, subjected to harassment of all sorts, and periodically arrested and mistreated, sometimes tortured and executed, in prison. Amr Khaled was too popular—more popular than Oprah Winfrey, he told a reporter!—to suffer this abuse, but others were not so fortunate. Abu'l-Ela Madi, Issam Hashish, and Mustafa Raslan were arrested and charged with terrorism when they broke from the Muslim Brotherhood and tried to establish a liberal Islamic party in 1996. A military court acquitted them after four months, but their application to register the party was rejected. In recent years, similarly groundless charges led to the arrest of Khaled Salam, a pro-democracy activist within the Muslim Brotherhood; Abdel Monem Abou al-Fattouh, one of the most senior reformists in the Brotherhood; and three young bloggers who had been promoting democratic reform both within the Brotherhood and within the Egyptian government. These and other arrests show that liberal Islam were not exempt from state repression and may even be treated more harshly than more conservative Islamic groups, out of concerns that it would have a greater chance of winning support among Egyptians and in the West.[42]

Despite this repression, despite the shutting of legal channels for dissent in Egypt and other authoritarian regimes, few liberal Islamic movements have abandoned their liberalism and taken up violence. The single most important instance of radicalization was the Islamic Salvation Front in Algeria, which won 80 percent of the seats in the country's first free parliamentary elections in 1991. The military stepped in, canceled the election, banned the party, and jailed its leaders. Abbassi Madani, the head of the Front and an outspoken supporter of democracy, was sentenced to a dozen years in prison. Some party activists who had gone into hiding to avoid arrest turned to armed insurrection, attacking security forces and bombing government buildings for several years. Even in rebellion, Madani and most of the Front's other leaders maintained liberal Islamic goals. Representatives of the group signed an accord in Rome committing the Front to multiparty democracy and respect for human rights. The Front avoided violence against civilians, while the military and Islamist terrorists escalated their conflict to grotesque levels, bombing cities and wiping out entire villages. Islamist terrorists also began to attack members of the Front, killing dozens of them. Disgusted with the violence, the Front declared a unilateral cease-fire in 1997 and disbanded in 1999. Many of the group's members were granted amnesty in 2000, but the liberal Islamic movement seems to have lost the widespread support that it had before the civil war. Several Islamic parties remain legal in Algeria, but they won only 13 percent of the vote in the most recent parliament election. Over the course of a decade, Islamists in Algeria went from electoral victory to armed rebellion to political marginality—the most dramatic victory and defeat that liberal Islam has experienced anywhere in the world.

While liberal Islam rarely turns radical, it is not uncommon for Islamist revolutionaries to turn to liberal Islam. The reformists in Iran had been revolutionaries in their youth and now attempted to undo some of the damage that their zeal had wreaked. Elsewhere, too, former revolutionaries have repented. Mansour al-Nogaidan is one of them. He dropped out of high school in Saudi Arabia to live and study with an isolated community of Islamic purists and issued his first fatwas—one of them against soccer—while still a teenager. Several years later, he and several friends decided to engage in direct action. They firebombed a video store for stocking Western filth and then a charity that they considered too supportive of women's rights. The Saudi government arrested and convicted him, and in prison he began to rethink his religious views, emerging eventually as an outspoken opponent of revolutionary Islamism. "No one owns the truth," he insisted. He became a newspaper columnist and challenged the revolutionaries on doctrine and strategy—until he aimed his critical barbs at the religious intolerance of the Saudi government as well. Then he was rearrested, sentenced to 75 lashes, and banned from publishing.[43]

The competition between liberal Islam and revolutionary Islamism is not symmetrical. Liberal politics has a following in the hundreds of millions, while the revolutionaries are able to recruit only thousands. If only 1 percent of liberal Muslims had radicalized over the past decade, the number of revolutionaries would have increased tenfold or more. But so long as the revolutionaries are willing to use violence, their visibility far outweighs their numbers. So revolutionary Islamists have responded to defections and declining public support with ever-more-heinous attempts to purify society through violence. They have targeted cafés that the revolutionaries consider decadent, weddings that do not observe the revolutionaries' rituals, even mosques that do not follow their creed. Every time that they do so, they drive more Muslims toward liberal Islam.

The backlash against violence can be witnessed in pop music. In 2003, after bombings in Casablanca, Mohammed Bahri, a Moroccan rapper who had been performing nearby, wrote a scathing song, "Who Are You?" that accused Islamist terrorists of playing into the hands of American imperialism: "Do you want peace, or do you want the politics of the CIA? You start to wear big trousers, and you grow your beard, and you wear tagia [a skullcap]. You speak of resistance but you are tamed monsters. If you understood the Quran, there wouldn't be bombs." After terrorist bombings in Bali, Indonesia's leading rocker, Ahmad Dhani, produced a best-selling album, *Warriors of Love*, to counter the ideology of the revolutionaries. When Islamists stepped up their violence in Pakistan, many of the country's top singers recorded an all-star song, "This Is Not Us (Say No to Terrorism)," which went platinum. Al-Qaida supposedly considered assassinating decadent Egyptian musicians but decided they were too popular to touch—yet another sign of how marginal the revolutionaries have made themselves.[44]

CHAPTER 5

❧

Uncle Sam versus Uncle Usama

In the weeks after September 11, 2001, even before the rubble had been removed from Lower Manhattan, a debate emerged about whether U.S. foreign policy was responsible for the attacks. This debate was not limited to crackpots and conspiracy theorists, although there were plenty of them to be heard. No, this debate occupied the center of American politics, and the side that won was: Yes. American foreign policy had indeed contributed to the tragedy of 9/11. A survey conducted at the end of 2001 estimated that three-quarters of Americans considered the United States partly responsible. Even the White House, led by President George W. Bush, agreed.[1]

At the same time, there was no agreement about *how* the United States was responsible, and what changes in foreign policy would prevent attacks in the future. President Bush insisted that the United States needed to adopt a stronger, more aggressive stance than it had in the past, so that Muslim terrorists would respect America rather than view it as a vulnerable "paper tiger," a phrase that the Bush administration used to characterize its opponents' approach. The administration's opponents, including almost every academic expert on Muslim societies, insisted that the United States needed to adopt more conciliatory and multilateral policies than it had in the past, so that Muslims would respect America as a fair broker rather than an imperialist meddler in world affairs.

Both sides in this debate were probably wrong. It turns out that Islamist revolutionaries are hardly affected at all by U.S. foreign policy. Whether the United States military bombs Muslim civilians or hands them emergency relief packages or stays in its bases—over the past two decades, the United States has tried all of these approaches and many others as well, singly and in combination—it does not make much difference.

In the language of economics, the "demand" for U.S. foreign policy is "inelastic." Elasticity refers to people's willingness to change their behavior in response to a change in their surroundings—if the price of Acme Widgets goes up, for example, elasticity means that people buy fewer Acme Widgets. If the price goes down, elasticity means that people buy more and more Acme Widgets. But when responses are *in*elastic, people keep on buying the same amount of Acme Widgets, no matter how high or low the price. Why would they do that? Well, instead of widgets, think of polio vaccines. Imagine that the price of polio vaccines doubled overnight, maybe because of some malfunction at the vaccine factory. Would you let your child go unvaccinated and risk being crippled or killed by polio, just because the price went up? Probably not. The desire for polio vaccine is relatively inelastic. Most people will pay whatever they can afford to keep their children healthy. That's why the price of polio vaccine is strictly regulated by the world's governments.

Let's examine attitudes toward government policies through the same lens as attitudes toward prices. When a policy shifts in one direction or another, how many people will change their views of the government? If the response is inelastic, very few people will change their views. That seems to be the case with Muslims' views of Uncle Sam. That is, most Muslims' views of the U.S. government are so entrenched that they do not change much in response to shifts in American policies. Polio vaccine is a startling example. In a few parts of the world, some parents do not want their children to be vaccinated against polio, not even for free. Resistance to vaccination is widespread enough in certain parts of West Africa and South Asia, populated mainly by Muslims, that polio remains endemic in these areas. Why would these families resist a harmless medication that could save their children from being painfully crippled or killed? The answer brings us back to elasticity of responses to U.S. foreign policy. In these communities, some Islamic leaders view polio vaccination as a plot by the United States and the Western world, according to a communiqué issued in 2003 by the Supreme Council for Shariah in Nigeria and the Kaduna State Chapter of Council of Imams and Ulama. "Our doctors have conducted extensive research on this," the groups announced, and they have found that the vaccination causes sterilization. The groups urged "the Muslim Ummah [to] be wary of the polio vaccination being aggressively and religiously pursued by the Federal Government [of Nigeria] and the United Nations agencies (World Health Organisation and UNICEF) because of its potential dangers to the Ummah." This opposition caused the governors of several states in northern Nigeria to suspend their anti-polio campaigns for a year, until new batches of the vaccine produced by Muslims in Indonesia were received and tested. Some parents in the region remained skeptical of the vaccine, and Nigeria now has the highest rate of unvaccinated children and the highest rate of polio infection in the world.[2]

Resistance to polio vaccination is a fringe position. Almost every Muslim scholar and political leader has endorsed the vaccine, and all but a few Muslim-majority countries have wiped out the disease entirely. But in some communities in northern Nigeria, distrust of the West ran so deep that medical assistance was considered more dangerous than polio. Whatever health officials said or did to reassure people about the humanitarian motives of the vaccination program was discounted as part of the plot. Even a humanitarian gesture like the campaign to eradicate polio failed to put a dent in this distrust. That is an extreme example of inelasticity of responses to American foreign policy.[3]

A similar attitude is visible on a far larger scale when it comes to other aspects of U.S. foreign policy. Many millions of Muslims believe that the American war on terrorism, its promotion of democracy, its advocacy of human rights and civil liberties are little more than window dressing for imperialism, at best. At worst, this activity is part of a plot to destroy Islam. No amount of goodwill gestures or civilizational dialogue has changed these people's minds. At the same time, many of the same Muslims safeguard their savings in dollar-denominated investments, enjoy American music and movies, support American ideals such as democracy and liberty, and aspire to send their children to college in the United States. No amount of saber-rattling and foreign intervention by the United States has changed their minds. On both dimensions—opposition to American foreign policy and admiration for American economic and cultural vitality—Muslims' views about America are relatively inelastic. These views are complex and sometimes contradictory, like any community's views about any other community, or even about itself, but they seem to change only over the course of decades, not over the course of a presidency or two.

Americans and their presidents can be impatient with foreign policy. We want instant results, or at least measurable progress by the next election cycle. This mismatch in timing between the frenetic activity of the U.S. government and the suspicious, wait-and-see attitude of the rest of the world can lead to frustration and misunderstandings. We Americans think we matter a great deal in fighting the battle against Islamist revolutionaries. Islamist revolutionaries, and the vast majority of Muslims who are not Islamist revolutionaries, are not so sure.

The image of the United States as a "paper tiger" comes from Chinese Communist leader Mao Zedong, who often spoke on this theme. "In appearance it is very powerful but in reality it is nothing to be afraid of, it is a paper tiger...unable to withstand the wind and the rain," Mao told reporters in the 1950s. "I believe the United States is nothing but a paper tiger." Notwithstanding the non-Islamic source, Usama Bin Ladin used the phrase in an interview with an American television reporter in 1998. The United States' brief intervention in Somalia in 1992–1993, Bin Ladin said, demonstrated that "the American soldier is a paper tiger that runs in defeat after a few blows." American right-wingers adopted the phrase as well, despite its communist origins. One particularly outspoken ideologue called for the United States to unleash "the most massive air and missile attack that our military can launch" against state sponsors of terrorism. "One attack like this should be enough to show the world that America is no longer a paper tiger."[4]

After 9/11, the "paper tiger" metaphor proliferated in the United States as a justification for military intervention in Afghanistan and elsewhere. Bernard Lewis, the best-selling Middle East historian in America, used this imagery in urging the United States to invade Iraq as well. Muslim terrorists "were encouraged by the opinion, often expressed by Osama bin Laden, among others, that America was a paper tiger," Lewis wrote in the fall of 2001. Lewis then went further: in order to dispel these impressions of American weakness, the United States should confront not just al-Qaida but other Muslims who were thumbing their noses at America. High on Lewis's list was Iraqi leader Saddam Hussein. "It may indeed be true that there is no evidence of Iraqi involvement...in the events of September 11th," Lewis wrote. (No credible evidence of this involvement has ever been produced.) "But it is difficult for Middle Easterners to resist the idea that this refusal to implicate Saddam Hussein is due less to a concern for legality than to a fear of confronting him." In Lewis's view, Muslims would respect the United States more for making a false accusation against Iraq, and even taking military action based on false pretenses, than for honest restraint.[5]

Over the next several months, Bernard Lewis met with Bush administration officials and helped to provide an intellectual buttress for the government's plans to remake the Middle East. Few in Washington acknowledged what a reversal this marked for Lewis. For decades, Lewis had published and republished a single book—with various revisions, under different titles—that spelled out why the Middle East could *not* be remade. According to Lewis, Muslims in the Middle East, and by extension Muslims all over the world, lacked the cultural and political heritage that would allow them to adopt Western mores and institutions. The very idea of nation-states "is alien and new in the world of Islam," Lewis wrote in 1964. "The division of the world into countries and nations, so important in the Western world's perception of itself and definition of its loyalties, is of comparatively minor importance in the world of Islam," he repeated in 1982. In his final pre-9/11 book, *What Went Wrong?*—already in page-proofs in September 2001—Lewis acknowledged that nationalism had "once commanded passionate support" among Muslims, but had since been "discredited" and "discarded." Moreover, he added, the idea of activities outside the scope of religious law "is alien to Muslim thought."[6]

Lewis is an eminent medievalist, but his work ignores virtually all of the evidence about Muslim attitudes and institutions in the modern world. He downplays the postcolonial school systems that have inculcated nationalism over the past century and makes no mention of the survey evidence showing persistent nationalist sentiment. Respondents in almost every Muslim-majority country surveyed on this subject over the past decade have indicated that they were "very proud" of their nationality, by more than a two to one margin—the one exception, Indonesia, was only half "very proud" of their nationality with another 45 percent saying they were "quite proud." Lewis makes almost no mention of Islamic debates about the limits of religious law and the inevitability of lay governance—debates that are hardly "alien to Muslim thought" but rather ancient and ongoing.[7]

Lewis did allow one single exception to his pessimistic view of Muslims' experience with modernity: Turkey. Turkey's path to modernization was successful, Lewis argued, because it had never been fully colonized by Western powers, and because its experiment with parliamentary democracy, on and off since the late nineteenth century, "rests on a far stronger, wider, and deeper base of experience" than in other Muslim societies. Even in Turkey, however, the goal of "achieving 'a synthesis of the best elements of West and East' . . . is a vain hope—the clash of civilizations in history does not usually culminate in a marriage of selected best elements." The most that can be hoped for, Lewis proposed, was that Turks "may yet find a workable compromise between Islam and modernism"—implying that after generations of Westernization, Turkey still has not yet found such a compromise.[8]

Even before *What Went Wrong?* appeared in print at the end of 2001, Lewis was repudiating its major points. He abandoned the book's restatement of his long-standing opinion that Muslims could never be like Westerners. Instead, he swapped his exaggerated Islamo-pessimism for an exaggerated Islamo-optimism: Muslims can indeed be just like Westerners, if only the West would apply enough force. The new Lewis summarily dismissed all of the old Lewis's objections. Turkey's long experience with democratic experiments and its freedom from extensive colonization by the West were no longer crucial factors in the modernization of Muslim society. Now Lewis pointed to the *lack* of these experiences as qualifying a country for imminent modernization: in

Iraq, Lewis told lecture audiences, British colonial tutelage in the first half of the twentieth century, and its long period of repression in the second half of the century, had readied the country for democratization. The secular nation-state and other Western values were not alien and discredited among Muslims, as he had previously written. Rather, in Iraq and many other countries, "there are people who share our values, sympathize with us, and would like to share our way of life. They understand freedom, and want to enjoy it at home." If the United States called on the Iraqi people to rise up, Lewis told television interviewer Charlie Rose in late 2001, the regime would be toppled easily. "While some military force might be necessary, I don't think that anything really extensive would be."[9]

This sudden optimism coincided with the new thinking in Washington. The Bush administration came into office in early 2001 determined to bulk up America's military posture and exorcise the demons of the War in Vietnam. The problem with U.S. foreign policy, administration officials said, was that leaders around the world did not believe that American positions would be supported, if push came to shove, by force. Everybody recognized that the United States had the world's most powerful military, but the American government was said to lack the political will to use its military effectively. Casualties among U.S. forces quickly turned American public opinion against military missions, and fear of casualties led American politicians to avoid significant military engagements. The U.S. envoy to Somalia in the 1990s heard this position stated confidently by a clan leader who believed that he knew how to defeat the world's only superpower: "We have studied Vietnam and Lebanon and know how to get rid of Americans, by killing them so that public opinion will put an end to things." As the Black Hawk Down episode proved, the warlord was right: a few dozen well-publicized casualties drove the U.S. military out of Somalia.[10]

In defense and foreign policy circles, this issue is known as "credibility": do foreign leaders consider the threat of force "credible" enough to deter them from antagonism? A group of conservative American foreign policy advocates, many of them officials from past Republican administrations, joined forces in the 1990s to argue that the American military, for all its strengths, had lost the credibility it needed to deter potential enemies. "American foreign and defense policy is adrift," announced the group, which called itself the Project for a New American Century. "We need to increase defense spending significantly," the group concluded. We need to "challenge regimes hostile to our interests and values." We need to "accept responsibility for America's unique role in preserving and extending an international order friendly to our security, our prosperity, and our principles." Among the signatories were Dick Cheney, who would soon be vice president; Donald Rumsfeld, who would soon be Bush's defense secretary; and a dozen more hawks who would serve as their aides and advisers.[11]

The most pressing short-term threat to American credibility, according to this group, was Saddam Hussein's Iraq. In 1998, the Project for a New American Century wrote to President Clinton to insist that his policy of inspection and containment was too weak to deter Hussein from developing weapons that would threaten America and its allies. The "only acceptable strategy," they argued, was "the removal of Saddam Hussein's regime from power.... That now needs to become the aim of American foreign policy." Within a week after taking office in January 2001, these same figures were working toward this goal. After 9/11, this planning was put on hold for two months.[12]

Instead, within hours of the attacks on September 11, the Bush administration turned toward Afghanistan. In a teleconference that afternoon with President Bush and other senior officials, CIA director George Tenet reported that al-Qaida was almost certainly behind the day's attacks. He was not alone in this belief. Speculation about al-Qaida's role was so widespread in Afghanistan that the Taliban's foreign minister held a press conference the same day in Kabul to condemn the killings, deny Taliban involvement, and ask for evidence of Bin Ladin's guilt so that the Taliban could arrest and try him. This offer would be repeated several times over the next month while the United States prepared to invade Afghanistan, but it was unlikely that the Taliban would honor the deal, even if the United States had cooperated. In previous years, the Taliban had been unwilling or unable to put Bin Ladin on trial or oust him from Afghanistan, even after al-Qaida had taken credit for violence against civilians. (For more on the distinctions between al-Qaida and the Taliban, please refer back to chapter 3.) Relations between the Taliban and al-Qaida were of little interest to policy-makers in Washington, in any event. Three days after 9/11, the United States Congress authorized the president to use military force against the whole lot of them: "those nations, organizations, or persons he determines planned, authorized, committed, or aided the terrorist attacks that occurred on September 11, 2001, or harbored such organizations or persons."[13]

This was the first time in the modern era that the United States had declared war on a nongovernmental organization. During the twentieth century, America's troops had generally been sent into battle against governments, from the German and Japanese governments in the 1940s to the Iraqi and Serbian governments in the 1990s. Even nongovernmental combatants were generally treated as proxies of some government sponsor, an approach that became official U.S. policy during the Reagan administration. This worldview was summarized in *The Terror Network*, a 1981 book by right-wing propagandist Claire Sterling. Sterling argued that seemingly unrelated terrorist movements around the world were being orchestrated secretly by the Soviet Union, and that CIA analysts and other experts were too timid to connect the dots. Reagan's CIA director, William Casey, told his staff to read Sterling's book and stop producing "mush." He fumed, "I paid $13.95 for this and it told me more than you bastards." International conflict, according to Cold Warriors like Sterling and Casey, was an affair of the state, not of freelance organizations. They viewed terrorism primarily through the lens of state sponsorship.[14]

On 9/11, the U.S. government broadened the Cold War focus on state "sponsorship" of terrorism in favor of a new, more flexible doctrine of counterterrorism targeting states that "harbor" terrorists. That evening, President Bush pledged to "make no distinction between the terrorists who committed these acts and those who harbor them." Congress used similar language in its authorization of force on September 14. So did the Department of Defense as it discussed options for responding to the attacks, according to the memoirs of military officials. Nobody suggested that the Taliban had attacked the United States or "sponsored" al-Qaida's attacks, but the United States was planning to retaliate against the Taliban nonetheless. There was no question of going after al-Qaida and leaving the Taliban intact.[15]

In the month between 9/11 and the U.S. invasion of Afghanistan, many of us who study Muslim societies—myself included—worried that American intervention would increase sympathy for al-Qaida and the Taliban. We wondered whether Muslims around the world would be radicalized, rather than intimidated, by a forceful Western response to terrorism.

I voiced these concerns at a peace rally in Chapel Hill, North Carolina, a week after 9/11. Peace movements were mobilizing all over the country, questioning whether al-Qaida's violence needed to be addressed with a violent response. Demonstrators toted signs with slogans such as the quotation often attributed to Mahatma Gandhi: "An eye for an eye leaves the whole world blind." At the rally in Chapel Hill, the auditorium overflowed with almost a thousand people, the largest audience I had ever spoken to. I began with the story of my godfather, whose office was across the street from the World Trade Center in New York, and his escape from lower Manhattan in a cloud of dust and ashes. "He survived. Thank God, he survived. He walked 90 blocks home, stopping every 30 blocks to find a phone that was working and call his family to tell them that he was okay. He got home and took a shower and watched it on television like the rest of us. But there are millions and millions of people around the country, who have stories of six degrees of separation or less, and their grief and their confusion has to be credited. It just has to, we can't deny that." Already, one week after 9/11, it seemed to me that many Americans were starting to regain their composure and consider the country's options. "People are starting to say, 'Yes, I'm angry, but I can deal with my anger in ways that don't involve the wholesale slaughter of other people.'" Others, however, were still so upset by 9/11 that they would only be satisfied by violent retribution. Some Americans were saying that all Muslims should suffer for the actions of a few, despite the fact that most Muslims abhorred the attacks. "If we let the most radical and militant Muslims define for us what Islam is, then we are just playing into their hands. We are also playing into the hands of our own militarists, whose interests always lie, I believe, in the exaggeration of threats, armed responses, and so on." Violence feeds off of violence. "I would argue that there is a tacit collusion among the militarists of all sides, that they are always providing atrocities that end up galvanizing their enemies, justifying their own budgets, and undermining the peaceniks in between. Those of us who don't hate each other and who want to get along end up being caught in the crossfire."[16]

Within days, a misquoted version of my comments was reported on right-wing websites around the country, making it sound as though I was blaming the attacks of 9/11 on the U.S. government. The misquotation then wound up on a conservative organization's list of 117 statements by professors and students questioning the wisdom of a full-scale attack on Afghanistan. The group called us "the weak link in America's response to the attack." I was number 100. Number 105 was Charles Tilly, one of the most influential social scientists of the era, who predicted that bombing the perpetrators of 9/11 would "increase incentives of unbombed activists to prove their mettle." This would lead to "increasing connection among Islamic oppositions across countries" and would ultimately "aggravate the very conditions American leaders will declare they are preventing."[17]

The CIA has a term for the negative byproducts of U.S. interventions in other countries: blowback. Originally, blowback referred to the poor publicity that the United States would suffer if the world learned about the American government's role in clandestine operations such as the coup against Iranian prime minister Mohammed Mossadeq in 1953. One of the lessons of that operation, a CIA official wrote in his classified history of the coup, was to avoid working with foreigners who might leak information about America's secret intervention. In the context of the Cold War, with the capitalist West and the socialist East competing for the hearts and minds of the postcolonial world, this sort of news would be disastrous. "Possibilities of blowback against the United States should always be in the back of the minds of all CIA officers involved in this type of operation," the CIA history concluded. Americans outside of the intelligence community learned about blowback in the 1970s, as the CIA's covert operations began to come to light. The term first appeared in the *New York Times* in 1977, with a slightly different meaning. Blowback meant false news items, secretly planted by the U.S. government in media outlets abroad, that migrated through foreign correspondents into American journalism: "The CIA accepts, as an unavoidable casualty of its propaganda battles, the fact that some of the news that reaches American readers and viewers is tainted with what the Russians call 'disinformation.' The agency has even coined terms to describe the phenomenon: blowback, or replay, or domestic fallout." Over the next several years, however, the term "blowback" expanded to include all sorts of negative side effects of American interventions, including the 1979 revolution in Iran, which was sometimes attributed to the coup of 1953, or the attacks of September 11, which were often viewed as blowback for U.S. support for Afghan mujahidin and their revolutionary Arab allies during the 1980s.[18]

This was the sense popularized by political scientist Chalmers Johnson, whose 2000 book *Blowback* accused the United States of repeatedly blundering into military interventions and occupations that fueled resentment and anger. Military interventions are supposed to "cause others to respect our power and authority—and hesitate to plunge into similar bloody strife in their own areas." That is the projection of "credibility" that national security experts consider so important. Johnson says it hardly ever works. Instead, retaliatory attacks—justified by the U.S. government as "'deterring' terrorism"—have the opposite effect. Rather than suppressing animosities, these interventions frequently generate new grievances and new enemies. "In this way, future blowback possibilities are seeded into the world." When blowback finally occurs, sometimes years or decades later, most Americans have already forgotten about their earlier behavior and the negative feelings it instilled. "It is typical of an imperial people to have a short memory for its less pleasant imperial acts, but for those on the receiving end, memory can be long indeed.... Even an empire cannot control the long-term effects of its policies. That is the essence of blowback."[19]

Writing a year before 9/11, Johnson picked Bin Ladin as a perfect example of blowback. Bin Ladin was an ally of the United States in the war against Soviet occupation of Afghanistan—a reluctant ally, given his ideological hostility toward the West, but in any case not an active combatant against the West. With the withdrawal of the Soviets from Afghanistan and the stationing of U.S. troops in Saudi Arabia, purportedly to deter Saddam Hussein's Iraqi troops from invading, Bin Ladin turned his sights on his former allies. Al-Qaida's bombing of the U.S. embassy buildings in Nairobi and Dar es Salaam was in this way blowback from American interventions in Afghanistan and Saudi Arabia. In retaliation against the embassy bombings, the U.S. government then launched missiles at a pharmaceutical plant in the Sudan and a training camp in Afghanistan, both of which were thought to be associated with Bin Ladin. Who knows what further blowback these actions might result in, Johnson wrote in 2000. "Blowback itself can lead to more blowback, in a spiral of destructive behavior."[20]

Johnson claimed that the attacks of September 11 confirmed his blowback theory with horrible accuracy. Writing the following month, Johnson warned that "the latest cycle of violence and reprisal has now begun," and "may even escalate out of control." American intervention in Afghanistan was likely to "boomerang back on to the American people themselves." It was not just American bombs that would alienate and radicalize Afghans, Johnson argued, but also America's blundering relief efforts. Johnson described food parcels that American airplanes were dropping in Afghanistan—metal boxes labeled, in English, "a food gift from the people of the United States of America." "The packages include 'beans and tomato vinaigrette,' together with peanut butter, strawberry jam, salt, pepper, a match (perhaps to help an Afghan heat his beans), and a napkin. The US Agency for International Development, which put the food parcels together, attached a paper wing to each metal box 'to help the packages survive the drop from the high-altitude planes.'" Johnson proposed that "there is obviously something contradictory about bombing the Afghans with lethal explosives and then with beans vinaigrette." He concluded: "I suspect that many [Afghans] will behave in an equally contradictory manner: they will eat the beans (if they can find them and are not blown up [by land mines while] retrieving them) and then join al-Qaeda."[21]

As it turned out, Johnson was wrong, and so was I. Afghans did not sign up with al-Qaida after eating American beans, and Muslims around the world did not protest in large numbers against the invasion of Afghanistan. Conflict between Muslims and the West did not escalate. A few incidents of terrorism were clearly provoked by the invasion—an American aid worker in Jordan was assassinated by a group claiming retaliation for the blood shed in Afghanistan—but the overall level of Islamist terrorism remained stable. According to the Global Terrorism Database at the University of Maryland, which is funded by the U.S. Department of Homeland Security, Islamist groups carried out 60 attacks per month in the year prior to 9/11 and 43 per month in the following year. Non-Islamist groups carried out a similar number of attacks during the same period.[22]

With his usual combativeness, conservative columnist Charles Krauthammer pointed out our error: "Just weeks ago the Middle East experts were warning that such violations of Islamic sensibilities would cause an explosion of anti-Americanism. Where, then, is the vaunted 'Arab street,' the pro-Osama demonstrations, the anti-American riots? Where are the seething masses rising up against America and its nominal allies from Egypt to Pakistan? Nowhere to be seen.... The Middle East experts, who a decade ago made identical warnings that war on Iraq would cause the Arab world to rise against us, don't get it. They never do."[23]

When the Bush administration started planning its next invasion of a Muslim society, this time in Iraq, I was careful enough not to go on record making predictions about the effects. Others were less circumspect. One reporter estimated that "every Middle East and Muslim affairs expert is saying that Al Qaeda's ranks will be fattened by new recruits right now and will have more of them when the United States attacks Iraq." A liberal group, the Institute for America's Future, took out a full-page ad in the *New York Times* with a drawing of Bin Ladin dressed up as Uncle Sam, pointing at the reader and saying, "I want you to invade Iraq. Go ahead. Send me a new generation of recruits. Your bombs will fuel their hatred of America and their desire for revenge. Americans won't be safe anywhere. Please, attack Iraq." Even al-Qaida agreed. One of its publications ran an article on U.S. military interventions in Iraq and elsewhere with the headline, "Thank You, Oh Zio-Crusaders." Again, predictions of backlash were mistaken, at least in the short run. Islamist terrorists carried out an average of 47 attacks per month in the year before the invasion and 44 per month afterward—34 per month if we only count attacks outside of Iraq.[24]

For a time, it looked as if the Bush administration was right. The U.S. military's "shock and awe" invasions made quick work of the governments of Afghanistan and Iraq, defeating each of them in a matter of weeks. Al-Qaida was on the run. "I'm sorry for getting you involved in this battle," Bin Ladin told his fighters at Tora Bora, Afghanistan, as he fled into hiding. "If you can no longer resist, you may surrender with my blessing." Speaking to American naval personnel on an aircraft carrier in December 2001, President Bush could brag: "Not long ago, al-Qaeda's leader dismissed America as a paper tiger. That was before the tiger roared."[25]

By the time that Bush left office in January 2009, braggadocio no longer seemed appropriate. Seven years of forceful foreign policy had not intimidated terrorists into giving up. "Our enemies are patient and determined to strike again," Bush said in his farewell address. "While our nation is safer than it was seven years ago, the gravest threat to our people remains another terrorist attack." Political violence had risen to horrific levels in Afghanistan and Iraq under occupation by tens of thousands of American troops. Al-Qaida and other Islamist terrorists worked hard to capitalize on images of Western violence, such as naked inmates being tortured by American guards at the Abu Ghraib prison in Iraq and wedding parties bombed by American missiles in Afghanistan. By 2007, the peak year in the Global Terrorism Database (as of this writing), Islamist attacks had jumped to 203 per month, 115 of them in Afghanistan and Iraq. Blowback seemed to be making a comeback.[26]

Still, the scale of blowback has been far less than many of us feared in the fall of 2001. Invasion of Afghanistan and Iraq did not trigger a cataclysm of civilizational conflict. Few Muslims joined Islamist revolutionaries, and outside of Afghanistan and Iraq, terrorist violence remains rare. It is not that Muslims around the world suddenly began to support or respect American foreign policy. The saving grace, it appears, was that their opinions couldn't get any more negative.

In April 1994, an American ambassador approached the imam of a small Balkan mosque and proposed an illegal gunrunning scheme. At the time, Bosniak Muslims were being slaughtered by Serbian militias. Tens of thousands had perished, and Sarajevo, the capital of newly independent Bosnia and Herzegovina, had been under siege for two years, with nearly constant sniper fire and shelling into civilian neighborhoods from the surrounding hillsides. A United Nations arms embargo, which the Serbian forces were able to evade, prevented the Bosniaks from defending themselves, and many Americans wanted to help. The United States government lobbied the Security Council to lift the embargo on the Bosniak side, but the council's European members vetoed the suggestion out of fear that their soldiers in the Balkans would become targets of Serbian forces. Unable to help the Bosniaks legally, President Bill Clinton opted to help them surreptitiously. Flying back to the White House from the funeral of former president Richard Nixon, Clinton ordered the military not to enforce the embargo on the Bosniaks. Planeloads of weapons and supplies began to arrive in Bosnia the following week, under the watchful gaze of American military surveillance.[27]

America's surreptitious role in rearming Bosniak Muslims became public knowledge almost immediately. The *Washington Post* and other newspapers reported on the arms pipeline one week after it started, and Bosnian Serbs protested loudly. "Muslim leaders in Bosnia will not rest until [they have] Bosnia in the grip of Islam," a Serb official told a press conference the day after the news broke. "What is curious is that the United States [is] doing exactly the same." Nonenforcement of the embargo became official U.S. policy in the fall of 1994, thanks to a congressional resolution. And in 1995, the U.S. and its allies intervened openly on the side of the Muslims, bombing Serbian positions in Bosnia and helping to bring the Serbians to the negotiating table to end the civil war.[28]

Muslims around the world desperately sympathized with the Bosniaks, whose plight was front-page news for more than four years in almost every Muslim community. Instant experts produced dozens of books on the subject, reflecting and fanning Islamic solidarity for the Bosniaks. Satellite television channels held fund-raisers. The Organization of the Islamic Conference—an intergovernmental forum for Muslim-majority countries—denounced the U.N. arms embargo and offered assistance, both military and humanitarian. Islamist militants complained that this was just words. They migrated by the hundreds from training camps in Afghanistan, where they had recently fought the Soviets, to form pan-Islamic battalions in Bosnia.[29]

Yet few Muslims gave the United States much credit for its support of the Muslims of Bosnia. Sure, the United States could have done much more to help the Bosniaks—if it had allowed them to acquire weapons two years earlier, thousands of lives might have been saved. But there is little evidence that the United States was in cahoots with Serbia to wage a genocidal war on

Balkan Islam—and that is the sort of accusation that was common at the time. "The West's role as co-conspirators with the Serbian war criminals becomes clearer with every passing day," wrote *Crescent International,* an Islamist magazine. Bin Ladin called this an example of America "killing the weaker men, women, and children in the Muslim world and elsewhere" through the "withholding of arms from the Muslims of Bosnia-Herzegovina, leaving them prey to the Christian Serbians who massacred and raped in a manner not seen in contemporary history."[30]

This kind of anti-American sentiment was not limited to Islamists. In Turkey, surveys by the U.S. Information Agency found that favorable opinions of the United States dropped from 57 percent in 1991, before the civil war in Bosnia, to 31 percent in 1994, when the United States had begun to allow weapons for the Bosniaks. It recovered partially the following year, to 48 percent favorable, after the United States and its allies stepped into the Bosnian conflict and forced the Serbs into truce negotiations. But Turkey has long been a "swing state" for U.S. foreign policy—attitudes toward America shift dramatically in Turkey from year to year, depending on the issues of the day. In the years before 9/11, favorable opinion about America had climbed over 60 percent in Turkey—and then dropped to 30 percent in 2002, after the U.S.-led invasion of Afghanistan. It dropped further, as low as 9 percent favorable, after the U.S.-led invasion of Iraq in 2003.[31]

Turkish views of the United States are deeply affected by what America *does,* not what America *is*—a distinction made by political scientists Peter Katzenstein and Robert Keohane in their recent book on global anti-Americanism. A similar shift is visible in Indonesia, where favorable views of America plummeted from 75 percent in 2000 to 15 percent in 2003. This evaporation of support for the United States is, ironically, a promising sign for U.S. foreign policy. It suggests that Turkish and Indonesian attitudes toward America are influenced by changes in U.S. policies—large portions of the populations in these countries may not have agreed with Bush administration policies, but a different set of policies might win them over. Very few Islamist terrorists come from these countries—approximately one per million residents.[32]

In many Muslim societies, by contrast, anti-Americanism may be so entrenched that changes in U.S. foreign policy do not make much difference. In Pakistan, for example, only 23 percent of respondents expressed a favorable view of America in 2000. At this low level there wasn't much room for decline during the Bush administration. So even though favorable responses dropped by more than half in 2002, this change only amounted to 13 percent of the sample—a far smaller proportion than the 50 percent of Turks and 60 percent of Indonesians who changed their minds about the United States during the same period. It is difficult to know how many societies exhibited a pattern similar to Pakistan's, because we don't have comparable pre-9/11 public-opinion data from many other Muslim societies—authoritarian governments such as Egypt and Saudi Arabia only began to allow extensive survey research after 9/11. However, the consistently low levels of support for the United States that emerged in surveys of these and many Muslim societies since 9/11 suggest that this pattern is fairly widespread. A significant portion of the world's Muslim population consistently opposes the United States, regardless of American foreign policy. A small portion consistently supports the United States, regardless of American foreign policy. And only a small portion—perhaps as little as 20 percent of the world's Muslims—is affected by shifts in American foreign policy.

Where does this unfavorable view come from? One week after 9/11, in a momentous speech to Congress, President Bush addressed the causes of anti-Americanism. The basic ideological difference, he proposed, was that America's enemies "hate our freedoms—our freedom of religion, our freedom of speech, our freedom to vote and assemble and disagree with each other." This

was inaccurate. Islamist terrorists do indeed oppose these freedoms but that is not why they hate America—they hate America
because of its foreign policy, which they view as an onslaught
against Islam. Prior to 9/11, Bin Ladin's statements did not dwell
much on America's domestic institutions; instead, he focused on
America's role in other countries, particularly in Muslim societies.
In a message released in 2004, Bin Ladin tried to rebut "Bush's
claim that we hate freedom." If that were the case, Bin Ladin wrote,
"perhaps he can tell us why we did not attack Sweden, for example?"
Rather, he conceived of the attacks as retaliation against "the
American-Israeli alliance's oppression and atrocities against our
people in Palestine and Lebanon," beginning in the 1980s. "I still
remember those distressing scenes: blood, torn limbs, women and
children massacred.... It was like a crocodile devouring a child,
who could do nothing but scream. Does a crocodile understand
anything other than weapons?" Bin Ladin's retrospective analysis
was probably just as fictional as Bush's analysis. Bin Ladin did not
exhibit much anti-American sentiment until the 1990s, and the
main grievance expressed in his statements of that period was the
U.S. military presence in Saudi Arabia, not the plight of Palestinians
and Lebanese. But Bin Ladin seemed to grasp one aspect of
Muslim public opinion that Bush did not: Muslims around the
world care more about American foreign policies than American
domestic conditions.[33]

Anti-Americanism in Muslim societies extends far beyond the
tiny number of terrorists, and this sentiment is not associated with
hatred of American freedoms. Surveys show that large majorities
of Muslims support American freedoms such as democracy and
free speech. (Freedom of religion is a different matter. Many
Muslims believe that apostasy should be illegal—but only in their
own societies. They are happy for Christians and Jews in the West
to have the freedom to convert to Islam.) Ironically, the American
freedoms that Muslims oppose most strongly are the same ones

that Bush and other conservative Christians also oppose, such as the freedom to be homosexual, to give birth out of wedlock, and to divorce. Cultural conservatives, both Christian and Muslim, denounce these freedoms as evidence of moral degeneration.[34]

In Muslim societies, the connection between cultural and political dimensions of anti-Americanism is stronger than in other countries around the world, but it is far from automatic. Political scientist Giacomo Chiozza has explored this connection in great statistical detail, analyzing surveys in dozens of countries. In the Middle East, disliking American music, movies, and television increases the odds of an unfavorable overall view of the United States by 18 percent—more than in other regions, but not a very powerful predictor. According to another set of surveys that Chiozza analyzes, Muslims who are ill disposed toward American culture and society tend to be ill disposed toward American foreign policy, but Muslims who favor American culture and society hold a huge variety of opinions about American foreign policy, both positive and negative. Similar results emerge in other surveys. In Algeria and Jordan, opinions about American culture were not correlated with attitudes toward terrorism against the United States. In nine Muslim societies surveyed by Gallup, four showed a slight correlation between concern about Western cultural influence and negative opinions of the United States; four countries exhibited no significant correlation; and in one country, Kuwait, apprehension about Western culture was associated with positive opinions of America. In more recent surveys of six Arab countries, political scientist Shibley Telhami asked respondents directly: "Would you say your attitudes toward the U.S. are based more on American values or American policy in the Middle East?" Three-quarters picked policy. The bottom line is this: many Muslims who like American culture oppose U.S. foreign policy. This combination of pro-Americanism and anti-Americanism may seem paradoxical to Americans, but it is common in Muslim societies, and it is persistent. Regardless of what strange turns American culture takes, from disco dancing to reality television, many Muslims come along for the ride. And regardless of how U.S. foreign policy shifts, many Muslims object.[35]

Many object to American foreign policy because they do not believe it is sincere. No matter how much the United States government claims that its actions around the world are principled and noble-minded, these actions are perceived as devious and self-serving. In a survey in 7 Muslim societies, most respondents agreed that "the U.S. tries to promote international laws for other countries, but is hypocritical because it often does not follow these rules itself." A Gallup poll in 35 Muslim societies found few places that considered the United States to be serious about establishing democratic systems around the world. The real objectives of American foreign policy, according to Telhami's surveys in six Arab countries, are to control oil (listed by one-half to five-sixths of respondents), protect Israel (listed by one-half to three-quarters), and weaken the Muslim world (listed by one-third to two-thirds). Kamilu Nasir, an illiterate grocer in Kano, Nigeria, voiced these concerns during President Bush's first visit to Africa in 2003: "His mission is to launch his war against Islam in Africa and also look for ways to exploit our oil resources."[36]

A large portion of the world's Muslims feel that the United States government is the most dangerous threat to their national security. Survey results are inconsistent on this subject—Telhami's surveys show overwhelming concern about an American threat in Arab countries, while the Pew Global Attitudes Project found half or fewer Arabs share this opinion. Regardless of which set of figures we believe, the numbers are substantial. Two-thirds of respondents named the United States as the greatest national threat in Bangladesh, Indonesia, Pakistan, and Turkey. In Pakistan, more than twice as many respondents named the United States as a greater threat to their personal safety than al-Qaida and the

Taliban, who have been bombing politicians, religious leaders, and ordinary citizens around the country for several years. It's not that Pakistanis support al-Qaida or the Taliban—large majorities opposed these groups and their agenda—but they distrust American foreign policy even more.[37]

Lower, but still considerable proportions of Muslims view the United States as a threat to Islam. In 2002, about one-third of Muslim respondents surveyed by the Pew Global Attitudes Project expressed concern that Islam was in danger; in subsequent years, that proportion rose to more than half. Still, only one-quarter of these respondents identified the United States as the primary threat to Islam. In Telhami's survey of six Arab countries, the proportion who considered weakening the Muslim world to be America's primary objective in the Middle East dropped from 59–69 percent in 2004–2006 to 30–38 percent in 2008–2010. However, other polls have found higher proportions. One survey research organization, World Public Opinion, reported that large majorities in eight Muslim societies felt that the United States was trying to spread Christianity in the Middle East and "weaken and divide the Islamic world." An average of 44 percent agreed that "the U.S. purposely tries to humiliate the Islamic world," with another 33 percent suggesting that "the U.S. is often disrespectful to the Islamic world, but out of ignorance and insensitivity." Only 12 percent felt that "the U.S. mostly shows respect to the Islamic world." These are alarmingly negative figures.[38]

These negative views swamped the Bush administration's "public diplomacy" project to convince Muslims that America is their friend. Islamists mocked these efforts as cover for the American "war on Islam." Mainstream media in Muslim societies focused far more on Bush's single unscripted remark that the United States was engaged in a "crusade" against terrorism than on his repeated insistence that the United States was *not* engaged in a religious war. Muslims are also well aware of the occasional

derogatory comments about Islam made by other American officials and religious leaders, such as the prominent Christian evan-
gelist, Franklin Graham, who called Islam "evil." (Fortunately,
there was only fleeting media coverage of the outrageous suggestion by failed presidential candidate Tom Tancredo that the United
States should deter terrorist attacks by threatening to bomb
Mecca.)[39]

Few Muslims thought Barack Obama's election as president of
the United States would shift the direction of American foreign
policy—approximately one-third, according to surveys by Telhami
and the Pew Global Attitudes Project. After Obama's election,
some Muslims expressed optimism, most notably in Saudi Arabia,
where 79 percent of respondents said they viewed Obama posi-
tively and were hopeful about American foreign policy—but
favorable attitudes toward the United States throughout the region
rose by only 3 percent, within the survey's margin of error. (By
2010, Arab opinion of Obama had turned upside down, with
positive ratings dropping by more than half, but favorable attitudes toward the United States dropped only by 6 percent.)
"Obama is a duplicate copy of Bush," al-Qaida editorialized after
the American presidential election. Many Muslims seem to
agree.[40]

Only a bold policy change might conceivably make a difference
in Muslim opinion of the United States. According to Muslim
survey respondents, one such step would be an Israeli-Palestinian
peace agreement—but it is not politically feasible in American
politics to pressure Israel into such an agreement, given Israel's
close alliance with America and its political clout in Washington. A
generation of American presidents, beginning with Jimmy Carter,
has attempted to negotiate Israeli approval for Palestinian
independence, but Barack Obama is no closer today than Carter
was in the 1970s. In some ways, a solution is even more distant
today than a generation ago, since Israel has moved hundreds of

thousands of its citizens into Palestinian territory in the West Bank over the past several decades. These settlers and their supporters seem to have veto power over Israeli negotiations, and Israel seems to have veto power over American policy toward the Palestinians. The obvious path to a two-state solution would be for the United States and the rest of the world to simply recognize the State of Palestine, regardless of Israeli objections, but no president has seriously contemplated taking that step. Even Obama, whose presidential campaign initially expressed sympathy for Palestinian national aspirations, backtracked during the primary elections. In a crucial speech to a high-profile American Jewish lobbying group, Obama stressed that he would not allow his sympathies for Palestinians to override his appreciation for the alliance with Israel. During his first months in office, Obama could not even convince the Israeli government to halt the expansion of Israeli settlements in Palestinian territories. A bold step such as recognition of Palestinian statehood seems to be out of the question. In the absence of a major shift in American foreign policy, Muslim public opinion toward the United States will likely remain inelastic.[41]

If Muslim attitudes toward the United States are largely stuck on negative, why should the United States even bother to take Muslim sensibilities into account? Why not just go after terrorist suspects with the full force of American military power, wherever they may be, and lock them up or execute them in secret prisons, regardless of the repercussions for Muslim public opinion? Why pretend that we care about the rights of Palestinians or the sovereignty of Pakistan? Why not embrace the self-interested, militaristic policies that most Muslims already accuse us of? Attitudes toward the United States government could not get much worse if we were to live up to the caricature.

Shirin Ebadi gives us two reasons not to go down this path. Ebadi is one of Iran's most prominent human rights advocates. She has spent decades representing political prisoners and campaigning for the rights of women, children, refugees, and political prisoners in Iran. The government fired her from her judgeship for being female, shut down her law office, accused her of treason, and allowed militants to threaten her life. Ebadi was not the only Iranian human rights activist to be harassed by the government, but she became the most famous of them in 2003, when she was awarded the Nobel Peace Prize—in large part for the symbolism of selecting a devout Muslim woman, the Nobel committee announced. Ebadi has energetically made the most of the international spotlight that the prize bestowed upon her, using every opportunity to promote the cause of reform in Iran. In her acceptance speech, Ebadi repeated her condemnation of the repressive rule of the Islamic Republic of Iran. As a Muslim, she decried the dangerous claim "that democracy and human rights are not compatible with Islamic teachings." On the contrary, she insisted, the message of Islamic revelation "cannot be in conflict with awareness, knowledge, wisdom, freedom of opinion and expression and cultural pluralism." In other words, Ebadi proposes an Islamic liberalism of the sort that the West would like to promote in Muslim societies. That's why right-wingers in Iran accuse her of being an agent of the United States.[42]

But Ebadi is no booster for United States foreign policy. In the same Nobel speech, she went out of her way to condemn the hypocrisy of American and Western imperialism: "If you consider international human rights law, including the nations' right to determine their own destinies, to be universal, and if you believe in the priority and superiority of parliamentary democracy over other political systems, then you cannot think only of your own security and comfort, selfishly and contemptuously." Ebadi condemned the U.S.-led invasion and occupation of Iraq, the American detention center at Guantánamo Bay, Cuba, and other U.S. actions that she said "violated the universal principles and laws of human rights by using the events of 11 September and the war on international terrorism as a pretext."

Ebadi's first objection to this sort of foreign policy is that it is morally wrong. It violates the ideals of justice and democratic self-determination that America wishes to embrace. This was one of the founding principles of American foreign policy, as elaborated by President George Washington: "Observe good faith and justice towards all nations; cultivate peace and harmony with all." The United States has not always stuck to these principles, but the ideals remain an important part of the story that America tells itself about itself. Americans want to believe that their country's foreign policy is not selfishly interventionist.[43]

Ebadi's second objection to American foreign policy is that it makes her work more difficult. "The concerns of human rights' advocates increase when they observe that international human rights laws are breached not only by their recognized opponents under the pretext of cultural relativity, but that these principles are also violated in Western democracies." Ebadi expects the Islamic Republic of Iran to claim that it is exempt from standards of human rights and democratic governance developed in the West, and she knows that these claims are failing. "The people of Iran, particularly in recent years, have shown that they deem participation in public affairs to be their right, and that they want to be masters of their own destiny." But when the West violates its own norms, it undermines Muslim support for reform. It makes people cynical and less likely to stick their necks out for ideals such as democracy and rights.

In effect, Muslim liberals suffer the secondhand smoke of American foreign policy. Muslim attitudes toward the United States are already so poisoned that a few more or a few less toxic policies may not make much of a difference, but the secondhand smoke from these policies is potentially disastrous for Muslim activists who share many of America's democratic ideals. That is why the Iranian reform movement has been so wary of allying itself with American sympathizers in recent years, and especially during the demonstrations in 2009 after the fraudulent reelection of President Mahmud Ahmadinejad. Iranians are well aware of the U.S. government's past interventions in Iran, from the coup of 1953 to the hundreds of millions of dollars that Congress has appropriated for "regime change" activities in Iran over the past two decades. The Republican leader of the House of Representatives, Newt Gingrich, insisted on $18 million for "covert" operations in 1995—"covert" is in quotation marks because the funding was publicized before it was ever signed into law. The Bush administration reportedly increased this funding to $400 million. According to cross-national surveys, Iranians have the most negative view of U.S. foreign policy of any country in the world, though, at the same time, a majority of Iranians also favor normalized relations with the United States.[44]

Iranian reformists walk a fine line in promoting American-style ideals while trying to avoid accusations that they are soft on the Great Satan. Every time that Iranian reformists have sought negotiations with the United States, hard-liners engineered international crises to disrupt relations with the West. In late 1979, just after the Islamic Republic came to power, student radicals took over the American embassy in order to undermine negotiations that Prime Minister Mehdi Bazargan was undertaking with the Carter administration. In 1986, Iranian hard-liners leaked news of the "Iran-Contra" affair in order to sabotage parliamentary leader Akbar Hashemi Rafsanjani's negotiations with the Reagan administration. In 1998, hard-liners assassinated a series of opposition intellectuals in order to prevent President Muhammad Khatami's "dialogue of civilizations" from becoming a dialogue of governments. "Our motive in having the officers of the [Writers'] Society and others killed was this," one of the suspects told Iranian investigators. "Human rights societies and centers would demand to come to Iran, Iran would again refuse, and from an international perspective Iran would remain isolated." Khatami's administration arrested the assassins and denounced their intentions, but it took their message to heart. Khatami did not pursue negotiations with the United States until the end of his administration, and then only through an opaque channel that he disavowed when it became public.[45]

When the Iranian reform movement revived in mid-2009 around the presidential campaign of Mir Hossein Musavi, reformists were once again wary of appearing to be pawns of the United States. At his first campaign press conference, Musavi announced, "We will definitely negotiate with them. Why not?" But he qualified his comments with a wait-and-see attitude toward the Obama administration. "We are studying the change advocated by Obama. If the change is also in action, we will negotiate; if not, then no."[46]

For his part, Obama avoided mentioning the upcoming election in Iran, presumably out of concern that his support for Musavi would backfire. When Iranian authorities shut down election monitors and hurriedly announced Ahmadinejad's reelection, and demonstrators took to the streets by the thousands to protest, Obama spoke out cautiously. "I want to start off by being very clear that it is up to Iranians to make decisions about who Iran's leaders will be; that we respect Iranian sovereignty and want to avoid the United States being the issue inside of Iran," Obama told reporters several days after the disputed election. "Having said all that, I am deeply troubled by the violence that I've been seeing on television. I think that the democratic process—free speech, the ability of people to peacefully dissent—all those are universal values and need to be respected."[47]

Obama took some flak from his political rivals in Washington, who felt he should encourage the Iranian opposition more forcefully. But the Iranian opposition itself appreciated Obama's restraint. Among demonstrators in Tehran, one reporter observed,

"Everyone understands that U.S. meddling would be the prover-bial kiss of death to the opposition's cause." Shirin Ebadi thanked Obama for his statement of support and basically told him to shut up: "What happens in Iran regards the people themselves, and it is up to them to make their voices heard. I respect his comments on all the events in Iran, but I think it is sufficient."[48]

Iranian authorities went ahead and blamed the protest movement on America and Europe anyway. To justify its violent repression of the reformists, the Ahmadinejad administration alleged a complex plot by the CIA, the British, and prominent Jews to manipulate the Iranian reform movement and wage a "soft war" against the Islamic Republic. One ludicrous smear campaign suggested that a friend of mine, a studious academic named Kian Tajbakhsh who had carefully avoided all political involvement since an earlier brush with the Iranian authorities, was the conduit of foreign influence over the reformists. He was arrested several weeks after the fraudulent election, forced to confess his supposed crimes, and sentenced to 15 years in prison.[49]

This debacle for the reform movement in Iran would hardly seem like a model for American foreign policy. Even many reform-ists in Iran came to regret Obama's hands-off approach to the crisis. By the fall of 2009, with the reformist movement reeling under heightened government repression, Ebadi no longer advised Obama to keep quiet about Iran. On the contrary, she told reporters, Obama should keep saying that "the voice of the people needs to be heard.... He needs to repeat the statement again and again, so that people in Iran hear him." Pro-democracy protestors in Tehran chanted, "Obama, Obama, is he with us or with them [the authorities]?"—a nice pun, since "U ba ma" in Persian means "he [is] with us."[50]

Despite this upsetting turn of events, the episode marks a vic-tory for American foreign policy. For once, the United States lis-tened to its Muslim allies—not its military allies, who are all too influential already, but its ideological allies, the pro-democracy movements that America claims to favor but often disregards. The Iranian reformists told the Obama administration not to get involved in the electoral crisis in Iran, and the administration did as they suggested, despite the political costs—criticism from activists on the left and the right in the United States, criticism from the Iranian regime, criticism even from some of the reformists themselves, after the fact. Think what would have happened if Obama had taken a different course of action, embracing the Iranian opposition more closely, or offering them funding, or ordering warships to lend military assistance. The reformists might have looked like stooges, handing over their country to American hegemony. That is what the reformists feared would happen—and who knows better than they do where their self-interest lies? Who knows better than they do what the United States can do to help them, or to hurt them? Perhaps the reformists miscalculated—perhaps not. We can't know whether the reform movement is down and out, or whether it is about to spring back and overwhelm the hard-liners in Iran, and we can't know how an alternative American policy would have affected this trajectory. But we do know one thing: the outcome of the Iranian election crisis was the Iranians' doing, not the result of American intervention. That is an accomplishment all by itself.

The precedent set in this episode may be more important than the immediate outcome in Iran. This precedent broaches the possibility of reorganizing American foreign policy around the interests of its allies. This would be a major change. Typically, American policy-makers ask: how is this policy going to affect the "national interest" of the United States? What they could be asking is: how is this policy going to affect the interests of the groups and movements that share American values, that care about democracy and rights? The national interest of the United States is not necessarily served by ignoring the interests of its allies. America may get its way in the short run—superpowers usually get their way in the short run—but at what cost? It is self-defeating to undermine one's future allies. They do not have a vote in U.S. elections, but they need to have a voice in American policy-making. Even if it means taking a hit, by narrow calculations of short-term self-interest, the marginal effect of this hit on U.S. interests in the world is generally tiny compared with life-and-death effects on pro-democracy movements in Muslim societies and elsewhere.

Don't expect that the United States would get credit for this approach. Whatever policy it adopts, there will be criticism. Inevitably, Muslim liberals will disagree among themselves about what the United States should do. They will change their minds as conditions shift. They may offer private advice that differs from their public positions. In public, they may distance themselves from the United States, or rail against the United States, if they see some political advantage in it. If they come to power, they may wind up leading weak governments and face challenges from radical groups. These are significant risks and complications, and it may sometimes seem confusing and frustrating to follow the advice of friends like these. But the alternative is far worse. The alternative is *not* to listen to the recommendations of the people that American foreign policy wants most to succeed. The alternative is to make a separate policy, contrary to their recommendations, as though Americans understood their situation better than they do. The alternative is to listen to the advice of *il*liberals, whose values are abhorrent and whose bloody repression fuels disgust with American hypocrisy.

If liberal movements ask the United States not to embrace them too closely, they deserve to be heard. Ironically, they may sometimes ask the United States to embrace dictators and radicals instead. If anybody is going to be discredited by association with American hegemony, Muslim liberals may prefer it to be their rivals. An Iranian blogger suggested as much in the aftermath of the 2009 election crisis: "Just imagine this: Tomorrow Obama comes to Tehran and shakes hands and has his picture taken with Ahmadinejad and [Iranian leader Ali] Khamenei. Ask yourself whether the day after tomorrow, when Khamenei can no longer say the word 'enemy' at Friday prayers, won't he die of sadness? Or if we take America away from Mahmud [Ahmadinejad], what will he have left to say?" The Iranian reform movement posted the blog on its main website.[51]

What would it be like, listening to the people that we hope to help? We might take a lesson from Greg Mortenson, an American adventurer whose life was saved by villagers in a mountainous region of northern Pakistan. After they rescued him from a glacier and nursed him back to health, Mortenson pledged to raise money for the village of Korphe and build it a schoolhouse. He spent the next year living in his car in the San Francisco Bay Area to save up enough money. He struggled to purchase supplies with his meager resources and deliver them to the village, which was so remote that it had no phones, no electricity, and no road. The village could only be reached by hoisting a basket along a cable stretched hundreds of feet above a river gorge. When Mortenson finally arrived, proudly bearing a truckload of building supplies, the village chief told him that they did not want a school. First, they wanted a bridge.

The news was devastating, Mortenson recalled in his best-selling memoir, *Three Cups of Tea*. But if that was what Korphe wanted, then who was he to impose his own priorities? "The people have spoken," he told himself. Mortenson set out to help build a bridge. And when that was completed, *then* the villagers accepted his gift of a schoolhouse, turning Korphe into a model of rural education in a region that has seen all too little of it. Mortenson applied this lesson in dozens of other remote villages around Pakistan and Afghanistan, where he built schools and community centers over the next decade: only help people who want you to help them, and only in the ways that they want you to help them. As one of his Pakistani associates taught him: "How can you know what the people need if you don't ask them?"[52]

Mortenson reminds me of Homer Atkins, the title character in the 1958 novel *The Ugly American*. Not that he is ugly—I was honored to meet him as he barnstormed through North Carolina raising money for still more schools in the mountains of Central Asia, and I can report that he is a fine-looking man. No, Mortenson reminds me of the Ugly American because both of them are role models for American foreign policy. Few people today remember that the original Ugly American character was a hero, not an ethnocentric imperialist. He was a successful engineer who signed on as a consultant to the U.S. embassy in Vietnam, when it was still a French colony. His job was to recommend where foreign donors should build roads, airstrips, and dams. But as he traveled around the countryside, talking with the Vietnamese, he realized that these things were not what people needed or wanted. They wanted small-scale projects to enhance village self-sufficiency, such as brick factories, canning plants, and irrigation pumps. Vietnamese, French, and American officials objected to Atkins's report. "It didn't tell us where the roads and dams should go," a French diplomat sputtered. Before storming out, Atkins retorted, "Just answer me: Have you been out in the boondocks?" The government officials sat in embarrassed silence.

One American diplomat followed Atkins out of the room and caught up to him. "I know you've had a rough time, and I know you've got plenty to keep you busy back in the States. But I think you could do some valuable things for me. And I'd give you a free hand." Atkins agreed to live in a remote town where he developed a cheap irrigation pump made of local scrap materials and powered by bicycle gears—no expensive foreign parts required, and no expensive foreign fuel. Then he negotiated with a village chief for permission to build a prototype and test it. A local mechanic came up with the final brainstorm: a rack for inserting the rear wheel of a bicycle, so that a poor family with only one bike could remove it and ride away. Atkins and Jeepo, the mechanic, formed a partnership and produced pumps to sell all over the region—a capitalist fairy tale in which ingenuity, sensitivity, and the can-do spirit manage to meet local needs, and make a profit in the process.[53]

Homer Atkins was fictional, but his character was based loosely on a pair of real-life Americans, Otto and Helen Hunerwadel. Otto lost his left foot to an infection as a young man, but that did not stop him from a successful career as a county agricultural agent, farmer, and businessman. After World War II, nearing retirement age, Otto and Helen left their comfortable lives behind and moved to northern Burma, where they ran educational programs for the International Cooperation Administration, a branch of the U.S. Department of State. Otto built his reputation in town by fixing and improving household appliances, then worked with local farmers to help them boost their yields. His proudest achievement was the introduction of broom corn and the invention of a jury-rigged broom-making device, using only local materials, that villagers were eager to adopt for themselves. Helen offered canning classes that were so popular she struggled to accommodate the demand. Both of them exemplified a can-do spirit of helpfulness that made them heroes in northern Burma—even bandits and insurgents left them alone as they traveled around the region. Otto died in Burma of complications from malaria; Helen went on to do further development work in Iran and elsewhere.[54]

These inspiring models—Mortenson in the early twenty-first century and the Hunerwadels in the mid-twentieth century—have an even longer history. Decades earlier, in the first years of the twentieth century, another American went abroad to serve the newly elected parliament in Iran, which was trying to gain public control over the monarchy's finances. Reformers in the Iranian government hired Morgan Shuster, a young attorney who had worked for U.S. colonial authorities in Cuba and the Philippines, as the treasurer-general of Iran. Shuster moved forcefully to limit the influence of Iran's traditional elites and their foreign allies. He forced the Imperial Bank of Persia to open its ledgers for accounting. He began negotiations to refinance Iran's foreign debt on nonconcessionary terms. He organized a gendarme force to protect the treasury and collect taxes from aristocrats who considered themselves exempt. These measures made Shuster one of the most popular people in Iran, but they also made him powerful enemies. Shuster was finally ousted when his gendarmes sought to exert their authority in the country's northern provinces, where Russia claimed a "sphere of influence." Russia gave the Iranians an ultimatum: fire Shuster or cede Iran's northern provinces to Russian occupation. Shuster resigned and left for America. A century later, Iran's parliament still has not managed to gain democratic oversight of the government's finances.[55]

Shuster, the Hunerwadels, and Mortenson are representatives of an American ideal, the energetic "everyman" whose practicality and altruism help to advance the causes of democracy and well-being in far-flung communities, not through imperial fiat but by listening to local priorities and acting on them. These "Ugly Americans" don't stand on ceremony, and they hate stuffed shirts. They resent red tape. For all these reasons, it is difficult to imagine replicating their individual initiatives on a large scale—implementing and overseeing hundreds or thousands of projects like these would require the very sort of administrative hierarchy that these independent souls resented. Still, U.S. foreign policy has much to learn from the heritage of "Ugly Americans." The basic idea is that America's "national interest" is often best served by putting its allies' interests first.

Contrast this with the United States' efforts at public diplomacy. Even before the term "public diplomacy" was coined in the 1960s, the United States Information Agency (USIA) was assigned the task of communicating with the people of the world. One of the agency's chief goals was to learn what the world thought—through pioneering public-opinion surveys as well as the standard methods of reading newspapers and chatting with locals in various countries—and bring this information to U.S. decision-makers. In the words of the USIA's first director, the famous television journalist Edward R. Murrow, the agency had to be "in on the take-offs as well as the crash landings" of American foreign policy. Very quickly, however, this noble ideal was compromised. Murrow was kept out of the loop in the planning for America's "Bay of Pigs" invasion of Cuba in 1961, and when he learned about it from a newspaper reporter, the White House ignored his objections and ordered him not to inform his staff. Public diplomacy became more about policy-promotion and less about policy-formation.[56]

In 2001, the Bush administration took this approach to its logical extreme, naming an advertising executive as director of the Office of Public Diplomacy. Charlotte Beers was hired for her expertise in marketing—not to listen to allies, but to get the American government's message across to them more effectively. Colin Powell, the secretary of state who hired Beers, made this clear in a speech to State Department employees: "I wanted one of the world's greatest advertising experts, because what are we doing? We're selling. We're selling a product. That product we are selling is democracy. It's the free enterprise system, the American value system. It's a product very much in demand. It's a product that is very much needed." Beers echoed this view, in politer language, soon after her confirmation in October 2001. Her goal, she said, is "to reach new audiences in different ways." This requires "a whole new level of dialogue between moderate Muslims and the United States," a dialogue that "can never be one-sided." What is the United States government planning to learn from its dialogue partners? It needs "to comprehend, to understand, and to walk in their shoes so we know how to draft those messages back to them." Public diplomacy did not apparently include the idea that dialogue might change U.S. foreign policy.[57]

Beers's most famous successor at the Office of Public Diplomacy was Karen Hughes, one of President Bush's closest advisers. She embarked on two high-profile "listening tours" in Muslim societies, where even the handpicked participants bristled at her promotion of American priorities. "Everybody who met her tried to give her a message for President Bush," an al-Jazeera journalist noted, though he—like many Muslim commentators at the time—was skeptical that Hughes's visits would "change the [United States'] image or [its] policy." Hughes stopped going on listening tours. She kept up pretenses ("our goal should be to have a dialogue with the world, not a monologue") but focused her office instead on "outreach"—media messages, foreign aid, exchange programs, and other activities that would improve Muslims' views of U.S. policies, rather than incorporate their views into U.S. decision-making.[58]

By contrast, Greg Mortenson has become something of a celebrity in the American military. General David Petraeus, President Bush's commander in Iraq, read *Three Cups of Tea* and wrote Mortenson a fan letter listing the main lessons he learned from the book: "Number one, we need to listen more; number two, we need to have respect, meaning we are there to serve the people; and number three, we have to build relationships." Admiral Mike Mullen, President Obama's chairman of the Joint Chiefs of Staff, instructed his top commanders to read the book, which is now required reading for officers deploying to Afghanistan. Colonel Christopher Kolenda is another big supporter of Mortenson's. He read the book on his wife's suggestion while he was commanding an American unit in eastern Afghanistan, and he was moved to try its approach. In one area, his troops were suffering repeated rocket attacks. Instead of forcibly searching the nearest village, Kolenda asked to meet with local elders. They were upset with an earlier American raid on their homes, and during the conversation they noted that what they really needed was a school. American troops soon returned with school supplies, and the shelling stopped. A delegation of villagers visited the American base and "they brought with them about 100 thank-you notes written in Pashtun from children," Kolenda told a reporter. His unit also helped to build roads, bridges, health clinics—whatever local villagers felt they needed most.[59]

This approach will not solve all of the problems of American foreign policy. Inevitably, America's allies will disagree about what the United States can and should do. There is no guarantee that their advice will generate the intended outcomes—and even if it does, there is no guarantee that they will remain allies. But if the U.S. military—the world's most lethal organization and one of the world's most bureaucratic labyrinths—can experiment with these ideas, perhaps the rest of the U.S. government can consider them as well.

CHAPTER 6

✦

Predicting the Next Attacks

Y ou might like to know, in a book on terrorism, what the author thinks will happen next. Are we in for more attacks, and if so, how many, and when, and where? I am often asked this sort of question when I present my research to community groups. On occasion, I get the same question from government officials. In early 2004, for example, I received an unsolicited e-mail from a contractor working for the Department of Homeland Security asking my view on when the "homeland" could expect another terrorist attack:

Please rate the below statements on the following scale:

> -2 Strongly Disagree -1 Disagree 0 Neutral +1 Agree +2 Strongly Agree

> Al-Qaida (or its affiliates) has not attacked the homeland since 9/11 because:
> A. It has a long planning cycle (e.g. attack plans are under way but just not yet executed).
> B. It has decided to focus short term on attacks abroad in Iraq and other countries.

C. It has made a longer-term strategic or ideological decision to take the US off the primary target list and focus on other enemies.

D. It never intended to launch another strike on the homeland.

E. Attack plans have been thwarted mainly because of US overseas operations and domestic security measures.

F. Attacks on domestic soft targets (with suicide bombers, VBIEDs [vehicle-borne improvised explosive devices], etc.) are too "unspectacular" for its taste.

G. AQ is content to increase anxiety via rumored threats rather than an actual attack.

H. AQ has become too weak and decentralized to organize such an attack.

I. Some other reason (please specify).
   Future Implications:

J. AQ is likely to launch an attack on the homeland this year (2004).

K. AQ is likely to launch an attack on the homeland within the next 5 years (by the end of 2008).

L. Such an attack will be large scale (such as 9/11).

M. Such an attack will succeed.

This information would assist in planning for a "red cell" exercise, in which a group of national security officials would play the role of enemy forces in a boardroom war game. America was the blue team, and the enemy was red—a holdover from the red-flagged Communists of the Cold War era. Back then, America was composed entirely of blue states.

I wasn't sure how to respond to the survey. It was an honor to be consulted, of course. I was surprised that anybody in the Department of Homeland Security had heard of me or my work, since I hadn't published much on terrorism. I couldn't help wondering whether I had come to the government's attention in some other way. Perhaps they were monitoring my computer as I researched terrorist websites? Perhaps they knew I had traveled to Iran and other countries in the Middle East? Perhaps they thought I had some inside information on the workings of al-Qaida? Could my answers be taken as evidence of illegal activity? In Britain, a graduate student writing his thesis on terrorism was arrested and detained for six days because he downloaded an al-Qaida document from the Internet—perhaps I was being set up for some sort of sting? I decided that these concerns were paranoid. The idea that I was being targeted for a secret operation was too flattering to be true.[1]

I decided to take the survey at face value: my government was reaching out to scholars for input on pressing issues that national security personnel worry about every day. Why didn't al-Qaida follow up with another attack in the United States after 9/11? When would it attack us again? Perhaps academics who study Islamic radicalism might have something to contribute to the national effort to prevent murderous attacks. I sent back my answers with brief explanations: A: 0, B: -2, C: -2, D: -2, E: 0, F: -2, G: -2, H: 0, J: +2, K: +2, L: 0, and M: ?. For Question I, I offered the observation—which forms the basis for this book—that al-Qaida has difficulty recruiting people who are willing to die for the cause. I never received a score from the Department of Homeland Security, but I suspect that I was so right about Question I that I was wrong about J and K: contrary to my pessimistic speculation, al-Qaida did not launch another attack in the United States by the end of 2008. The next al-Qaida attack—perpetrated by an affiliate group in Yemen—occurred on Christmas 2009. Instead of 19 men on four planes, like 9/11, the next attack involved a single man, Umar Farouk Abdulmutallab, on a single plane. He tried to set fire to his underwear, which was packed with explosives, but was subdued by the flight's passengers and crew.

Apparently he didn't want to die enough to lock himself into the lavatory until he got it right.

I would answer the survey the same way today. Al-Qaida and other Islamist terrorists are still furious at the United States for what they see as its "war on Islam," and their literature is full of threats against Americans. I assume that some of them are plotting attacks in the United States and that they will carry them out eventually if they get the chance. But they are struggling even more than in 2004 to find capable recruits. Despite the missteps of U.S. foreign policy, the terrorists' missteps have been even worse. That's why I believe that our fears of terrorism are exaggerated. There just aren't many terrorists, thank goodness.

This conclusion puts me in the awkward position of undermining the importance of my own expertise. Many of us who chose to study Islamic subjects prior to 2001 find it somewhat disconcerting that our field is suddenly in demand. The more that non-Muslims fear Islam, the more that security threats are hyped, the more attention Islamic studies gets. It's not just that the field benefits from Muslims committing atrocities, but that it benefits also from non-Muslims' ignorance and paranoia. As a result, responsible scholars of Islamic studies spend much of their time in the limelight trying to dispel the very stereotypes that helped bring them to prominence.

For their efforts, scholars in Middle East and Islamic studies have come in for heavy criticism from right-wing think tanks and politicians. One of the silliest critiques came from Lynne Cheney, wife of Vice President Dick Cheney and founder of the group that called academics the "weak link" in America's response to 9/11, as I described in the last chapter. In the same pamphlet that called me "weak link" number 100, Lynne Cheney suggested that expertise on Islam was overrated and possibly even counterproductive. "To say that it is more important now [to study Islam] implies that the events of Sept. 11 were our fault, that it was our failure... that led to so many deaths and so much destruction." Cheney proposed that universities encourage the study of American history rather than Islamic history, because it is more important to know what America stands for than to understand others. Apparently she was not concerned about training the next generation of experts on foreign affairs.[2]

A more serious challenge to Middle East and Islamic studies in the United States came from Martin Kramer, a think-tank expert on the Middle East, whose scathing *Ivory Towers on Sand: The Failure of Middle Eastern Studies in America* was written before 9/11 and published, with quickly updated material, one month afterward. Kramer argued that scholars were so blinded by their liberal, multicultural, and Third Worldist political biases that they failed to notice the emergence of Islamist terrorism: "Twenty years of denial had produced mostly banalities about American bias and ignorance, and fantasies about Islamists as democratizers and reformers. These contributed to the public complacency about terrorism that ultimately left the United States vulnerable to 'surprise' attack by Islamists." At the same time, Kramer charged, Middle East specialists profited from the Islamist violence that they downplayed: "How many resources within the university could they command if their phones stopped ringing and their deans did not see and hear them quoted in the national newspapers and on public radio? And how would enrollments hold up if Muslim movements failed to hit the headlines?"[3]

How right he was! Not about scholars' responsibility for complacency—we have no evidence that Middle East studies has had much of an effect on government policy or public opinion in the United States. (I gather from academic colleagues around the world that the situation is similar in other countries, but this chapter focuses primarily on the United States.) In any case, few scholars in Middle East studies ever denied that Islamist terrorism was a threat. The question is usually posed as a contest within

Islam—between revolutionary and reformist movements, between states and oppositions, between violence and nonviolence. Some scholars were more optimistic about the prospects for nonviolence, and some were more pessimistic (very few rooted for violence). Pessimists like Kramer claim to be vindicated on days when mass violence occurs. Should optimists claim to be vindicated on days when mass violence does not occur?

Rather, Kramer was right about the benefits that Middle East experts derive from public anxiety. Of course, university scholars are not the only ones to benefit from this anxiety. Kramer and other think-tank commentators have profited too from widespread attention to Islam. Just like university deans, think-tank administrators and the donors who finance them allocate resources based in part on quotations in national newspapers and on public radio. Kramer's position fits consistently within this system. Every alarm that he sounds helps both to raise public vigilance about threats that he considers severe and to increase funding for the think tank where he works.

The rising tide of public interest has floated both boats in Middle East studies, the think tanks and the universities. Both sides complain about the other, but only the think tanks have actually tried to do something about the situation. In 2003, several right-wing think tanks managed to get legislation introduced in Congress to subject universities' international programs to oversight by political appointees. This oversight committee would make recommendations to Congress and the U.S. Department of Education to ensure that international studies programs "reflect diverse perspectives and represent the full range of views on world regions, foreign language, and international affairs." By "diverse," the bill clarified, it meant greater emphasis on perspectives that prioritized "homeland security and effective United States engagement abroad." The bill's supporters charged that federally funded university programs in Middle East studies "are committed to a narrow point of view at odds with our national interest," that they "tend to purvey extreme and one-sided criticisms of American foreign policy," and that many of them have "acted to undermine America's national security."[4]

Fortunately for academia, the think tanks overreached. Their harsh criticism of universities generated howls of protest from academic organizations and their supporters, who saw political oversight as a threat to the autonomy of the scholarly peer review system. Perhaps even more damaging to their cause, the think tanks made a bold bid for federal resources. The bill authorized the oversight board "to secure directly" any information that it desired "from any executive department, bureau, agency, board, commission, office, independent establishment, or instrumentality." The board was even authorized to work with federal agencies to utilize "the services, personnel, information, and facilities of other Federal, State, local, and private agencies with or without reimbursement." The idea of political appointees in the Department of Education demanding the assistance of national security professionals, rather than the other way around, violated the status hierarchy in Washington, and the bill was dropped.

The think tanks failed in their takeover bid. In its place, they settled for a requirement that federally funded university programs on the Middle East and other world regions prove that their campuses "reflect diverse perspectives and a wide range of views and generate debate on world regions and international affairs," and "encourage government service in areas of national need."[5] As it happens, I wound up writing these sections for a University of North Carolina application for federal funding last year, in conjunction with our Middle East studies partners at Duke University. It was easy to document how we encourage government service—from the State Department to the Peace Corps to the U.S. Agency for International Development, in addition to the military and intelligence agencies that the right-wingers had in mind. It was easy to demonstrate diverse perspectives and debates on our campuses, a far cry from the narrow and one-sided image that the think tanks tried to pin on us. Our campuses have courses and events where hawks and peaceniks square off against each other; we have courses and events where Israeli and Palestinian perspectives are aired and compared; we have courses and events that juxtapose theocratic and secularist ideologies and movements. I challenge any think tank in the world to offer perspectives as diverse as at any research university.

That may be why national security agencies have continually called upon Middle East scholars to help fight the war on terrorism. In 2003, as Congress was considering punishing scholars for supposedly anti-American views, the Department of Defense was inviting them to help predict the future of the Middle East. The Defense Advanced Research Projects Agency (DARPA)—the office that invented the Internet—funded an experimental online market that would allow experts to bet on the likelihood of various events occurring in the region, such as terrorist attacks or revolutions. DARPA hoped to test the theory, developed by several economists, that even small amounts of real money would motivate experts to make better guesses than they would otherwise and that a market-style mechanism would cumulate expert judgments and "provide an early warning system to avoid surprise." Days before the experiment was to begin recruiting participants, two Democratic senators denounced the plan to the *New York Times*, calling it unethical to bet on tragedies in other countries. The senators also worried that terrorists would sign up as experts and profit from market manipulation, though I never understood why terrorists would risk blowing their cover and undermining their own plots for a few dollars in winnings. In any case, DARPA canceled the program the day that the story broke. I never got to sign up and bet on my research findings.[6]

Other government programs have continued to call on scholarly expertise. Beginning in 2003, its first year of operation, the Department of Homeland Security has spent more than $100 million on university-based Centers of Excellence as "an integral and critical component of the new 'homeland security complex' that will provide the nation with a robust, dedicated and enduring capability that will enhance our ability to anticipate, prevent, respond to, and recover from terrorist attacks." In 2008, the Department of Defense launched a large-scale academic research program, the Minerva Initiative, to improve "elements of national power beyond the guns and steel of the military" using "untapped resources outside of government—resources like those our universities can offer."[7]

It is gratifying to see government officials value the expertise of scholars in Middle East and Islamic studies. There is even a frisson of excitement at being the target of right-wing denunciation, which I enjoy all the more so long as these campaigns keep failing. But I worry that both government funders and right-wing critics are asking too much of us. In particular, I am concerned that our fans and our critics are overly focused on our skills at prediction, especially prediction of terrorist attacks. Kramer and colleagues say we are bad at prediction. In their view, pessimistic think-tankers were the only ones to predict 9/11 (in the broadest sense of predicting that Bin Ladin would continue to target Americans), and only pessimistic think-tankers are able to predict subsequent calamities (though they missed one of the biggest calamities since 9/11, the United States' bungled occupation of Iraq). By contrast, the departments of defense and homeland security seem to be investing considerable funds on the proposition that university scholars may help the government to predict and prevent terrorist violence.

Of course, expertise does help us anticipate the future—so long as the future remains similar to the past. Take language skills, for example. An Arabic specialist can tell us how Arabic-speakers are likely to respond to a given phrase. Language training consists largely of learning these patterns so that we can generate the responses we want. But languages change over time, sometimes suddenly. A phrase or a manner of speaking can fall out of style; new expressions constantly emerge; and the patterns that we dutifully memorized as students may no longer generate the desired responses. A really knowledgeable linguist may even be able to anticipate some of the changes that a language undergoes. After conquest by a foreign army, for example, a country's language tends to incorporate vocabulary and calques from the occupation forces, such as *dush* in Moroccan Arabic (from the French word for shower, *douche*) and *narsi* (nurse) in Palestinian Arabic under British colonial administration in the middle of the twentieth century, or *baj* (badge) and *stob* (stop) in the Iraqi dialect of Arabic since the U.S.-led invasion in 2003.[8] But this general prediction doesn't tell us how many borrow-words will enter the language, much less *which* borrow-words. That level of detail can only be tracked after the fact.

During the American occupation of Iraq, the U.S. Department of Defense realized it had a major deficit in Arabic language skills. On top of its traditional language training programs, the military also funded a series of high-tech solutions, including a handheld translation device (sample sentence chosen by the developers to illustrate the system: "Get out of the car"/"Inzil min al-siyara") and a language-learning video game called *Tactical Iraqi* (sample sentence: "Maaku luzuum lil-teftiish hna"/"There is no need to search here"). These computer programs are based on glossaries, grammatical rules, and statistical patterns derived from linguistic expertise on the Iraqi dialect of Arabic—a reasonable approach for teaching the language to beginners. This is the same approach that underlies government enthusiasm for scholarly expertise on culture and society more generally. DARPA and other funders view human interaction as a rule-based system involving inputs, mechanism, and outputs that they want experts to specify. In this grand vision of society, knowing the rules of conduct allows one to predict people's responses and therefore to act effectively. *Tactical Iraqi* offers numerous examples of this sort of "cultural awareness instruction," such as taking off your sunglasses and looking Iraqis of your gender directly in the eye during conversation. Green plus signs floating above the virtual Iraqi characters "indicate the Iraqi's opinion of you just went up, because you showed cultural sensitivity," the developers' promotional video explains. "Bad move!" the video chastises after a cultural blunder. The Iraqi character "had no connection to militias, but he may now consider joining."[9]

DARPA's vision for the social sciences aimed to develop a rule-based model of society as a whole. "Imagine that you are the commander leading coalition forces to accomplish an important mission," a DARPA official suggested at a military research conference in 2005. "You will have to deal with mixed communities and cultures. You're equipped with a host of resources that includes the traditional military capabilities and funds for projects to help the local populace, but these resources are not unlimited....What you don't have today are really effective decision tools to help you assess the most likely outcomes of the courses of action available to you." With new theoretical approaches and massive computing power, he predicted, it is not unreasonable to expect the social sciences "to develop a set of rules that govern the interactions among agents." The challenge is to synthesize these rules in a computer simulation that will allow the military to identify enemies and anticipate their actions. Beyond anticipation, another DARPA official proclaimed, today's national security challenges require "social engineering skills and an understanding of the cultures and motivations of potential adversaries. Indeed, we need to be able to shape the attitudes and opinions of entire societies, with predictable outcomes." A similar vision was expressed by the White House's National Science and Technology Council. "No one can be expected to fully predict or prevent future terrorist attacks on American soil," the panel acknowledged in a 2005 report on counterterrorism research priorities. Nonetheless, the report concluded, the social sciences "can model extremist and socially marginalized group and organizational behaviors, which can help explain why certain people become sympathizers, followers, members, or leaders of terrorist and extremist groups; and how these behaviors change over time." In this way, social scientists can "help predict, prevent, prepare for and recover from a terrorist attack."[10]

DARPA did not invent this mechanical image of society. In fact, this is the founding image of social science. We find this view of society spelled out almost two centuries ago by Auguste Comte, the megalomaniacal visionary who coined the term "sociology" (and later went on to found the Church of Positivism, with himself as chief priest). "We now possess a celestial physics, a terrestrial physics, both mechanical and chemical, a vegetable physics, and an animal physics: we are yet due one last one, a social physics, for our system of natural sciences to be complete," Comte wrote in 1825. "I understand by *social physics* the science that has as its object of study social phenomena, considered in the same spirit as astronomical, physical, chemical, and physiological phenomena, that is to say, subject to invariable natural laws whose discovery is the special aim of its research." The results of this research "will become, in turn, the positive point of departure for the work of the man of state, ... so as to avoid, or at least soften as much as possible, the crises, more or less grave, that are spawned by spontaneous and unforeseen developments. In a word, in this class of phenomena as in all others, science leads to prediction, and prediction permits the regularization of action." In Comte's vision, the ability to discover and apply the laws of human interaction warrants a powerful role for social scientists as advisers to rulers and "spiritual directors" of society.[11]

Some social scientists still claim this role. Among the boldest of these claimants is Bruce Bueno de Mesquita, a political scientist who has developed sophisticated mathematical models of international relations and government policies. BDM, as he is known to his colleagues, speaks openly of his extensive work for the Central Intelligence Agency. He claims to be able to predict all things political, based on expert judgments of the goals and power of selected political leaders, and he has bragged consistently since the mid-1980s about a 90 percent accuracy rate—a far better record, BDM insists, than the predictions of the experts on whose judgments his statistical models are based. I was a bit uncomfortable listening to BDM dismiss the insights of Iranian studies specialists at a recent public lecture about the future of Iran, where he encouraged bright students not to bother learning foreign languages but rather to hone their statistical skills instead. I had just served on a panel of Iran specialists for one of his recent projects, and I won't be doing that again.[12]

Like Comte, BDM proposes that discovering the laws of society will help governments to control and improve society: "If you can predict what people will do, you can engineer what they will do. And if you engineer what they do, you can change the world, you can get a better result." This optimistic view of social science's capacity to engineer change—always for the better, never self-interested or venal—has long prompted government funding for academia. It was one of the guiding principles for the founding of academic departments of social science in the late nineteenth century, and it helped finance the expansion of the social sciences in the mid-twentieth century. The current system of university centers in Middle East studies, along with other world regions, was established explicitly for its pragmatic value to U.S. government policies. The National Defense Education Act of 1958 allocated money for these centers on the grounds that "the national defense needs of the United States" require far more experts than the country was currently producing in order to provide "a full understanding" of societies around the world.[13]

Over the past generation, however, the social sciences have largely abandoned the vision of invariant social mechanisms that would allow specialists to predict and control human interaction. This vision has been replaced by two countercurrents that make much more modest promises. The first countercurrent is the now-dominant view that social patterns are inherently probabilistic. Society is not governed by underlying "laws" that determine outcomes the way that gravity or other physical laws determine outcomes in the material world. All that social sciences can do is calculate the likelihood of particular outcomes, based on theoretical and methodological assumptions that are built into each analysis. Technically, this is how BDM presents his forecasts, with the caveat that his predictions are statistically the most likely outcomes. In early 2009, for example, BDM offered his view of the evolving power struggles in Iran. Based on expert judgments about major decision-makers inside and outside of Iran, he suggested that the most likely scenario was for Iranian business interests and moderate religious scholars to gain steadily in power over the course of the subsequent two years, at the expense of President Mahmud Ahmadinejad and his hard-line allies. Ahmadinejad "is getting weaker, and while he gets a lot of attention in the United States, he is not a major player in Iran. He is on the way down." Four months later, the presidential election in Iran (absent in BDM's forecast) resulted in massive social unrest (unforeseen in BDM's forecast) that Ahmadinejad managed to suppress (contrary to BDM's forecast). Ahmadinejad remains, as of this writing, a major player in Iran—arguably *more* of a major player than in early 2009, according to many observers.[14]

Two weeks after the presidential elections in Iran, BDM met with a reporter from the *New York Times* and stood by his predictions. Repression seemed to have quelled street protests already, but BDM insisted that the dissidents were growing in power and would rival Khamenei by October 2009, when the protest movement was going to "really perk up again." That prediction was wrong too. BDM might defend his failed predictions by pointing out, correctly, that his models make no claim of certainty, only of likelihoods. Unlikely outcomes may still occur from time to time. By this logic, forecasts can be right even when they are wrong. BDM has managed to do the opposite, as well—his proudest prediction was wrong even though it was right. In 1984, BDM published a forecast, based on expert judgments about the relative power of major players in Iran, that Ali Khamenei would succeed Ruhollah Khomeini as the country's leader. Five years later, when Khomeini died, this actually came to pass. While BDM brags about this success, however, he neglects to note that his forecast was "predicated on the assumption that Khomeini will leave the scene soon enough so that the preferences and power of the various groups will remain as it was specified in this analysis." As it happened, Khamenei succeeded Khomeini for the opposite reason—because Khomeini stayed on the scene long enough to fire his appointed successor, Hossein Ali Montazeri, several months before dying. Surely BDM didn't predict that?[15]

BDM deserves credit for going public with these predictions, putting himself at risk of falsification. I hope that picking on him won't seem petty—he is one of the most prominent social-scientific forecasters working today, and I happen to know a little about one of the countries whose future he keeps trying to predict. The problem is not that BDM is bad at what he does, but that what he does is inherently error-prone. BDM's "game theory" models assume that the players in tomorrow's game are the same players as in today's game, and models like this run into trouble when major players exit the stage and new ones enter. A further problem is that the people we study may respond to our analyses—when counterterrorism specialists say that they expect (or don't expect) attacks in a particular area, terrorists may read these analyses and adjust their targets to take advantage of presumed security lapses. How does it make sense for Fox television's "intelligence" expert David Hunt to rant in public that "we aren't even pretending to protect our rail transportation infrastructure"? Fortunately, nobody seems to pay him any attention. Instead, Al-Qaida and other terrorist organizations obsess over serious counterterrorism experts like Jarret Brachman, who are sophisticated enough to recognize that their public statements are in fact public.[16]

An even bigger problem for forecasters is that people change. Their preferences can shift dramatically. They start to want different things; they try out new ways of getting what they want; and they interact with people differently than they did before. During the Iranian Revolution, which I examined in an earlier book, these sorts of shifts seem to have been common. People who had considered revolution unthinkable because of the seeming stability of the monarchy began to entertain the idea that political change was a realistic possibility and then to act on that idea, making demands on the regime that they would not have imagined making months earlier. Others underwent cathartic conversions that turned their preferences upside down. One young Iranian, a leftist university graduate, told an interviewer that she disdained religion as a backward ideology—until she witnessed and joined the massive anti-shah demonstrations of early September 1978, which were organized around the observation of an Islamic holiday, Eid al-Fitr. The holiday had never before been the occasion of protest, and many senior religious leaders objected to its politicization in 1978, but the sight of the crowds impressed this young woman immensely, so much so that she abandoned her faith in socialism. "I was very surprised," she reported shortly after the event. "I saw

that Islam is a great religion, because it makes all things possible."
A forecast made on the basis of her preferences a month earlier
would have miscalculated her new preferences and behaviors.[17]

Really dramatic change like this doesn't occur very often, and
even when it does, a person doesn't change entirely. Much of
human activity is relatively routine and can be forecast with some
confidence. For most things, it is a good bet that the way things are
this year will be the way things are next year. For example, it is
likely that there will be approximately 16,000 murders in the
United States next year, give or take a thousand—that's how many
there have been each year for more than a decade, according to the
U.S. Department of Justice. Somehow, with several hundred million potential killers and victims in the United States, the country
manages to produce a consistent rate of around 16,000 murders
per year. Even phenomena that change over time can do so consistently. For example, it seems likely that federal complaints about
Internet crime will increase next year, just as they have increased
almost every year for the past decade. The most thrilling predictions, though, are of phenomena that are unprecedented. The trick
to this sort of prediction is to make an analogy to past phenomena.
For example, it is a safe bet that China will make ambitious new
demands on its trading partners at some point in the near future.
This prediction is not based on China's past demands, but rather
on the expectation that China will behave like other major
industrial producers who have reshaped international relations in
the past.[18]

Prediction involves judgments about which characteristics and
mechanisms will continue to operate in the future. So long as the
pattern holds, prediction remains possible. When the pattern
breaks down, so does our ability to predict. The holy grail of social
science is the prediction of these disruptions. If we could know in
advance the circumstances under which patterns break down, we
could at least sketch out the limits within which our forecasts are

relatively reliable. But we can't. At any given moment, patterns may change. All we can say is that predictions work until they stop working. The number of murders in the United States, for example, is uncannily stable from year to year—but a mass-casualty attack like 9/11 could change that overnight. From 1993 to 2000, murders dropped steadily from more than 24,000 to around 16,000 a year—but that information could not help us predict the violence of 9/11. China might behave like the Great Powers of the past, or it might not—perhaps Chinese leaders will feel constrained by the country's economic interdependence with its trading partners, or they might value international stability more than maximizing current terms of trade, or they might lack some new weapon system that changes the balance of international relations. We can't know in advance what kind of game-changing developments will or will not emerge.

This does not mean that we should stop predicting the future. We can't stop. All sentient creatures must predict the future—at the very least, they try to predict which plants are poisonous and could kill them, which animals are dangerous and could kill them, which mates are compatible and could help them propagate the species. Human societies require elaborate skills at prediction, including estimates about the return on educational investments, the projected value of one's house in 30 years (and the value of all other houses one might consider buying), the amortization schedule of clothes and pots and pans, and a million other calculations that we make every day with an eye toward future utility. Predicting next year's fashion styles may seem far afield from predicting terrorist attacks, but they are basically the same intellectual activity: taking what we know now and imagining how this will play out in the future.

In some fields, experts can be sued for false predictions. An engineer who fails to calculate a bridge's load-bearing capacity can be held accountable. A lawyer or a doctor who makes an egregious error of prediction can be accused of malpractice. But in other fields, there is no expectation of accuracy. Investment consultants, for example, tell their clients in writing that past performance is no guarantee of future success so that they can't be sued if their predictions turn sour. Hollywood producers have a terrible track record at predicting a film's popularity—most movies lose money—but investors pour billions of dollars into the industry nonetheless.[19] So what kind of experts are social scientists? Are we more like engineers or more like Hollywood producers? I think we're Hollywood producers. We may dress more like engineers and get paid more like engineers, but the social scientific phenomena that we study can be fickle like movie audiences. This is particularly true for rare and high-risk phenomena like terrorism, where a few "blockbuster" predictions can make or break a career. The experts who warned about Bin Ladin prior to 9/11 will always look prescient, even if they never get another prediction right.

In the study of terrorism, experts walk a fine line between down-playing expectations of predictive accuracy and selling their own expertise. Walter Laqueur, one of the most respected terrorism specialists in the United States, expressed this tension vividly in a 2004 essay with the soothsaying title, "The Terrorism to Come." Laqueur acknowledged that predicting terrorist incidents is impossible: "To make predictions about the future course of terrorism is even more risky than political predictions in general. We are dealing here not with mass movements but small—sometimes very small—groups of people, and there is no known way at present to account for the movement of small particles either in the physical world or in human societies." At the same time, Laqueur made a series of predictions, couched in the language of likelihoods: Islamist terrorism "certainly has not yet run its course. But it is unlikely that its present fanaticism will last forever.... More likely the terrorist impetus will decline as a result of setbacks.... There are likely to be splits among the terrorist groups even though their structure is not highly centralized.... That terrorist attacks are likely to continue in the Middle East goes without saying; other main danger zones are Central Asia and, above all, Pakistan.... Europe is probably the most vulnerable battlefield." If small groups are hard to account for, as Laqueur suggests, then these predictions are also hard to account for. So far, his record appears to have been right about Pakistan, wrong about Central Asia and Europe, and mixed on setbacks and splits.[20]

The one deterministic prediction Laqueur made illustrates his dilemma. He proposed that the region he knows best, Europe, is particularly vulnerable to Islamist terrorism because of the growth of a second generation of Muslim immigrants, born and raised in Europe, who suffer feelings of "deep resentment" and "free-floating aggression" because of discrimination and failure in education and the workplace. Laqueur described this as something of a social-scientific law: "This is a common phenomenon all over the world: the radicalization of the second generation of immigrants. This generation has been superficially acculturated (speaking fluently the language of the host country) yet at the same time feels resentment and hostility more acutely." As it happens, the Pew Global Attitudes Project conducted a survey of European Muslims two years later. The second generation did indeed feel more resentment than the first generation—but only slightly. Twenty-two percent of the second generation said they felt that most Europeans were hostile to Muslims, as compared with 18 percent of first-generation immigrants. This hardly represents a sea-shift in attitudes. Nineteen percent of the second generation said that suicide bombing was sometimes or often justified, as compared with 12 percent of the first generation. At the same time, 78 percent of the second generation said they identified more with moderate Muslims than with Islamic fundamentalists, as compared with 73 percent of the first generation. These figures do no confirm an iron law of radicalization—and according to security officials, sec-ond-generation Muslims are not the primary source of terrorism in the European Union. Notwithstanding a number of high-profile cases, the second generation constitutes as little as one-fifth of Islamist terrorist suspects in Europe in recent years.[21]

Not every prediction fails, of course. The problem is that we don't know in advance which ones will fail. This raises an ethical question for those of us who are asked to peer into the future. We may phrase our predictions as likelihoods, but what responsibility do we have toward the people whose actions we are predicting, most of whom will do nothing to deserve the suspicion that we cast upon them?

The ethical dilemmas of predicting terrorism are on display in the strange career of *The Arab Mind*, a book published in 1973 by Raphael Patai. Like Walter Laqueur, Patai was a Central European Jew who emigrated to Palestine in the 1930s, surviving the Holocaust and later settling in the United States. In addition to training as a rabbi, Patai was fluent in Arabic, and his book offered a sympathetic critique of the Arab psyche, drawing on Arab sources from the Middle Ages to present-day social science. Patai recognized that there was no single "Arab mind," of course, but he offered his book as a portrait of certain frequently observed traits. Along the same lines, he published a book on *The Jewish Mind* several years later.

The Arab Mind would have fallen into obscurity, as most books do, but for the efforts of two part-time Middle East experts who considered the book iconic. The first was Edward Said, one of the most influential scholarly figures of the late twentieth century. Said, who taught at Columbia University until his death in 2003, special-ized in the study of European literature, but he is best known for his book *Orientalism*, which examined European images of Arabs, and the relationship of these images to European colonial and neocolonial intervention in the Middle East. This book—hugely important in Middle East studies and in cultural studies more generally—took *The Arab Mind* as a paragon of twentieth-century Orientalism: demeaning, overgeneralizing, and designed to serve imperialist interests. Said was not himself a Middle East specialist, though he grew up in the region, and he did not offer evidence that Patai's analysis was incorrect. Instead, he attacked the book's underlying goals as illegitimate. "The Oriental is given as fixed, stable, in need of investigation, in need even of knowledge about himself.... [T]he result is to eradicate the plurality of differences among the Arabs (whoever they may be in fact) in the interest of one difference, that one setting Arabs off from everyone else. As a subject matter for study and analysis, they can be controlled more readily."[22]

Said's critique of Patai was part of a broad move among scholars away from the study of culture, in the singular, to the study of cultures, in the plural—the debate, contestation, rebellion, and change that all cultures experience, to a greater or lesser degree, at all times. Patai recognized this. One of his earliest publications was an essay on culture change in the Middle East. But throughout his career, Patai preferred to focus on culture as a singular whole rather than on cultural variety. As scholars abandoned monolithic visions of culture in favor of a more complex image of multiple moving parts, Patai's book was doomed to be considered outmoded. Thanks to Said's critique, however, the book was not forgotten. Said turned *The Arab Mind* into a poster child for Western Orientalism. At the same time, Said's critique has come to be considered outmoded as well, on the same grounds—his own fans in Middle East studies frequently turn Said's approach against Said himself. They charge that Said treated Western Orientalism as monolithic, without exploring the variety of Western debates about imperialism and the Orient.[23]

The second individual working to maintain the memory of *The Arab Mind*, U.S. Army colonel Norvell B. De Atkine, shares this critique of Said. Said and his followers charge that "Eurocentric Orientalists believe in an 'essentialist' and monolithic Islamic world," and then "engage in the same stereotyping they reject in Orientalist writings." De Atkine is an artillery officer who also has a background in Middle East studies, having studied at the American University in Beirut and serving several tours of duty in the region. He was stationed in Jordan during the "Black September" war of 1970, replacing an officer who was killed by Palestinian revolutionaries. He was stationed in Egypt during the assassination of President Anwar Sadat in 1981—in fact, De Atkine and his wife were seated 100 feet away when Sadat was gunned down by Islamist revolutionaries. He served in Iraq after the U.S.-led invasion of 2003, working with a psychological operations unit. But he has spent most of the past quarter century at Fort Bragg, North Carolina, preparing American troops for deployment in the Middle East. De Atkine's specialty is cultural training, and *The Arab Mind* is central to his curriculum. "Raphael Patai's *The Arab Mind* is a 'field tested' book—and I mean those words in an entirely positive sense," De Atkine wrote in a preface to a reprint of *The Arab Mind*. "In my 18 years of teaching at the Special Warfare School at Ft. Bragg, many of my former students, returning from assignments in the Middle East, would comment on how useful the cultural education they had received was and how much they had benefitted from it." Other students of his, officers who had served in Iraq, said they "found their cultural instruction to be invaluable and related to me many examples of Iraqi cultural traits described by Patai. The instruction helped them work with Arab leaders and better understand their ambivalence, methods of conflict resolution, sensitivities to loss of face, proclivities to excessive rhetoric and habit of substituting words for action, disinclination to accept responsibility, as well as their traits of hospitality and generosity." Patai and De Atkine present no systematic evidence that these characteristics are more common among Arabs than in any other group. Nevertheless, enough military officers agree with De Atkine about the value of *The Arab Mind* that it has been placed on the "Cultural Awareness Reading List" of the Command and General Staff College at Fort Leavenworth. Patai's book formed the basis for the training of American military interrogators at the infamous Abu Ghraib prison in Iraq.[24]

According to De Atkine, Patai's critics in Middle East studies suffer from an anti-American political agenda and a "demand for conformity to group-think that for some years has constricted academic work in area studies, especially when the area is as controversial a one as the Middle East." In an article cowritten with Daniel Pipes, a think-tank critic of Middle East scholarship, De Atkine denounced Middle East studies for its "pronounced leftist bias," its "proclivity toward apologetics for enemies of the United States," as well as its "postmodern practice of stuffing the complexities of political science and history into bottles labeled race, gender, and class." Another problem with the field, they propose, is that there are too many Middle Easterners in it. This has transformed the field's leading professional organization, the Middle East Studies Association of North America, "from an American organization interested in the Middle East to a Middle Eastern one that happens to meet in the United States." Middle Easterners "display a hypersensitivity to criticism that nearly shuts off debate," and "the same applies to scholars of the Middle East, who infuse intense emotions and hyperbole into their scholarship." De Atkine has gone even further in recent years, indulging in a little hyperbole of his own in an e-mail to an Islamic studies electronic mailing list in North Carolina: "The reason the US Middle Eastern academic community is held is such low repute is that it is always wrong, has tunnel vision, is still living in a socialist 60's daze, and basically knows very little about the region it purports to teach (indoctrinate) young impressionable students."[25]

In De Atkine's view, *The Arab Mind* is not just a useful introduction to Middle Eastern culture. In the wake of 9/11, it also provides crucial insight into the causes of Islamist terrorism. "To begin a process of understanding the seemingly irrational hatred that motivated the World Trade Center attackers, one must understand the social and cultural environment in which they lived and the modal personality traits that make them susceptible to engaging in terrorist actions. This book does a great deal to further that understanding. In fact, it is essential reading," De Atkine wrote in November 2001. He added in 2007: "A careful reading and understanding of Patai twenty years ago would have answered the question still being asked, 'Why did they do it?'"[26]

What are we supposed to do with this explanation? If we accept De Atkine's claim that Arab men are psychologically "susceptible to engaging in terrorist actions," what ethical debt do we incur toward Arab men who have never committed such acts of violence? Leave aside that the attacks contradicted Patai's characterization of Arab men as lacking in the ability to engage in decisive action (a characteristic due to on-demand breastfeeding and late weaning of Arab boys, Patai proposed). Leave aside the fact that this explanation ignores non-Arab terrorists, including the chief organizer of 9/11, Khalid Sheikh Mohammed, who was Pakistani (though raised in Kuwait, perhaps nursed according to Arab custom?). Are a hundred million Arab men to be considered "susceptible to engaging in terrorist actions"? If so, why have so few of them actually engaged in such actions?[27]

This sort of question emerges in many social-scientific studies of terrorism, which frequently invoke large-scale causes for relatively small-scale outcomes. One famous analysis by political scientist Robert Pape focuses on suicide bombing as a strategic response to foreign military occupation—yet most populations that experience this intervention produce little or no terrorist activity. The United States has stationed thousands of soldiers in

Turkey for half a century, yet there has been little anti-American terrorism (so far) by Turks. Even in Saudi Arabia, where American troop presence since 1990 has been one of al-Qaida's prime grievances, very few residents have ever responded with violence. Of course, it only takes a few individuals to produce a dramatically violent act of terrorism, and these few may have had help from a larger number of compatriots, but a theory that is accurate for a few dozen or a few hundred individuals, and inaccurate for millions, seems like an overly blunt explanatory instrument. The same problem arises with the "geometric" theory of terrorism proposed by sociologist Donald Black. Terrorist violence "is unpredictable and unexplainable only if we seek its origins in the characteristics of individuals (such as their beliefs or frustrations) or in the characteristics of societies, communities, or other collectivities (such as their cultural values or level of inequality)." The "geometry of terrorism," by contrast, is intended to be predictive and precise. It narrows down potential sites of terrorism to conflicts where two sides are socially polarized, highly unequal in power, and physically close. In the modern world, air travel makes all of us physically close—which is why we see more terrorism in the modern world than in previous eras, Black argues. But if we have all become physically close, then every polarized, unequal conflict in the world—and there are hundreds of them—ought to degenerate into terrorism. Yet few of them have done so.[28]

We could continue the list of overly broad explanations for terrorism—globalization, belief in otherworldly rewards, resentment, pride, and many more factors have been proposed by an industry of terrorism experts that generates new theories all the time. The market for these theories never seems to be saturated. At an academic conference several years ago, a well-meaning government official asked me to produce a theory to fill a niche that he had identified. Two economists had just published a paper debunking the idea that poverty breeds terrorism—it turned out that poor communities were statistically no more likely to produce terrorists than rich ones. The government official had read the study and was looking for a terrorism expert to debunk the debunking. His reasoning was that Congress would increase international development assistance for poor countries if these programs could be marketed as a deterrent to terrorism. He saw hundreds of billions of dollars being allocated to the military each year and was hoping to divert some small portion of this sum to development aid. All he needed was an academic theory to help legitimize the pitch to Congress. Aside from the ethics of fudging the data, I worried about a theory that presented all of the world's poor people as potential terrorists. That's just the sort of overgeneralization that has made people so disproportionately afraid of terrorism.[29]

Any discussion of a public threat walks a fine line between complacency and panic. On one hand, we want the public to take the threat as seriously as it deserves; on the other hand, we don't want to panic people into overreacting. This is a common dilemma in the field of public health. Perhaps you remember severe acute respiratory syndrome (SARS). This was a huge concern in the winter and spring of 2003, as it spread outward from China and threatened to generate a global pandemic. SARS was transmitted by coughs or sneezes and killed a tenth or more of the people who were infected. There was no known cure. In April 2003, according to one survey, a third of Americans said they were more worried about their family catching SARS than falling victim to terrorism. (Only 15 percent said they were not worried about either threat.) One in 14 respondents said they were avoiding public events for fear of contracting the disease. And the United States was not even near the top in fear of SARS: 90 percent of Nigerians said they were worried about their family contracting the disease, as did 83 percent of Russians and 80 percent of Brazilians, despite the fact that there had been no cases of SARS in any of these countries. Public health officials tried not to fan hysteria as they dealt with the crisis. In Nigeria, this meant press conferences promising to quarantine people who had come into contact with people suspected of having SARS and test incoming passengers at the country's international airports.[30]

Even before the SARS virus receded, public health professionals began to debate whether government responses had overly panicked the world's population. A prominent physician in Canada, one of the countries that was most proactive in fighting the spread of the disease, cautioned that "the response should not be worse than the disease." The government's initial reaction, including shutting down two hospitals and ordering the quarantine of thousands of people who had casual contact with SARS patients, "fueled public fears" and wasted health-care resources. Instead, the physician concluded, "Public health officials must show leadership in restoring calm and balance to the battle against SARS." In the United States, as well, leading public health specialists urged the government to weigh the duty of protecting the public from disease with the duty of protecting individuals from excessive government intrusion. This ethical dilemma "does not require public health authorities to adopt measures that are less effective but does require the least invasive intervention that will achieve the objective." The director of the Centers for Disease Control gave regular press briefings on the disease, detailing the precautionary measures that the government was taking and, at the same time, trying to communicate "common sense and prudent recommendations from a public health perspective without causing unnecessary fear and panic or overreaction in the public."[31]

The discussion of terrorism could use more debate like this. Compare the U.S. government's statements on SARS—warning against "unnecessary fear and panic or overreaction"—with its statements on smallpox, another deadly virus. Smallpox was eradicated in the wild by 1979 and contained in two highly secure labs, one in the United States and one in Russia. Still, the Bush administration worried that terrorists might somehow obtain and use it as a biological weapon. Once the disease was linked with terrorism, it left the realm of public health and entered the realm of national security, where there is less concern about fear and panic. In the fall of 2002, seeking to justify an invasion of Iraq, the Bush administration leaked secret intelligence assessments that Iraq might have a stock of smallpox. (These assessments later turned out to be based primarily on false information from Iraqi defectors.) "We believe that regimes hostile to the United States may possess this dangerous virus," President Bush announced. "To prepare for the possibility that terrorists would kill indiscriminately," using smallpox obtained from hostile regimes such as Iraq, the U.S. government ordered half a million military personnel to be vaccinated and reassured Americans that the government "has stockpiled enough vaccine...to inoculate our entire population in the event of a smallpox attack." Bush stressed that a mass-scale biological attack was not imminent, but his announcement nonetheless stoked public fear—surveys in the following months found that 60 percent of respondents were worried about a smallpox attack and 11 percent considered it somewhat or very likely that their family would contract smallpox in the coming year. Behind the scenes, public health officials were relieved that they had warded off an even more alarmist policy of vaccinating the entire country immediately, which Vice President Dick Cheney's staff had proposed.[32]

Fear of smallpox evaporated when American troops failed to find any biological weapon programs in Iraq, but terrorism itself has morphed into a virus in the public consciousness—deadly and highly contagious. One month after 9/11, a State Department official encouraged Americans to "view international terrorism as analogous to a terrible, lethal virus." Like a virus, it can live dormant for lengthy periods and then explode into virulence, leaping across borders and becoming "particularly malevolent when it can find a supportive host." We can never fully eradicate this virus, so we must be on permanent watch: "take steps to prevent it, protect ourselves from it, and, when an outbreak occurs, quarantine it, minimize the damage it inflicts, and attack it with all our power." This was hardly the first invocation of the analogy between terrorism and viral disease, but in the new era of heightened national security concerns, the analogy has itself "gone viral"—a phrase that suggests something omnipresent and unstoppable. For example, a frightening cover story in the *New York Times Magazine* warned in 2005 that al-Qaeda had become a "viral movement" with a "large and growing supply" of terrorists plotting do-it-yourself attacks that are "nearly impossible to prevent." Viral analogies tend to be worst-case scenarios, with little concern for the balancing act between alertness and panic that public health professionals consider when they confront actual viruses.[33]

These worst-case scenarios feed the worldview that civilization is precarious and constantly at risk of extinction. "Unless it keeps its citizens safe, the modern metropolis may go the way of ancient Rome," author Joel Kotkin predicted in 2005, likening today's terrorists to the nomadic brigands who overran ancient centers of civilization. "If cities are to survive in Europe or elsewhere, they will need to face this latest threat to urban survival with something more than liberal platitudes, displays of pluck and willful determination." Only "harsh measures" like preventive detention will "protect the urban future." Kotkin downplayed evidence that cities have endured far worse injuries than a few thousand deaths by terrorist attack. For example, large sections of Hamburg, London, Tokyo, and other cities were destroyed during World War II, yet these cities have bounced back. Over the past two centuries, American cities have survived pandemics, civil war, mass rioting, crime waves, and other grievous threats to urban life. Even 9/11, with the country's worst single-day death toll since 1862, failed to topple New York City. After a period of mourning and economic recession, the Big Apple has indeed relied on pluck and willful determination to recover its vitality and appeal, without unconstitutional measures like preventive detention. Kotkin and other doomsayers contribute to a broader "culture of peril," as sociologist Robert Wuthnow has phrased it. For generations, this culture has obsessed over nuclear annihilation, viral pandemics, devastating terrorist attacks, and other threats. Too many of us have become recidivist millenarians, constantly anticipating a new Armageddon—and when each doomsday fails to materialize, we move on to dread about the next one. Even when the threats are real, an exaggerated sense of existential angst prevents us from considering our response in proper perspective.[34]

On the question of terrorism, our response invokes two distinct goals, both of them cherished American ideals. One is security—we need people to take the threat seriously, even as the memory of September 11 fades and other concerns replace terrorism as public fear number one. The other goal is liberty—we don't want overblown fears to justify overly intrusive or discriminatory government programs. The debate over terrorism has gotten so intemperate at points that we sometimes forget to acknowledge the importance of *both* goals. One side dismisses libertarian concerns on the grounds that we are living through an emergency and can't afford to play by the usual rules. In this view, shackling the government's hands with legal niceties is dangerous, possibly even treasonous. The other side dismisses security concerns as exaggerated, possibly even manipulated for partisan political gain. This view sometimes lapses into apologetics or denial.

Disagreement is not necessarily a problem—that's what democracy is all about, brokering civil solutions when people disagree. But it is a problem when one-sided positions dominate public debate over terrorism. Counterterrorism policy suffers from zigs and zags, and our political life suffers from incivility. Each side accuses the other of harboring secret fascist plots to undermine the Constitution and the American way of life. Each side denies that its opponents have anything reasonable to contribute to public discussion of terrorism. That sort of sniping is inaccurate and unhelpful. Each side needs to admit that its opponents share *both* goals, security and liberty. Libertarians care about law and order, and securitarians care about liberty, even if they disagree about where to locate the balance.

What sort of criteria should we use to establish this balance and to evaluate whether any particular policy lies too far in one direction or the other? One factor to consider might be the death toll. First we would examine the past record of deaths by terrorism, as compared with other causes of death—as noted in chapter 1, terrorism turns out to be quite low on the list, accounting for fewer than 1 in 1,000 of the world's deaths each day and far fewer in the United States. (The authors of *SuperFreakonomics* estimate that an American's chances of dying from terrorism are about 1 in 5,000,000, though I don't know how they calculated this.) Next, we examine worst-case scenarios for the future—according to scenarios prepared by the Bush administration, this would be hundreds of thousands dead from a 10-ton nuclear device or a massive influenza attack. Keep in mind that this would be a hundred times more fatalities than any terrorist attack in modern history—9/11 killed almost 3,000 people; the next most deadly attack killed 1,000; the next one was in the 500s, the next two in the 400s, and the next 10 in the 300s, all horrible, terrible events, but nothing like hundreds of thousands. Now multiply the casualties by the likelihood of these worst-case scenarios actually occurring. This likelihood is probably very low, since weapons this deadly are extremely difficult to obtain—terrorists have expressed an interest in getting their hands on these weapons for years, and none have ever managed to come close. But for the purposes of our calculations, let's imagine the opposite. Let's imagine that the likelihood is 100 percent—that it is absolutely certain that terrorists will have the capacity for an attack of this magnitude within the next several years. Now we need to calculate the odds that a shift in policy will prevent this attack. If the attack is going to happen no matter what we do, then there is no sense trying to prevent it—we might as well focus our efforts on recovering from the attack instead. Imagine that some new policy has a 100 percent chance of preventing the attack. In other words, the policy is guaranteed to save several hundred thousand lives over the next several years. Who wouldn't support this policy? But what if the policy meant violating your deeply held values—for example, what if it meant detaining and torturing thousands of people? If the policy were easy and unproblematic, you can be sure that we'd already have tried it. Are these values worth several hundred thousand lives? This is the sort of question that counterterrorism debates should be raising: how many lives are we willing to sacrifice to maintain our core values of individual liberty?[35]

Of course, we have no way of knowing the actual probabilities of future terrorist attacks or of our preventative measures. If the likelihood of a massive attack was only 1 percent, instead of 100 percent, and the likelihood of prevention was only 1 percent, then the new policy would reduce the risk from 1 in 100 to 1 in 101. This hardly seems worth violating core values for. That may be why Dick Cheney objected to this sort of calculation. At a national security meeting in late 2001, Cheney reportedly spelled out a different view. The issue at hand was an intelligence report that Pakistan's nuclear program may have cooperated with al-Qaida. "With a low-probability, high-impact event like this...we're going to have to look at it in a completely different way," Cheney told his colleagues, according to journalist Ron Suskind. "If there's a one percent chance that Pakistani scientists are helping al Qaeda build or develop a nuclear weapon, we have to treat it as a certainty in terms of our response."[36]

Al-Qaida has shown no signs of actually having nuclear or biological weapons capability on a scale large enough to carry out such a massive attack, despite 15 years of on-and-off attempts to develop this capacity. It seems more likely that terrorists will engage in far less devastating attacks, using firearms and conventional explosives, like the ones that we've seen over the past several years. If the death toll from these attacks remains low—even if it were to rise tenfold into the hundreds each year—it would not be a leading cause of death in the U.S. America suffers that many fatalities on the road on a typical holiday weekend. We suffer far more murders at the hands of relatives each year.[37]

Over time, the Bush administration relaxed some of its most controversial antiterror measures. It stopped using "enhanced interrogation," partially suspended its registration system for legal visitors from designated countries, and invaded no more countries after 2003. At the same time, the Bush administration maintained many of the counterterrorism policies that it introduced during the scariest moments after 9/11, including the domestic surveillance mechanisms of the USA PATRIOT Act and the "enemy combatant" status of alleged foreign terrorists, which denied them the rights either of prisoners of war or of criminal suspects.

Barack Obama's presidential campaign challenged these and other aspects of Bush's security policy. Obama argued that the balance could be shifted toward greater liberty with no loss of security—that the trade-off was a "false choice" foisted on America and the world by the Bush administration. In office, however, the Obama administration has made no major changes to the national security policies it inherited. Obama has extended provisions of the USA PATRIOT Act and defended the detention of "enemy combatants," two measures that he specifically denounced during his campaign. Perhaps Obama learned of serious threats that the rest of us still don't know about, when he came into office. Or perhaps he concluded that responsibility for a major terrorist attack would be politically debilitating. A considerable segment of the American population considers Obama to be soft on terrorism, even though he has kept Bush's security policies in place. In recent surveys, a quarter of respondents say that Obama has made the country less safe from terrorism. Then again, a quarter of respondents say that Obama has made the country *more* safe. These ratios appear to be relatively stable—they did not budge even after Faisal Shahzad's failed car bomb in Times Square in May 2010, and respondents have been evenly split for more than four years on a related survey question: which political party, the Democrats or the Republicans, do you trust to do a better job handling the U.S. campaign against terrorism?[38]

The political calculation for any administration is: how many citizens will change their votes when the next terrorist attacks occur? I don't know how big this swing vote might be and how it might be affected by perceptions of government laxity when more competent terrorists eventually surface—a Taheri-Azar who picks a sidewalk with room for acceleration, an Abdulmutallab who stays in the airplane lavatory until his underwear explodes, a Shahzad who uses a reliable detonator instead of firecrackers. If a few hundred Americans die in the next successful attack, how many current Obama supporters will turn on him? This sort of political concern may prevent the administration from tweaking counterterrorism policy—unless public opinion shifts to allow a more honest and realistic debate about terrorism.

That's what this book aims for:

1. Turn down the volume on terrorism debates. This is a serious subject, too serious for name-calling and partisan exaggeration. We are talking about fine-tuning the balance between security and liberty, not ditching either of them.

2. Put the threat of Islamist terrorism in perspective. This is not one of the major causes of death in the world, especially not in the United States. Taking the threat seriously does not mean fixating on it to the neglect of other public concerns.

3. Give credit to Muslims as the primary defense against Islamist revolutionaries. The revolutionaries themselves are frustrated with Muslims' lack of support for terrorist violence—"scum

of the flood," one al-Qaida supporter called today's Muslims (see chapter 1). Instead of viewing Muslim societies as potential enemies, it may be more effective to view them as current allies. Like many allies, Muslims around the world have issues with U.S. foreign policy, and they are entitled to their views. In fact, we would do well to listen to the views of our allies—they know better than we do what sort of support would be most helpful in the struggle against terrorism.

4. Accept uncertainty. Don't ask me to predict how many terrorist attacks there will be or where they will be. I can't tell you, and neither can any other so-called expert—but that's okay. Life is uncertain. In the meantime, let's act responsibly and live up to our ideals.

5. Be brave! Don't abandon your values just because terrorists kill a few thousand of us. Terrorists want us to panic—they want us to overreact. Let's not give them that satisfaction. Let's get through this challenge by living up to our national anthem—"the land of the free and the home of the brave."

ACKNOWLEDGMENTS

This book was conceived in the days after 9/11, when I wondered—as everybody did—what the world was in for. Was 9/11 the bloody signal of an impending cataclysm? As years passed and cataclysm did not occur, I began to ask why not. I asked in a faculty working group with Mark Crescenzi, Robert Jenkins, Anthony Oberschall, Jeffrey Sonis, and other colleagues, who sent me back to the drawing board on several occasions. I asked in a research project with David Schanzer and Ebrahim Moosa, supported by the National Institute of Justice, which allowed us to collect data on terrorism and terrorism prevention. I asked my students, including Marium Chaudhry, Keegan De Lancie, Matthew Garza, Sarah Grossblatt, Timur Hammond, Ali Kadivar, Sherine Mahfouz, Lara Moussa, Ijlal Naqvi, and Yekta Zülfikar, who scoured the Internet for evidence of "radical sheik," conducted interviews for me around the world, and helped me with translations. I asked community groups that invited me to speak about terrorism, and I asked friends and family, who rarely invited me to speak on the topic but were usually polite when I spoke anyway. Most importantly, I asked my godfather, Ralph X. P. who survived both the Holocaust and 9/11 and is still open-hearted enough, despite witnessing such evil, to believe in human goodness.

NOTES

CHAPTER 1

1. Taheri-Azar described the event and his preparations in detail in letters of May 2 and 3, 2006, to reporter Shannon Bowen at the *Daily Tar Heel*, the student newspaper at the University of North Carolina at Chapel Hill. I thank Ms. Bowen and the editors of the newspaper for sharing Taheri-Azar's letters with me.

2. Audio recording of 911 call, March 3, 2006, released by Orange County Emergency Services.

3. *Herald-Sun* (Durham, N.C.), March 25, 2006.

4. Roy Cooper and John J. Aldridge III, *North Carolina Firearms Laws* (Raleigh: North Carolina Department of Justice, Law Enforcement Liaison Section, 2006).

5. Mike Davis, *Buda's Wagon: A Brief History of the Car Bomb* (London, England: Verso, 2007); C. P. Berry, *The Law of Automobiles*, 2nd ed. (Chicago, Ill.: Callaghan, 1916), p. 997. Gillo Pontecorvo, *La Battaglia di Algeri* (Algiers, Algeria: Casbah Films; Rome, Italy: Igor Film, 1966); this film is not included in Taheri-Azar's list of his 15 favorite movies, which is heavy on science-fiction action heroes (letter of May 7, 2006). Copycats: Omeed Aziz Popal, an Afghan-American, killed one man and injured more than a dozen pedestrians in Fremont and San Francisco, California, in August 2006 (Superior Court of California, San Francisco County, case number 2281252; Alameda County, case number 160861). Ismail Yassin Mohamed, a Somali-American, smashed a stolen car into several vehicles in Minneapolis in January 2007, injuring one woman; he was found not guilty by reason of mental incompetence (Minnesota Fourth District Court, case number 27CR07007209). Muhammad Khalil al-Hukayma, "How to Fight Alone," 2006, translated by the Combating Terrorism Center, United States Military Academy. See also Yahya Ibrahim, "The Ultimate Mowing Machine," *Inspire*, number 2, 2010, p. 54: "use a pickup truck as a mowing machine, not to mow grass but mow

down the enemies of Allah. You would need a 4WD pickup truck. The stronger the better. You would then need to weld on steel blades on the front end of the truck."

6. Bin Ladin: Untitled As-Sahab audio file, May 18, 2008, translated by the NEFA Foundation as "Usama Bin Laden: 'Message to the Islamic Nation on 60th Anniversary of Israel.'" Ayman Zawahiri, *Al-Mu'adala al-Sahiha* (*The Correct Equation*), As-Sahab video, January 2007.

7. "Al-Azhar: The Lion's Den: Interview with Shaykh Ayman al-Zawahiri," As-Sahab video, October 2008, www.archive.org. The quotations are from the video's English subtitles.

8. Harakat ul-Mujahedeen, "Jihad: The Forgotten Obligation," date unknown, posted at jihadunspun.org and harkatulmujahideen.org. *Mu'askar al-Battar*, number 7, March-April 2004, p. 2. Abu Musab al-Suri: Brynjar Lia, *Architect of Global Jihad: The Life of al-Qaida Strategist Abu Mus'ab al-Suri* (New York: Columbia University Press, 2008), p. 245. Dadullah: "Liqa' ma' al-Qa'id al-Mujahid al-Mulla Dadullah," As-Sahab, December 28, 2006.

9. Sayyid Qutb [transliterated in this edition as Sayed Qutb], *Milestones* (Lahore, Pakistan: Kazi Publications, [1964] 1981), pp. 9, 53–76.

10. Muhammad Abd al-Salam Faraj, *al-Farida al-Ghaiba*, ed. Muhammad 'Imara (Cairo, Egypt: Dar Thabit, 1982), translation adapted from Johannes J. G. Jansen, *The Neglected Duty* (New York: Macmillan, 1986), pp. 199–200. Abdullah Azzam, *Defense of Muslim Lands*, trans. Ahl al-Sunna wa'l-Jama'a, publication date and location unknown, chapter 3. Usama Bin Ladin, Ayman Zawahiri, and Rifa'i Taha, "Nas Bayan al-Jabha al-Islamiyya al-'Alamiyya li-Jihad al-Yahud wa-'l-Salibiyun," *Al-Quds al-'Arabi* (London, England), February 23, 1998. On recent treatments of jihad as an individual duty, see Shmuel Bar, *Warrants for Terror: Fatwas of Radical Islam and the Duty of Jihad* (Lanham, Md.: Rowman & Littlefield, 2006), pp. 36–45.

11. Azzam: al-Qaida recruitment video, 2001, Reel 3, excerpts posted and translated by Columbia International Affairs Online, ciaonet.org. Bin Ladin interview with al-Jazeera reporter Taysir Alluni, October 21, 2001, translated in Bruce B. Lawrence, ed., *Messages to the World: The Statements of Osama Bin Laden* (London, England: Verso, 2005), p. 107. Poem: *New York Times*, November 18, 2005. Al-Muhajiroun: Kylie Baxter, *British Muslims and the Call to Global Jihad* (Clayton, Australia: Monash University Press, 2007), p. 107. Muhammad bin Zayyid al-Muhajir, *Harb al-I'lam 'ala Ahl al-Islam* (n.p.: Al-Jabha al-I'lamiyya al-Islamiyya al-'Alamiyya, 2008), p. 25.

12. These figures were estimated from *Terrorist Organization Profiles* (Oklahoma City, Okla.: National Memorial Institute for the Prevention of Terrorism, 2008). This database is now hosted at start.umd.edu, but it has not been updated since March 2008. The denominator, the number of Muslims in the world, is estimated at 1.5 billion: Pew Forum on Religion and Public Life, *Mapping the Global Muslim Population*, October 2009, pewforum.org.

13. Khalid Sheikh Mohammed: Yosri Fouda and Nick Fielding, *Masterminds of Terror* (Edinburgh, Scotland: Mainstream Publishing, 2003), p. 114; "Substitution for

the Testimony of Khalid Sheikh Mohammed," *U.S. vs. Zacarias Moussaoui*, defendant's exhibit DX-0941, introduced March 28, 2006, pp. 26–27, 51. The U.S. government described these comments as "made under circumstances designed to elicit truthful statements from the witness." Frances Fragos Townsend, assistant to the president for homeland security and counterterrorism, "Press Briefing on the West Coast Terrorist Plot," February 9, 2006. Former al-Qaida member Abu Jandal told a reporter that he also heard the plot was supposed to be larger than four planes (*Al-Quds al-'Arabi*, August 3, 2004, p. 4, translated by the U.S. government's Foreign Broadcast Information Service, FBIS-NES-2004-0803).

14. Taliban-era training camps: *The 9/11 Commission Report* (Washington, D.C.: National Commission on Terrorist Attacks on the United States, 2004), pp. 67, 470. Pakistan training camps: Sami Yousafzai and Ron Moreau, "The Taliban in Their Own Words," *Newsweek*, October 5, 2009, p. 39; Sami Yousafzai and Ron Moreau, "Inside Al Qaeda," *Newsweek*, September 13, 2010, pp. 30-37; Peter Bergen, "Where You Bin?" *New Republic*, January 29, 2007, pp. 16–19; *New York Times*, February 19 and September 10, 2007, and July 10 and August 13, 2008; S. H. Tajik, "Insight into a Suicide Bomber Training Camp in Waziristan," *CTC Sentinel*, March 2010, p. 10. Bergen also quoted a former U.S. intelligence official as estimating that there are more than 2,000 foreign fighters in the region, though this seems at odds with the small size of the camps, as estimated by a U.S. military intelligence official whom Bergen quotes. Another article in the *New York Times* (June 30, 2008) quoted a retired CIA officer—perhaps the same unnamed source as in Bergen's article?—estimating "as many as 2,000 local and foreign militants" in the region. Another author suggests that there are 2,000 foreign fighters in Afghanistan as of 2006 and tens of thousands in Waziristan—Antonio Giustozzi, *Koran, Kalashnikov, and Laptop: The Neo-Taliban Insurgency in Afghanistan* (New York: Columbia University Press, 2008), pp. 34–35, 132. This estimate was contradicted by American national security officials, who estimated that there are fewer than 100 al-Qaida members in Afghanistan, and fewer than 500 in the entire region—Associated Press, October 4, 2009; *New York Times*, July 1, 2010. A video of portions of the large graduation ceremony was posted online by ABC News, "Inside the Taliban Graduation," June 28, 2007. Somalia: *Somaliland Times* (Hargeysa, Somaliland, Northern Somalia), April 29, 2009; *Garowe Online* (Garowe, Puntland, Northern Somalia), May 19 and 25, 2009, garoweonline. com; *Guardian* (London), June 11, 2009; *New York Times*, June 12, 2009.

15. "Interview with Shaykh Ayman al-Zawahiri," As-Sahab, May 2007. Robert S. Mueller III, testimony before the Select Committee on Intelligence, United States Senate, February 11, 2003. Less responsible observers: Steven Emerson, *Jihad Incorporated: A Guide to Militant Islam in the US* (Amherst, N.Y.: Prometheus Books, 2006), pp. 431–447; Laura Mansfield, *One Nation Under Allah: The Islamic Invasion of America* (n.p.: Greene Leaf Pub., 2005); Daniel Pipes, *Militant Islam Reaches America* (New York: W. W. Norton, 2003), p. 146. Al-Qaida-related convictions in the U.S.: *Counterterrorism White Paper* (Washington, D.C.: United States Department of Justice, 2006); *Terrorist Trial Report Card: U.S. Edition,*

September 11, 2001–September 11, 2006 (New York: Center on Law and Security, New York University School of Law, 2006); *Transactional Records Access Clearinghouse* (Syracuse, N.Y.: Syracuse University, 2007). Muslim terrorist plotters in the United States: David Schanzer, Charles Kurzman, and Ebrahim Moosa, "Anti-Terror Lessons of Muslim-Americans," National Institute of Justice Working Paper, 2009. Mueller in North Carolina: *Charlotte Observer*, April 25, 2006.

16. *Crime in the United States, 2009* (Washington, D.C.: Federal Bureau of Investigation, 2010); *Terrorism Knowledge Base* (Oklahoma City, Okla.: National Memorial Institute for the Prevention of Terrorism, 2008); *Global Terrorism Database* (College Park, Md.: National Consortium for the Study of Terrorism and Responses to Terrorism, University of Maryland, 2009); *Terrorism, 2002–2005* (Washington, D.C.: Federal Bureau of Investigation, 2006), p. 29. Casualties from Islamist terrorism in the United States include murders by John Allen Muhammad and Lee Boyd Malvo, the convicted Washington-area snipers (10 dead, 2001); Hesham Mohamed Hadayet in Los Angeles, California (2 dead, 2002); Naveed Haq in Seattle, Washington (1 dead, 2006); Omeed Aziz Popal in Fremont, California (1 dead, 2006); Sulejmen Talovic in Salt Lake City, Utah (5 dead, 2007); Abdulhakim Mujahid Muhammad in Little Rock, Arkansas (1 dead, 2009); and Nidal Malik Hasan at Fort Hood, Texas (13 dead, 2009). It is not clear whether some of these attacks were motivated by Islamist terrorist intentions. The Washington-area snipers identified themselves as Muslim, but by this they meant the Nation of Islam, a tiny African-American messianic movement that draws on selected elements of Islam as other Muslims understand it. Reporters in the United States were not always aware of the distinction. Sari Horwitz and Michael E. Ruane, *Sniper: Inside the Hunt for the Killers Who Terrorized the Nation* (New York: Random House, 2003), pp. 19, 28, 219, 235; Angie Cannon, *23 Days of Terror: The Compelling True Story of the Hunt and Capture of the Beltway Snipers* (New York: Pocket Books, 2003), pp. 38, 41. For a list of Muslim-American terrorist plots, see Schanzer et al., "Anti-Terror Lessons of Muslim-Americans," and Charles Kurzman, "Muslim-American Terrorism Since 9/11: An Accounting," January 2011, www.unc.edu/~kurzman.

17. David L. Altheide, *Terror Post 9/11 and the Media* (New York: Peter Lang, 2009), pp. 99–116; Ian S. Lustick, *Trapped in the War on Terror* (Philadelphia: University of Pennsylvania Press, 2006), pp. 29–47; John Mueller, "Is There Still a Terrorist Threat? The Myth of the Omnipresent Enemy," *Foreign Affairs*, September–October 2006, pp. 2–8. Margaret Mead attribution: Nancy Lutkehaus, *Margaret Mead: The Making of an American Icon* (Princeton, N.J.: Princeton University Press, 2008), p. 261.

18. Daily deaths from Islamist terrorism are estimated from the maximum annual figure of 15,669 fatalities in 2007 in Muslim-majority countries and provinces, plus Israel, plus attacks attributed to "Islamic extremists," as listed in National Counterterrorism Center, *Worldwide Incidents Tracking System*, wits.nctc.gov. Similar figures emerge from the *Global Terrorism Database*. Global mortality figures are drawn from the *Revised Global Burden of Disease, 2002 Estimates*

(Geneva, Switzerland: World Health Organization, 2004). Iraqi mortality: Gilbert Burnham et al., *The Human Cost of the War in Iraq: A Mortality Study, 2002–2006* (Baltimore, Md.: Bloomberg School of Public Health, Johns Hopkins University; Baghdad, Iraq: School of Medicine, Al Mustansiriya University, 2006); *Iraq, August 2007* (London, England: Opinion Research Business; Baghdad, Iraq: Independent Institute for Administration and Civil Society Studies, 2008).

19. Fox News, July 12, 2002, and August 16, 2007, foxnews.com. Column 9, "Media on Terror: A Column 9 Report on Terror Reporting in Karnataka," October 2008, ninthcolumn.blogspot.com.

20. Bin Ladin on satellite television: Ahmad Muwaffaq Zaydan, *Bin Ladin bi-la-Qina'* (Beirut, Lebanon: al-Sharika al-'Alamiyya li'l-Kitab, 2003), pp. 142–143. The disease of screens: Alan Cullison, "Inside Al-Qaeda's Hard Drive," *Atlantic Monthly*, September 2004, p. 59. Obsessed: Fawaz A. Gerges, *The Far Enemy* (Cambridge, England: Cambridge University Press, 2005), p. 194. Electronic jihad: Muhammad bin Ahmad al-Salim, *39 Wasila li-Khidmat al-Jihad wa'l-Musharaka fihi*, 2003, faroq.net.

21. Nasra Hassan, "Al-Qaeda's Understudy," *Atlantic Monthly*, June 2004, p. 44. Walter Laqueur, ed., *Voices of Terror: Manifestos, Writings, and Manuals of Al-Qaeda, Hamas and Other Terrorists from Around the World and Throughout the Ages* (New York: Reed Press, 2004). Taheri-Azar wrote to several journalists asking for this book to be brought to him in jail. Taheri-Azar letters of May 3 and 7, 2006. Laqueur recounts his personal and family history in *Thursday's Child Has Far to Go: A Memoir of the Journeying Years* (New York: Scribner, 1993).

22. Interview with law-enforcement officer assigned to Taheri-Azar's case, February 2008.

23. Taheri-Azar letters of May 2 and 3, 2006. On Iran, the Shia, and al-Qaida, see Bruce Riedel, "The Mysterious Relationship Between Al-Qa'ida and Iran," *CTC Sentinel*, July 2010, pp. 1–3; *Wall Street Journal*, July 27, 2010, reporting on U.S. military and intelligence reports released in Wikileaks.org's *Afghan War Diary*, July 26, 2010; and Bernard Haykel, "Jihadis and the Shi'a," in Assaf Moghadam and Brian Fishman, eds., *Self-Inflicted Wounds: Debates and Divisions Within al-Qa'ida and Its Periphery* (West Point, N.Y.: Combating Terrorism Center, U.S. Military Academy, 2010), pp. 202-223. Taheri-Azar's spelling of "al-Quaeda" might also have been influenced by the Pakistani practice of adding a "u" in the transliteration of phrases such as "Quaid-e-Azam" (the Great Leader, a title bestowed on the founder of Pakistan, Muhammad Ali Jinnah), though his letters give no indication of familiarity with Pakistan. On Khalifa's murder: Editorial Team of submission.org, "Dr. Rashad Khalifa: The Man, the Issues, and the Truth," undated.

24. The Global Terrorism Database lists 12 Islamist attacks in 1970–2007 causing 200 or more deaths, along with 30 non-Islamist attacks; the Worldwide Incidents Tracking System lists four Islamist terrorist attacks in 2004–2009 with this death toll, along with five non-Islamist attacks.

25. Americans' fear of terrorism: McLaughlin & Associates, "National Survey Results," May 19, 2009, mclaughlinonline.com; see also *The Language of Nuclear Terrorism* (Alexandria, Va.: Luntz, Maslansky Strategic Research and Saga Foundation, 2007). Other surveys report far lower figures: Gallup, "The Decade in Review: Four Key Trends," December 23, 2009, and "Most Important Problem," November 2010, gallup.com; *Findings of the 2007 International GfK Survey on Personal and Societal Fears* (Nuremberg, Germany: GfK Custom Research, 2007). Fanning fear: John Mueller, *Overblown: How Politicians and the Terrorism Industry Inflate National Security Threats, and Why We Believe Them* (New York: Free Press, 2006). U.S. budget: Amy Belasco, *The Cost of Iraq, Afghanistan, and Other Global War on Terror Operations Since 9/11* (Washington, D.C.: Congressional Research Service, 2007); Jennifer Kates, *U.S. Federal Funding for HIV/AIDS: The FY 2009 Budget Request, April 2008* (Menlo Park, Calif.: Henry J. Kaiser Family Foundation, 2008).

26. Shahzad's potential death toll: *New York Post*, July 20, 2010; Associated Press, July 20, 2010.

27. Neil Englehart and Charles Kurzman, "Welcome to World Peace," *Social Forces*, volume 84, 2006, pp. 1957–1967; Charles Kurzman and Neil Englehart, "Farewell to World Peace?" *Christian Science Monitor*, August 29, 2008. Number of terrorist attacks: *Terrorism Knowledge Base, Global Terrorism Database*.

CHAPTER 2

1. I have not been able to locate transcripts or video of al-Jazeera's coverage of 9/11. However, its coverage was reported on other networks—the FBI comments were repeated on CBS News, September 11, 2001, 9:44 a.m.; the feed from Kabul was rebroadcast on ABC News, September 11, 2001, 6:01 p.m.

2. Interview by Matthew Garza, Cairo, Egypt, November 20, 2007. On similar cafés, see Anouk de Koning, "Café Latte and Caesar Salad: Cosmopolitan Belonging in Cairo's Coffee Shops," pp. 221–233 in Diane Singerman and Paul Amar, eds., *Cairo Cosmopolitan* (Cairo, Egypt: American University in Cairo Press, 2006).

3. Fatin, shamela.net, September 16, 2001. I thank Lara Moussa for locating and translating this item. Sadik J. Al-Azm, "Time Out of Joint: Western Dominance, Islamist Terror, and the Arab Imagination," *Boston Review*, October-November 2004, p. 6.

4. French literary scholar: Edouard Launet, "Elementary School," *Harper's*, May 2008, p. 26. Greek soccer fans: Brigitte L. Nacos, "Terrorism as Breaking News: Attack on America," *Political Science Quarterly*, volume 118, 2003, pp. 46–47. Russian politicians: Andrei Piontkovsky, "A Selective Sort of Sorrow," *Globe and Mail* (Toronto), October 4, 2001. British conversations: Eva Hoffman, "Such a Facile Response to Terrorism," *Independent* (London), September 27, 2001, p. 5. Celebrations on September 11: Daniel Pipes, "A Middle East Party," *Jerusalem Post*, September 14, 2001; Cameron S. Brown, "The Shot Seen Around the World: The Middle East Reacts to September 11th," *MERIA Journal* (Middle East Review of International Affairs), volume 5, December 2001. *Gallup Poll of the Islamic*

World, 2002: Subscriber Report (Princeton, N.J.: Gallup Organization, 2002), pp. 4 and 33.

5. Datafiles from *Gallup Poll of the Islamic World, 2002*; *Global Terrorism Database* (four terrorist incidents by Kuwaitis, 2001–2007); *Worldwide Incidents Tracking System* (zero terrorist incidents by Kuwaitis, 2004–2009).

6. The Pew Research Center for the People and the Press, *2002 Global Attitudes Survey*, December 4, 2002, p. T-39, and associated datafile, pewglobal.org. Americans on attacking civilians: WorldPublicOpinion.org, "Public Opinion in Iran and America on Key International Issues," January 24, 2007, p. 10. Hiroshima: *The Gallup Poll*, August 5, 1995, pp. 111–112.

7. Pew Global Attitudes Project, *Wave 2 Update Survey*, 2003, p. T-158, and associated datafile. Respondents from Lebanon (15 percent) and Nigeria (31 percent) were not identified by religion.

8. Tom Wolfe, "Radical Chic: That Party at Lenny's," *New York*, June 8, 1970, pp. 26–56; revised version published in *Radical Chic and Mau-Mauing the Flak-Catchers* (New York: Farrar, Straus and Giroux, 1970). Headline writers: William Safire, "On Language," *New York Times Magazine*, September 6, 1981, p. 6. Conservative journalists: Shelby Steele, "Radical Sheik: John Walker Was Looking for Authentic Victimhood: He Found It in Treason," *Wall Street Journal*, December 10, 2001; Christopher Tennant, "Lefty Pitchers: Call It 'Radical Sheik': The War on Terror Shakes the Dust off the SDS Crowd," *New York*, September 30, 2002; Terry Golway, "Radical Sheik at CUNY Law," *New York Observer*, May 5, 2003, on a student group that wanted to honor Lynne Stewart, convicted bomb-plot conspirator Shaykh Umar Abd al-Rahman's attorney, as public-interest lawyer of the year.

9. Bin Ladin T-shirts: Kazi Mahmood, "Osama Fever Hits Cellular Phones in ASEAN Countries," Islam-Online, October 3, 2001 (Southeast Asia); Thomas L. Friedman, "Foreign Affairs: In Pakistan, It's Jihad 101," *New York Times*, November 13, 2001, p. 17 (Peshawar, Pakistan); Deutsche Presse-Agentur, August 8, 2002 (Tajikistan); *Herald Sun* (Melbourne, Australia), October 26, 2002, p. 7 (Lombok, Indonesia); Greg Powell, "Hat Yai Happy New Year, Thailand," bootnall.com, November 2002 (Hat Yai, Thailand); Mark Moxon, "Burkina Faso: Ouagadougou," moxon.net, December 12, 2002 (Burkina Faso); *Tribune* (Chandigarh, India), February 24, 2003 (Pakistan); Charles Bowden, "Outback Nightmares and Refugee Dreams," *Mother Jones*, March-April 2003 (Lombok, Indonesia); Agence France Presse, July 10, 2003 (Kano, Nigeria); Jason Burke, *Al-Qaeda: Casting a Shadow of Terror* (London: I. B. Tauris, 2003), p. 239 (Indonesia); *Washington Post*, May 15, 2004, p. A1 (Suso, Thailand). The only one resisting: *New York Times*, April 23, 2004.

10. Michael Casey, *Che's Afterlife: The Legacy of an Image* (New York: Vintage, 2009); Michael Eric Dyson, *Making Malcolm: The Myth and Meaning of Malcolm X* (New York: Oxford University Press, 1996). Basayev: Georgi M. Derluguian, *Bourdieu's Secret Admirer in the Caucasus* (Chicago, Ill.: University of Chicago Press, 2005), pp. 38, 42.

11. Coldplay: Shy_grrl, muziqpakistan.com, September 16, 2002. I thank Marium Chaudhry for locating and translating this item. Our shaykh: Mafia_sub7, 3asfh. net, April 20, 2005. I thank Sherine Mahfouz for locating this item. If he is a terrorist: Sefere_Niyet, ihvanforum.org, April 13, 2007. I thank Yekta Zülfikar for locating and translating this item.

12. Shia leader: *Sunday Times*, August 30, 1998; see also Simon Reeve, *The New Jackals: Ramzi Yousef, Osama bin Laden, and the Future of Terrorism* (Boston, Mass.: Northeastern University Press, 1999), pp. 203–204, 213. Dawood Gustave: British Broadcasting Company, August 4, 2005. Aki Nawaz: Fun-Da-Mental, *All Is War (The Benefits of G-Had)* (London, England: 5 Uncivilised Tribes, 2006); see also Ted Swedenburg, "Fun^Da^Mental's 'Jihad Rap,'" in Linda Herrera and Asef Bayat, eds., *Being Young and Muslim* (New York: Oxford University Press, 2010), pp. 291–307. The first Islamist terrorist pop song may have been Sheikh Terra and the Soul Salah Crew, "Dirty Kuffar," 2004. Al-Qaida music: "If You Have a Jihad Nasheed Please Post It Here," Ummah.com, June 2005; Mr. Roach, "Al Qaeda's Soundtrack," ManSizedTarget.com, March 15, 2006; Vladimir, "Nasheeds (Updated)," InfoVlad. net, undated.

13. Katie Brayne, "Osama bin Cool: What Do Indonesian Students Think about Osama bin Laden?" *Inside Indonesia*, number 67, January-March 2002. Lyrical Terrorist: British Broadcasting Company, November 8, 2007. Her conviction on grounds of possessing "information of a kind likely to be useful to a person committing or preparing an act of terrorism" was later overturned on appeal. Jessica Stern, "Jihad: A Global Fad," *Boston Globe*, August 1, 2006.

14. Gangster rap: Eithne Quinn, *Nuthin' but a "G" Thang: The Culture and Commerce of Gangsta Rap* (New York: Columbia University Press, 2005); on the lack of evidence that listening to gangster rap spurs criminality, see Katheryn Russell-Brown, *Underground Codes: Race, Crime, and Related Fires* (New York: New York University Press, 2004), pp. 44–50. Tamer Nafar: *Guardian*, March 11, 2005; Charles Kurzman, "Da Arabian MC's," *Contexts*, Fall 2005, pp. 70–72; Lisa Goldman, "Who's the Terrorist? The Leading Palestinian Hip-Hop Group Finds an Unlikely Fan Base," *Nextbook*, November 6, 2007; Jackie Reem Salloum, director, *Slingshot Hip Hop* (New York: A Fresh Booza Production, 2008).

15. Abu Jandal: *Al-Quds al-'Arabi*, August 3, 2004, p. 4. Al-Muhajiroun: Baxter, *British Muslims and the Call to Global Jihad*, p. 73. Jihobbyists: Jarret M. Brachman, *Global Jihadism: Theory and Practice* (Abingdon, England: Routledge, 2009), p. 19.

16. Gabriele Marranci, *Jihad Beyond Islam* (Oxford, England: Berg Publishers, 2006), pp. 113–114. *Signs of the Hypocrites* (Karachi, Pakistan: Darul Ishaat, 2005), p. 113. Zawahiri: al-Sharq al-Awsat, April 23, 2001, translated by BBC Worldwide Monitoring, quoted in Lawrence Wright, *The Looming Tower: Al-Qaeda and the Road to 9/11* (New York: Alfred A. Knopf, 2006), p. 336. Anwar al-Awlaki: "Thawaabit 'ala Darb al-Jihad: Constants on The Path of Jihad by Shaykh Yusuf al 'Uyayree, Lecture Series Delivered by Imam Anwar al Awlaki," transcribed and edited by Mujahid Fe Sabeelillah.

17. Amel Boubekeur, "Post-Islamist Culture: A New Form of Mobilization?," *History of Religions*, volume 47, 2007, pp. 75–76, 82.

18. Abu Bakr Naji, *Idarat al-Tawahush* (2004), p. 46, translated by William McCants as *The Management of Savagery* (Cambridge, Mass.: John M. Olin Institute for Strategic Studies, Harvard University, 2006), p. 108. Jordan: Pew Global Attitudes Project, *Spring 2006 Survey*, June 22, 2006, p. 57; Fares Braizat, "Post Amman Attacks: Jordanian Public Opinion and Terrorism," Public Opinion Polling Unit, Center for Strategic Studies, University of Jordan, 2006; Pew Global Attitudes Project, *Global Public Opinion in the Bush Years (2001–2008)*, December 18, 2008, p. 7. Morocco: Pew Global Attitudes Project, *Spring 2005 17-Nation Survey*, p. 46. Pakistan attacks: Pak Institute of Peace Studies, *Pakistan Security Report 2008*, January 2009, p. 4, san-pips.com. Pakistan surveys: Terror Free Tomorrow, "Pakistani Support for Al Qaeda, Bin Laden Plunges," January 2008, p. 50, and "Pakistanis Strongly Back Negotiations with Al Qaeda and Taliban over Military Action; Public Support for Al Qaeda Gaining Ground," July 2009, pp. 80–81, terrorfreetomorrow.org; Pew Global Attitudes Project, *Global Public Opinion in the Bush Years (2001–2008)*, December 18, 2008, p. 7. Britain: *Sunday Times*, November 4, 2001; Munira Mirza, Abi Senthilkumaran, and Zein Ja'far, *Living Apart Together: British Muslims and the Paradox of Multiculturalism* (London, England: Policy Exchange, 2007), pp. 62–63. Iraq: Mansoor Moaddel, "What the Iraqi Study Group Missed: The Iraqi People," *Footnotes* (American Sociological Association), January 2007; Ronald Inglehart, Mansoor Moaddel, and Mark Tessler, "Xenophobia and In-Group Solidarity in Iraq: A Natural Experiment on the Impact of Insecurity," *Perspectives on Politics*, volume 4, September 2006, pp. 495–505. See also *Human Security Brief 2007* (Vancouver, Canada: Human Security Research Group, 2008), p. 17.

19. Interview by Ijlal Naqvi, Islamabad, Pakistan, April 3, 2008. On communal violence in Pakistan, see Musa Khan Jalalzai, *Sectarianism and Ethnic Violence in Pakistan*, 3rd ed. (Lahore: Iszharsons, 1996), pp. 377–398; Muhammad Qasim Zaman, "Sectarianism in Pakistan: The Radicalization of Shi'i and Sunni Identities," *Modern Asian Studies*, volume 32, July 1998, pp. 689–716.

20. Marsul al-'Ayn and Milak al-Layl, www.tedlal.com, March 29, 2007; Fuksiyya Dala' and Zauba'a www.foxarab.com, October 21 and 22, 2007; Murhaf al-Ihsas, kuwait60.com, April 18, 2008.

21. John C. Lamoreaux, *The Early Muslim Tradition of Dream Interpretation* (Albany: State University of New York Press, 2002), p. 4. The quotation from Bin Ladin is drawn from the translation by George Michael and Kassem M. Wahba, "Transcript of Usama Bin Laden Video Tape," U.S. Department of Defense, defenselink.mil, December 13, 2001. (The authenticity of this videotape is in question; I have no way to confirm or deny its authenticity.) Iain R. Edgar, "The Inspirational Night Dream in the Motivation and Justification of Jihad," *Nova Religio*, volume 11, number 2, November 2007, pp. 59–76. Apocalyptic texts: David Cook, *Contemporary Muslim Apocalyptic Literature* (Syracuse, N.Y.: Syracuse University Press, 2005), pp. 173–183; Jean-Pierre Filiu, *L'Apocalypse dans l'islam* (Paris,

France: Fayard, 2008), pp. 270–289; Timothy R. Furnish, *Holiest Wars: Islamic Mahdis, Their Jihads, and Osama bin Laden* (Westport, Conn.: Praeger, 2005), pp. 111–117, 150–158.

22. Ilyas's dream: Muhammad Manzur Nu'mani, *Malfuzat-i Hazrat Maulana Muhammad Ilyas* (Lucknow, India: Kutub-Khanah-yi al-Furqan, n.d.), p. 50. More recent Tablighi dream premonitions: Farish A. Noor, "Pathans to the East! The Development of the Tablighi Jama'at Movement in Northern Malaysia and Southern Thailand," *Comparative Studies of South Asia, Africa and the Middle East,* volume 27, 2007, pp. 14. On Tablighi Jamaat politics and beliefs: Yoginder Sikand, *The Origins and Development of the Tablighi Jama'at (1920–2000)* (Hyderabad, India: Orient Longman, 2002). Preparing soldiers: Muhammad Khalid Masud, "Ideology and Legitimacy," in Masud, ed., *Travellers in Faith: Studies of the Tablighi Jama'at as a Transnational Islamic Movement for Faith Renewal* (Leiden, Netherlands: Brill, 2000), p. 105. Weak Muslims: Salahuddin al-Bengali, "Tableeghi Jama'ah on the Strategic Spectrum," *Jihad Recollections,* number 3, 2009, pp. 8–9.

23. Musa Khan Jalalzai, *Sectarian Violence in Pakistan and Afghanistan* (Lahore, Pakistan: System Books, 1999), p. 36; Terry McDermott, *Perfect Soldiers: The Hijackers: Who They Were, Why They Did It* (New York: HarperCollins, 2005), p. 74; Alex Alexiev, "Tablighi Jamaat: Jihad's Stealthy Legions," *Middle East Quarterly,* Winter 2005; Jessica Stern, "The Protean Enemy," *Foreign Affairs,* July-August 2003; Nicholas Howenstein, "Islamist Networks: The Case of Tablighi Jamaat," United States Institute of Peace Briefing, October 2006.

24. Hathout: Paul M. Barrett, *American Islam: The Struggle for the Soul of a Religion* (New York: Farrar, Straus and Giroux, 2007), p. 95. Revolutionary *takfir*: Gilles Kepel, *Jihad: The Trail of Political Islam* (Cambridge, Mass.: Harvard University Press, 2002), p. 273; Quintan Wiktorowicz, "The Salafi Movement: Violence and the Fragmentation of Community," in Miriam Cooke and Bruce B. Lawrence, eds., *Muslim Networks: From Hajj to Hip Hop* (Chapel Hill: University of North Carolina Press, 2005), pp. 223–224. *Takfir* and marriage annulment: Maurits S. Berger, "Apostasy and Public Policy in Contemporary Egypt," *Human Rights Quarterly,* volume 25, 2003, pp. 720–740; Susanne Olsson, "Apostasy in Egypt: Contemporary Cases of Hisbah," *The Muslim World,* volume 98, 2008, pp. 95–115; *Times of India,* September 5, 2006.

25. Lawrence, *Messages to the World,* p. 28.

26. Carrie Rosefsky Wickham, "Pro-Democratic Learning in Islamist Groups: Lessons from Egypt, Jordan and Kuwait," Annual Meeting of the Middle East Studies Association, 2004. 17th International Congress of Muslim Communities Union, May 29–30, 2008, Istanbul, hosted by the Ekonomik ve Sosyal Araştırma Merkezi, esam.org.tr. "Interview with Shaykh Ayman al-Zawahiri," as-Sahab video, May 2007.

27. Shaykh of al-Azhar: Muhammed Sayyid al-Tantawi, Agence France Presse, September 14, 2001. Qaradawi et al.: untitled fatwa of September 27, 2001. Hamas, Muslim Brotherhood, etc. statement of September 14, 2001: *al-Quds al-'Arabi,* September 14, 2001, translated at MSANews.mynet.net. These and dozens

of similar statements are available at www.unc.edu/~kurzman/terror.htm. Al-Qaida's critique of its critics: Quintan Wiktorowicz and John Kaltner, "Killing in the Name of Islam: Al-Qaeda's Justification for September 11," *Middle East Policy*, volume 10, Summer 2003, pp. 76–92.

28. Interviewed by the author in Istanbul, Turkey, May 7, 2008.

29. On conspiracy theories in the region, see Daniel Pipes, *The Hidden Hand: Middle East Fears of Conspiracy* (New York: St. Martin's Press, 1996). On the distinction between conspiracy theories and actual conspiracies, see Jeffrey M. Bale, "Political Paranoia *v.* Political Realism: On Distinguishing Between Bogus Conspiracy Theories and Genuine Conspiratorial Politics," *Patterns of Prejudice*, volume 41, 2007, pp. 45–60.

30. *Gallup Poll of the Islamic World, 2002*; Pew Global Attitudes Project, *Spring 2006 Survey*, June 22, 2006, p. 60; WorldPublicOpinion.org, "Muslim Public Opinion on US Policy, Attacks on Civilians and al Qaeda," April 24, 2007, p. 17; Pew Research Center, *Muslim Americans: Middle Class and Mostly Mainstream*, May 22, 2007, p. 5; WorldPublicOpinion.org, "Who Was Behind 9/11?," September 10, 2008; WorldPublicOpinion.org, "Public Opinion in the Islamic World on Terrorism, al Qaeda, and US Policies," February 25, 2009, p. 24. *A New Antisemitic Myth in The Middle East Media: The September 11 Attacks Were Perpetrated by the Jews* (Washington, D.C.: Middle East Media Research Institute, 2002). Scripps Howard News Service and Scripps Survey Research Center, Ohio University, August 1, 2006, and November 23, 2007.

31. Ayman Zawahiri, *Al-Luqa' al-Maftuh ma' al-Shaykh Ayman al-Zawahiri* (Part 2), As-Sahab Media, April 2008, p. 41. Al-Manar: Bryan Curtis, "4,000 Jews, 1 Lie: Tracking an Internet Hoax," October 5, 2001, slate.com. Nasrullah's popularity: Shibley Telhami, *2008 Annual Arab Public Opinion Poll* (College Park: Anwar Sadat Chair for Peace and Development, University of Maryland, 2008), pp. 95–97.

32. Shibley Telhami, *2005 Annual Arab Public Opinion Survey* (College Park, Md.: Anwar Sadat Chair for Peace and Development, 2005), p. 19; Telhami, *2008 Annual Arab Public Opinion Poll*, p. 21; Telhami, *Annual Arab Public Opinion Survey*, 2009, p. 43. WorldPublicOpinion.org, "Muslim Public Opinion on US Policy, Attacks on Civilians, and al Qaeda," April 24, 2007, p. 11, and "Muslim Publics Oppose Al Qaeda's Terrorism, But Agree With Its Goal of Driving US Forces Out," February 24, 2009, p. 23.

33. Gary G. Sick, Columbia University, Gulf/2000 electronic mailing list, October 11, 2001.

34. Ira Silverman, "An American Terrorist," *New Yorker*, August 5, 2002; Jean-Daniel Lefond, director, *American Fugitive: The Truth About Hassan* (Montreal, Canada: InformAction, 2006).

35. *Durus 'Askariyya fi Jihad al-Tawaghit*, translated by British police as "Military Studies in the Jihad Against the Tyrants," p. 16. *Al-Mu'askar al-Battar*, number 1, December 2003–January 2004, pp. 26–27.

36. Saudi extradition efforts: Wright, *The Looming Tower*, pp. 288–289. The most substantive public allegations of Saudi support for al-Qaida come from the CIA's interrogation of al-Qaida operative Abu Zubayda, as reported in Gerald Posner,

Why America Slept: The Failure to Prevent 9/11 (New York: Random House, 2003), pp. 181–194. These interrogations involved "waterboarding" and other treatment that the U.S. government used to call torture. Michael Hayden, director of the Central Intelligence Agency, testimony before the U.S. Senate Select Committee on Intelligence, February 5, 2008. Saudi arrests: Bruce Riedel, "Al Qaeda Strikes Back," *Foreign Affairs*, May-June 2007, p. 36. Prisoner reeducation program: Christopher Boucek, "Extremist Reeducation and Rehabilitation in Saudi Arabia," *Terrorism Monitor*, August 16, 2007.

37. Akil N. Awan and Mina Al-Lami, "Al-Qa'ida's Virtual Crisis," *RUSI Journal*, volume 154, 2009, pp. 56–64. Alfirdaws.org, July 18, 2006, quoted in Anne Stenersen, "The Internet: A Virtual Training Camp?," *Terrorism and Political Violence*, volume 20, 2008, p. 229. Other observers consider Internet communication to be relatively safe for militants: Gary R. Bunt, *iMuslims: Rewiring the House of Islam* (Chapel Hill: University of North Carolina Press, 2009), pp. 177-274; Hanna Rogan, "Jihadism Online: A Study of How Al-Qaida and Radical Islamist Groups Use the Internet for Terrorist Purposes," Norwegian Defence Research Establishment, 2006, rapporter.ffi.no; Manuel R. Torres Soriano, "Maintaining the Message: How Jihadists Have Adapted to Web Disruptions," *CTC Sentinel*, November 2009, pp. 22–24; Sajjan M. Gohel, "The Internet and Its Role in Terrorist Recruitment and Operational Planning," *CTC Sentinel*, December 2009, pp. 12–15; Evan Kohlmann, "A Beacon for Extremists: The Ansar al-Mujahideen Web Forum," *CTC Sentinel*, February 2010, pp. 1–4.

38. *Oregonian*, September 19, 2003; September 13, 2006.

39. Human Rights Watch, *No One Is Safe: Insurgent Attacks on Civilians in Thailand's Southern Border Provinces*, August 2007, p. 89.

40. Tantawi: "Whoever Wants to Go to Iraq to Fight, Can Go: Tantawi," IslamOnline. net, April 5, 2003; Yotam Feldner, "Sheikh Tantawi's Positions on Jihad Against Coalition Forces, Saddam's Resignation, and The War in Iraq," Middle East Media Research Institute, April 8, 2003. Number of foreign fighters in Iraq: *Washington Post*, May 15, 2005; Abu Ayyub al-Masri quoted by Associated Press, September 28, 2006; *New York Times*, July 10, 2008. Usama Bin Ladin, "Ila Ahlina fi'l-'Iraq," October 22, 2007, translated by the NEFA Foundation.

41. Sinjar records: Combating Terrorism Center, U.S. Military Academy, *Al-Qa'ida's Foreign Fighters in Iraq: A First Look at the Sinjar Records*, December 19, 2007, and associated Harmony Document Database hosted at ctc.usma.edu. For per-capita analyses of this dataset, see Clint Watts, *Beyond Iraq and Afghanistan: What Foreign Fighters Reveal About the Future of Terrorism*, Part 1, "Where Are They Coming From" (PJ Sage, Inc., 2008); Joseph Felter and Brian Fishman, "Becoming a Foreign Fighter: A Second Look at the Sinjar Records," in Brian Fishman, ed., *Bombers, Bank Accounts, and Bleedout: Al-Qa'ida's Road In and Out of Iraq* (West Point, N.Y.: Combating Terrorism Center, U.S. Military Academy, 2008), pp. 35–42. One-tenth of the young men: Estimated on the basis of the proportion of 15–25-year-old males in Libya as a whole (10 percent of the population, from the U.S. Census Bureau's *International Data Base*, census.gov)

times the population of Darnah (approximately 50 to 80 thousand). Kevin Peraino, "Destination Martyrdom: What Drove So Many Libyans to Volunteer as Suicide Bombers for the War in Iraq? A Visit to Their Hometown—The Dead-End City of Darnah," *Newsweek*, April 28, 2008, pp. 24–30. Detained insurgents: William Selby, "Detained Terrorists Reveal Al Qaeda Recruiting Process," American Forces Press Service, defense.gov, March 18, 2008. Al-Qaida in the Arabian Peninsula: *Sawt al-Jihad*, number 1, 2003, quoted in Thomas Hegghammer, "The Failure of Jihad in Saudi Arabia," Occasional Paper Series, Combating Terrorism Center at West Point, February 25, 2010, p. 22. Families travel to training camps: S. H. Tajik, "Insight into a Suicide Bomber Training Camp in Waziristan," *CTC Sentinel*, March 2010, p. 10.

42. Audencia Nacional, Sala de lo Penal, Sección Segunda (Madrid, Spain), "Sentencia número 65/2007," October 31, 2007, pp. 222–223. Andrea Elliott, "Where Boys Grow Up to Be Jihadis," *New York Times Magazine*, November 25, 2007, pp. 70–81, 96–100. Afghanistan notebook, September 2000, translated by the Combating Terrorism Center, U.S. Military Academy, *Harmony and Disharmony: Exploiting Al-Qa'ida's Organizational Vulnerabilities*, document AFGP-2002–801138, ctc. usma.edu.

43. "Obtaining Parents' Permission to Participate in Jihad," IslamOnline.net, April 8, 2003. Ayman Zawahiri, *Al-Tabri'a: Risala fi Tabri'at Ummat al-Qalam wa al-Sayf min Manqasat Tuhmat al-Khawar wa al-Da'f*, As-Sahab Media, March 2008, pp. 83–87.

44. Book on recruitment: Abu Amr al-Qaidi, *Daura fi Fann al-Tajnid*, September 2008, p. 45. Sayf al-Adl: *Mu'askar al-Battar*, number 4, January-February 2004, pp. 30–32. Wali al-Haqq, Ekhlaas.com, April 27, 2008, archived by William McCants, Jihadica.com, May 11, 2008.

45. Marc Sageman, *Understanding Terrorist Networks* (Philadelphia: University of Pennsylvania Press, 2004), pp. 101, 108, 115, 125, 157. Dina Temple-Raston, *The Jihad Next Door: The Lackawanna Six and Rough Justice in the Age of Terror* (New York: Public Affairs, 2007).

46. Mao Tse-tung, *On Guerrilla Warfare* (Champaign: University of Illinois Press, [1937] 2000), p. 93.

CHAPTER 3

1. Charles Kurzman and Ijlal Naqvi, "Who Are the Islamists?," in Carl W. Ernst and Richard C. Martin, eds., *Contemporary Islam Between Theory and Practice* (Columbia: University of South Carolina Press, 2010), pp. 133–158.

2. Sayyid Jamal ad-Din al-Afghani, *An Islamic Response to Imperialism: Political and Religious Writings of Sayyid Jamal ad-Din al-Afghani*, trans. Nikki R. Keddie (Berkeley: University of California Press, 1968), p. 107. For other modernist Islamic critiques of the *ulama*, see Charles Kurzman, ed., *Modernist Islam, 1840–1940: A Sourcebook* (New York: Oxford University Press, 2002), p. 11. Bin Ladin: Lawrence, *Messages to the World*, pp. 17, 33–34, 198. Muhammad Khalil al-Hakayma, *Toward a New Strategy in Resisting the Occupier*, 2006, translated by the

Combating Terrorism Center, U.S. Military Academy, p. 9. Maudoodi: Seyyed Vali Reza Nasr, *Mawdudi and the Making of Islamic Revivalism* (New York: Oxford University Press, 1996), p. 19, 29. Khomeini: Charles Kurzman, *The Unthinkable Revolution in Iran* (Cambridge, Mass.: Harvard University Press, 2004), pp. 44–45. Abd al-Rahman: Malika Zeghal, *Gardiens de l'islam: les oulémas d'Al Azhar dans l'Égype contemporaine* (Paris, France: Presses de la Fondation Nationale des Sciences Politiques, 1996), p. 354; Malika Zeghal, "Religion and Politics in Egypt: The Ulema of al-Azhar, Radical Islam, and the State (1952–94)," *International Journal of Middle East Studies*, volume 31, 1999, pp. 391–396.

3. Saad Eddin Ibrahim, "Anatomy of Egypt's Militant Islamic Groups: Methodological Note and Preliminary Findings," *International Journal of Middle East Studies*, volume 12, 1980, pp. 423–453. Saad Eddin Ibrahim, "The Changing Face of Islamic Activism" (1995), in *Egypt, Islam and Democracy: Twelve Critical Essays* (Cairo, Egypt: American University in Cairo Press, 2002), pp. 69–79. Carrie Rosefsky Wickham, *Mobilizing Islam: Religion, Activism, and Political Change in Egypt* (New York: Columbia University Press, 2002). Review of 22 studies: Kurzman and Naqvi, "Who Are the Islamists?," Bin Ladin: Lawrence, *Messages to the World*, p. 27.

4. Donald Rumsfeld, memo of October 16, 2003, posted by globalsecurity.org. Thomas L. Friedman, "Origin of Species," *New York Times*, March 14, 2004.

5. Harvard dataset: Robert J. Barro and Jong-Wha Lee, "International Data on Educational Attainment: Updates and Implications," Harvard Center for International Development, April 2000. Pakistan: *Social Development in Pakistan: Annual Review, 2002–03: The State of Education* (Karachi, Pakistan: Social Policy and Development Centre, 2003), p. 157; Tahir Andrabi, Jishnu Das, Asim Ijaz Khwaja, and Tristan Zajonc, "Religious School Enrollment in Pakistan: A Look at the Data," *Comparative Education Review*, volume 50, 2006, pp. 446–477; C. Christine Fair, *The Madrassah Challenge: Militancy and Religious Education in Pakistan* (Washington, D.C.: United States Institute of Peace Press, 2008), p. 30. Indonesia: Ronald A. Lukens-Bull, *A Peaceful Jihad: Negotiating Identity and Modernity in Muslim Java* (New York: Palgrave Macmillan, 2005), p. 18.

6. Harry S. Truman, "Inaugural Address," *Public Papers of the President*, 1949, p. 114.

7. Muslim Student Association, University of Southern California, "Compendium of Muslim Texts," www.usc.edu/dept/MSA.

8. Abdullahi Ahmed An-Na'im, *Islam and the Secular State* (Cambridge, Mass.: Harvard University Press, 2008); Abdulaziz Sachedina, *The Islamic Roots of Democratic Pluralism* (Oxford, England: Oxford University Press, 2001). On the introduction of Shiism at al-Azhar, see Kate Zebiri, *Mahmud Shaltut and Islamic Modernism* (New York: Oxford University Press, 1993), pp. 24–26. Pew Research Center for the People and the Press, Global Attitudes Project, "Views of a Changing World 2003," Final Topline Results, June 3, 2003, p. T-95.

9. Bin Ladin: Lawrence, *Messages to the World*, p. 104. Ayman Zawahiri, *Realities of the Conflict Between Islam and Unbelief*, As-Sahab Media, December 2006. Survey

in Egypt, Indonesia, Morocco, and Pakistan: WorldPublicOpinion.org, "Muslim Public Opinion on US Policy, Attacks on Civilians and al Qaeda," April 24, 2007, p. 15.

10. Bin Ladin on commander of the faithful: Lawrence, *Messages to the World*, pp. 86, 98, 101, 110. Bin Ladin on equality of blood: Lawrence, *Messages to the World*, pp. 117–118.

11. Qurayshi precedence: Asma Afsaruddin, *Excellence and Precedence: Medieval Islamic Discourse on Legitimate Leadership* (Leiden, Netherlands: Brill, 2002), pp. 36–79; Asma Afsaruddin, *The First Muslims* (Oxford, England: Oneworld, 2008), pp. 20–22.

12. Bruce B. Lawrence, *Defenders of God*, 2nd ed. (Columbia: University of South Carolina Press, 1995); Mark Juergensmeyer, *Terror in the Mind of God* (Berkeley: University of California Press, 2000).

13. Abdessalame Yassine, *Islamiser la modernité* (Rabat, Morocco: al-Ofok Impressions, 1998).

14. Bookkeeping: Alan Cullison, "Inside al-Qaeda's Hard Drive," *Atlantic Monthly*, September 2004, p. 64. Transponders: *Aviation Week and Space Technology*, January 27, 2003. Revolutionaries' tips on Internet privacy: *Washington Post*, April 13, 2006. Revolutionary techniques online: *Washington Post*, August 7, 2005.

15. *Durus 'Askariyya fi Jihad al-Tawaghit* (Military Lessons in the Jihad against the Tyrants), undated, translated by the British government and posted online by thesmokinggun.com, p. 19.

16. Taliban constitutional revisions: Agence France Presse, July 19, 1998; Kamal Hossain, "Interim Report on the Situation of Human Rights in Afghanistan, Prepared by the Special Rapporteur of the Commission on Human Rights," United Nations document A/54/422, September 30, 1999, paragraphs 37, 58; *Telegraph*, September 29, 2007. Taliban government offices and decrees on women: Ahmed Rashid, *Taliban: Militant Islam, Oil and Fundamentalism in Central Asia* (New Haven, Conn.: Yale University Press, 2000), pp. 100–102, 105–116, 217–218. Women in Iran: Charles Kurzman, "A Feminist Generation in Iran?," *Iranian Studies*, volume 41, 2008, pp. 297–321. Khamene'i and Jannati: *New York Times*, October 13, 1996.

17. David B. Edwards, *Before Taliban: Genealogies of the Afghan Jihad* (Berkeley: University of California Press, 2002), pp. 191–198; Barnett R. Rubin, *The Fragmentation of Afghanistan: State Formation and Collapse in the International System*, 2nd ed. (New Haven, Conn.: Yale University Press, 2002), pp. 95–97. IQ test: John Miller and Michael Stone, with Chris Mitchell, *The Cell: Inside the 9/11 Plot, and Why the FBI and CIA Failed to Stop It* (New York: Hyperion, 2002), p. 282.

18. "Frequently Asked Questions about the Taliban," undated, islamicawakening. com.

19. Ahmad Rashid, *Taliban* (New Haven, Conn.: Yale University Press, 2000), p. 42; *New York Times*, December 19, 2001.

20. Abdullah Azzam, *Defense of the Muslim Lands*, undated, translated by "Brothers in Ribatt," p. 40. Uneasy toward jihad: Afghanistan notebook, AFGP-2002-801138,

p. 140, and translation, p. 20 (other criticisms of the Taliban by al-Qaida recruits are cited in Lia, *Architect of Global Jihad*, p. 239). Yes, there are cases: Afghanistan notebook, AFGP-2002-003472, p. 3, and translation, pp. 3–5.

21. On the diverse history of Islamic treatment of human images, see the entries on "Sura" and "Taswir" in *The Encyclopedia of Islam*, 2nd ed. (Leiden, Netherlands: Brill, 1997, 2000), volume 9, pp. 889–892, and volume 10, pp. 361–366. Bin Ladin letter: Afghanistan notebook, AFGP-2002-600321, p. 2; the letter refers to the ongoing civil war in Tajikistan, which ended in June 1997.

22. Rahimullah Yusufzai, "Osama bin Laden: The Man and his Cause," *Gulf News*, September 24, 2001; Rahimullah Yusufzai, "Face to Face with Osama," *Guardian*, September 26, 2001. Abu Musab al-Suri and Abu Khalid al-Suri, letter of July 19, 1998, in Lia, *Architect of Global Jihad*, pp. 284–291, drawing on material from Cullison, "Inside al-Qaeda's Hard Drive," p. 59. Abu Hudhayfa, minutes dated June 20, 2000, AFGP-2002-003251, p. 7, and translation, p. 3. Video of Muhammad Atta and Ziad Jarrah, January 8, 2000: *Sunday Times* (London), October 1, 2006. Shutting down camps: Lia, *Architect of Global Jihad*, pp. 287, 293–294.

23. "Substitution for the Testimony of Khalid Sheikh Mohammed," p. 26. Afghanistan notebook, AFGP-2002-801138, p. 170, and translation, p. 34.

24. Bin Ladin conversation and rumors: Vahid Mozhdeh, *Afghanistan va Panj Sal-e Solteh-ye Taleban* (Tehran, Iran: Nashr-e Ney, 2003), pp. 160–161, 74. Taliban warning about 9/11: *Independent*, September 7, 2002.

25. United Nations Security Council Resolution 1267, October 15, 1999. Davis, *Buda's Wagon*, p. 194; George Crile, *Charlie Wilson's War: The Extraordinary Story of How the Wildest Man in Congress and a Rogue CIA Agent Changed the History of Our Times* (New York: Grove Press, 2003), pp. 201, 318, 335, 348; Steve Coll, *Ghost Wars: The Secret History of the CIA, Afghanistan, and Bin Laden, from the Soviet Invasion to September 10, 2001* (New York: Penguin Books, 2004), pp. 128–129, 132–134. Taliban commander: *Newsweek*, October 5, 2009, p. 42.

26. Umar statement, December 2006: *Newsweek*, March 5, 2007, p. 46. Umar exchange with journalists: *New York Times*, January 5, 2007. Anonymous commander: *New York Times*, October 22, 2009. Umar statement: "Message of Felicitation of Amir-ul-Momineen on the Occasion of Eid-ul-Fitre," September 19, 2009, ansarnet.info.

27. Dadullah beheading video: *Sunday Times* (London), October 15, 2006. Dadullah boasting: video interviews posted by the NEFA Foundation, April 8 and May 10, 2007. Leaked his location: "Geopolitical Diary: Examining Mullah Dadullah's Death," May 14, 2007, stratfor.com; Ahmed Rashid, *Descent into Chaos: The United States and the Failure of Nation Building in Pakistan, Afghanistan, and Central Asia* (New York: Viking, 2008), p. 399; and allegations by Muhibullah Mahajir, quoted by the Associated Press, December 30, 2007. Mansur Dadullah fired: "Statement from the Islamic Emirate of Afghanistan (Taliban)," translated by the NEFA Foundation, December 29, 2007. Mansur Dadullah press conference: ABC News, June 18, 2007. Mansur Dadullah interview: *World Politics Review*,

July 3, 2007. Rumors about Mansur Dadullah negotiations: *Independent* (London), July 25, 2008. Prisoner swap: *News* (Islamabad), May 28, 2008; denied by Pakistani officials who said that Mansur Dadullah was still in prison in Pakistan, *Jang* (Rawalpindi), June 19, 2008, translated by BBC Monitoring International Reports.

28. *Newsweek*, October 5, 2009, p. 42. No al-Qaida training camps in Afghanistan: U.S. National Security Adviser James L. Jones, quoted by the Associated Press, October 4, 2009.

29. Ghassan Dau'ar, *Al-Muhandis: Al-Shahid Yahya 'Ayyash, Ramz al-Jihad* (London, England: Flistine al-Muslemah, n.d.), hosted at http://www.palestine-info.info; Samuel M. Katz, *The Hunt for the Engineer* (New York: Fromm International, 1999).

30. Azzam, *Defense of the Muslim Lands*, chapter 2.

31. Palestinian Afghans: Yoram Schweitzer and Shaul Shay, *The Globalization of Terror* (Herzliya, Israel: The Interdisciplinary Center; New Brunswick, N.J.: Transaction Publishers, 2003), pp. 35–38; *New York Times*, June 15, 2006; Zaki Chehab, *Inside Hamas: The Untold Story of the Militant Islamic Movement* (New York: Nation Books, 2007), p. 194; Lia, *Architect of Global Jihad*, pp. 74, 90. Pew Global Attitudes Project, *Global Opinion Trends 2002–2007*, July 24, 2007, p. 57, pewglobal.org.

32. Training camps: Lia, *Architect of Global Jihad*, pp. 237–250. U.S. Department of Defense, "List of Individuals Detained by the Department of Defense at Guantanamo Bay, Cuba, from January 2002 through May 12, 2006," May 15, 2006. Reuven Paz, "Arab Volunteers Killed in Iraq: An Analysis," *PRISM Series of Global Jihad*, March 2005, p. 2; Murad Al-Shishani, "The Salafi-Jihadist Movement in Iraq: Recruitment Methods and Arab Volunteers," *Terrorism Monitor*, December 2, 2005, p. 6; Combating Terrorism Center, *Al-Qa'ida's Foreign Fighters in Iraq*, p. 8.

33. Video testaments: Anne Marie Oliver and Paul F. Steinberg, *The Road to Martyrs' Square: A Journey into the World of the Suicide Bomber* (New York: Oxford University Press, 2005). Educated cadres: Claude Berrebi, "Evidence about the Link Between Education, Poverty and Terrorism Among Palestinians," *Peace Economics, Peace Science and Public Policy*, volume 13, 2007, p. 19. Yasin: Chehab, *Inside Hamas*, p. 108.

34. Chehab, *Inside Hamas*, p. 108. Hamas, Muslim Brotherhood, etc. statement of September 14, 2001: *al-Quds al-'Arabi*, September 14, 2001, translated at MSANews.mynet.net. Hamas militant: Jeffrey Goldberg, "Letter from Gaza: The Forgotten War," *New Yorker*, September 11, 2006, p. 44.

35. Hamas, "The Charter of God" (1988), trans. Raphael Israeli, article 14. Saudi bus tour: *Washington Post*, September 14, 1990.

36. Hamas, "The Charter of God" (1988), article 12; see also Khalid Amayreh, "Hamas and al-Qaida," *Conflicts Forum*, October 2007; E. Alshech, "Hamas: Between Liberating Palestine and Restoring the Global Islamic Caliphate," Middle East Media Research Institute, December 27, 2007; Reuven Paz, "Jihadis

and Hamas," in Assaf Moghadam and Brian Fishman, eds., *Self-Inflicted Wounds: Debates and Divisions Within al-Qa'ida and Its Periphery* (West Point, N.Y.: Combating Terrorism Center, U.S. Military Academy, 2010), pp. 183–201. Azzam, *Defense of the Muslim Lands*, p. 36. Zawahiri: "Tremendous Lessons and Events in the Year 1427 AH—An Audio Speech by Dr. Ayman al-Zawahiri," translated by the SITE Institute, February 12, 2007.

37. Ernest Renan, "What Is a Nation?" (1882), in Geoff Eley and Ronald Grigor Suny, eds., *Becoming National: A Reader* (New York: Oxford University Press, 1996), p. 52. Language and *pays* in France: Eugen Weber, *Peasants into Frenchmen: The Modernization of Rural France, 1870–1914* (Stanford, Calif.: Stanford University Press, 1976). Gauls: Suzanne Citron, *Le mythe national: L'histoire de France en question*, 2nd ed. (Paris, France: Éditions Ouvrières; Études et Documentation Internationales, 1991).

38. Debate over boundary delimitation; Basheer M. Nafi, *Arabism, Islamism and the Palestine Question, 1908–1914* (Reading, England: Ithaca Press, 1998), pp. 67–71. Palestinian borders: Gideon Biger, *The Boundaries of Modern Palestine, 1840–1947* (London, England: Routledge, 2004). Palestinian nationalism: Rashid Khalidi, *Palestinian Identity: The Construction of Modern National Consciousness* (New York: Columbia University Press, 1997).

39. Zionism: David Vital, *The Origins of Zionism* (Oxford, England: Clarendon Press, 1975). Claiming ancient heritages: Charles Kurzman, "Weaving Iran into the Tree of Nations," *International Journal of Middle Eastern Studies*, volume 7, 2005, pp. 137–166; Neil Asher Silberman, *Between Past and Present: Archaeology, Ideology, and Nationalism in the Modern Middle East* (New York: H. Holt, 1989); James F. Goode, *Negotiating for the Past: Archaeology, Nationalism, and Diplomacy in the Middle East, 1919–1941* (Austin: University of Texas Press, 2007).

40. Number of questions: Jarret Brachman, Brian Fishman, and Joseph Felter, *The Power of Truth? Questions for Ayman al-Zawahiri* (Combating Terrorism Center, U.S. Military Academy), April 21, 2008, pp. 4–5, 18. Zawahiri, *The Open Meeting with Shaykh Ayman al-Zawahiri*, Part 1, As-Sahab Media, 2008, pp. 4, 5, 12, 35, 37. Later statements by Zawahiri criticizing Hamas are discussed in Vahid Brown, "Al-Qa'ida and the Afghan Taliban: 'Diametrically Opposed'?," October 21, 2009, jihadica.com. Al-Qaida in Iraq: Abu 'Umar al-Baghdadi, "Al-Din al-Nasiha," February 14, 2008, selections translated by Nibras Kazimi, talismangate.blogspot. com. Apostate apes: Alkhidr, clearinghouse.infovlad.net, September 17, 2008. On the bad blood between al-Qaida and Hamas, see also Kim Cragin, "Al Qaeda Confronts Hamas: Divisions in the Sunni Jihadist Movement and Its Implications for U.S. Policy," *Studies in Conflict and Terrorism*, volume 32, 2009, pp. 576–590; and Mary Habeck, "Al-Qaida and Hamas: The Limits of Salafi-Jihadi Pragmatism," *CTC Sentinel*, February 2010, pp. 5–7.

41. Chehab, *Inside Hamas*, pp. 187–192; Benedetta Berti, "Salafi-Jihadi Activism in Gaza: Mapping the Threat," *CTC Sentinel*, May 2010, pp. 5–9. *New York Times*, July 8, 2006; Middle East Media Research Institute, Islamist websites monitor number 116, June 27, 2007, special dispatch number 1946, June 3, 2008. Curry

favor: Spiegel Online International, July 17, 2008. Jaysh al-Islam, "Taudih wa I'lam li-Ummat al-Islam" and "Da'wa li'l-Mubahala ma' Qiadat Harakat Hamas," September 16, 2008.

42. Hizbullah cooperation with al-Qaida: Ali Mohamed, guilty plea statement in *U.S. vs. Ali Mohamed*, U.S. District Court, Southern District of New York, October 20, 2000, p. 28, posted at cryptome.org. Hizbullah popularity among Sunnis: *New York Times*, July 28, 2006; Shibley Telhami, *2006 Annual Arab Public Opinion Survey* (College Park: Anwar Sadat Chair for Peace and Development, University of Maryland, 2007), p. 65. Hizbullah popularity declines after 2006: Shibley Telhami, *2008 Annual Arab Public Opinion Poll* (College Park: Anwar Sadat Chair for Peace and Development, University of Maryland, 2008), p. 58; Pew Global Attitudes Project, *Unfavorable Views of Jews and Muslims on the Increase in Europe*, September 17, 2008, pp. 27–28. Debate among Sunni militants: Evan Kohlmann, "Zawahiri's New Message: A Landmark Call for Unity or a Tempest in a Teapot?," July 27, 2006, counterterrrorismblog. org. "A Video Speech from Dr. Ayman al-Zawahiri Regarding the Events in Lebanon and Gaza," July 27, 2006, translated by the SITE Institute.

43. Sunni Islamist militants migrating to Lebanon: Bernard Rougier, *Everyday Jihad: The Rise of Militant Islam among Palestinians in Lebanon* (Cambridge, Mass.: Harvard University Press, 2007), pp. 108–109, 161. Iraq veterans: *Al-Akhbar* (Beirut), October 10, 2007, translated by Nibras Kazimi at talismangate.blogspot. com; *New York Times*, October 15, 2007. An alternative assessment of Victory of Islam, downplaying the role of Iraq veterans, is provided by Samer Abboud, "The Siege of Nahr Al-Bared and the Palestinian Refugees in Lebanon," *Arab Studies Quarterly*, volume 31, 2009, pp. 31–48. Assassination attempts: Bilal Y. Saab and Bruce O. Riedel, "Hezbollah and Al Qaeda," *International Herald Tribune*, April 9, 2007. Couple of hundred militants: Bilal Y. Saab, "Al-Qa'ida's Presence and Influence in Lebanon," *CTC Sentinel*, December 2008, p. 6; Bilal Y. Saab, "Lebanon at Risk from Salafi-Jihadi Terrorist Cells," *CTC Sentinel*, February 2010, pp. 8–11. Al-Absi: *Gulf News*, June 10, 2008.

CHAPTER 4

1. Mike McDonell, Royal Canadian Mounted Police news conference, June 3, 2006, rcmp.ca. Canadian Broadcasting Corporation, June 11, 2008, cbc.ca; *National Post*, June 18, 2008, and October 9, 2009; *Globe and Mail*, June 19, 2008, and October 9, 2009.

2. Muslim Canadian Congress, June 3, 2006, and September 26, 2008, muslimcana-diancongress.org. Muslim Association of Canada, June 4, 2006, macnet.ca. Canadian Broadcasting Corporation, February 13, 2007, cbc.ca.

3. Thomas L. Friedman, "If It's a Muslim Problem, It Needs a Muslim Solution," *New York Times*, July 8, 2005. "Public Statements by Senior Saudi Officials Condemning Extremism and Promoting Moderation," May 2004, saudiembassy. net. Condemnations of the September 11 attacks: I have posted dozens of these statements at http://www.unc.edu/~kurzman/terror.htm.

4. Islamic Thinkers Society, "Press Release on FCNA [Fiqh Council of North America] and Their Pathetic Fatwa," September 3, 2005, and "Muslim Day Parade, 2008," October 12, 2008, islamicthinkers.com. Other Muslim-American groups that support violence abroad include Revolution Muslim, revolutionmuslim.com; and the producers of the online magazine *Jihad Recollections*. Surveys of American Muslims: Project MAPS and Zogby International, *Muslims in the American Public Square*, October 2004, project-maps.com; Council on American-Islamic Relations, *American Muslim Voters: A Demographic Profile and Survey of Attitudes*, October 24, 2006, cair.com; Pew Research Center, *Muslim Americans: Middle Class and Mostly Mainstream*, May 22, 2007, pewresearch.org; Gallup, *Muslim Americans: A National Portrait*, 2009.

5. Charles Kurzman, ed., *Liberal Islam: A Source-Book* (New York: Oxford University Press, 1998).

6. Khayr al-Din, *The Surest Path*, trans. Leon Carl Brown (Cambridge, Mass.: Center for Middle Eastern Studies, Harvard University, 1967), excerpted in Charles Kurzman, ed., *Modernist Islam, 1840–1940: A Sourcebook* (New York: Oxford University Press, 2002), pp. 40–49.

7. *Teraqqi* (Tashkent, Russian Turkistan), August 12, 1906; Necip Hablemitoğlu, *Çarlık Rusyası'nda Türk Kongreleri (1905–1917)* (Ankara, Turkey: Ankara Üniversitesi Basımevi, 1997); Ahmet Kanlıdere, *Reform Within Islam: The Tajdid and Jadid Movements Among the Kazan Tatars (1809–1917)* (Istanbul, Turkey: Eren Yayıncılık, 1997), pp. 107–112; Hakan Kırımlı, *National Movements and National Identity Among the Crimean Tatars, 1905–1916* (Leiden, Netherlands: E. J. Brill, 1996), p. 71.

8. Charles Kurzman, *Democracy Denied, 1905–1915* (Cambridge, Mass.: Harvard University Press, 2008). Abdul-Hadi Hairi, *Shi'ism and Constitutionalism in Iran* (Leiden, Netherlands: E. J. Brill, 1977), p. 242. Cemaleddin Efendi, *Siyasi Hatıralar, 1908–1913* (Istanbul, Turkey: Tercüman, 1978), pp. 20–21.

9. Michelle U. Campos, "A 'Shared Homeland' and Its Boundaries: Empire, Citizenship and the origins of Sectarianism in late Ottoman Palestine, 1908–1913," doctoral dissertation, Stanford University, 2003, pp. 25, 42; Kurzman, *Democracy Denied*, pp. 5, 53–54.

10. Mahdi Ansari, *Shaykh Fazlullah Nuri va Mashrutiyat* (Tehran, Iran: Amir Kabir, 1997), p. 306; Osman Selim Kocahanoğlu, *Derviş Vahdeti ve Çavuşların İsyanı* (Istanbul, Turkey: Temel Yayınları, 2001), p. 73.

11. Kurzman, ed., *Liberal Islam*, pp. 29–36.

12. Charles Kurzman, "The Globalization of Rights in Islamic Discourse," in Ali Mohammadi, ed., *Islam Encountering Globalization* (London: RoutledgeCurzon, 2002), pp. 131–133.

13. Kurzman, ed., *Liberal Islam*, pp. 245–246. On Soroush's intellectual trajectory, see Mahmoud Sadri and Ahmad Sadri, eds., *Reason, Freedom, and Democracy in Islam: Essential Writings of 'Abdolkarim Soroush* (New York: Oxford University Press, 2000); and Behrooz Ghamari-Tabrizi, *Islam and Dissent in Postrevolutionary*

Iran: Abdolkarim Soroush, Religious Politics, and Democratic Reform (London: I. B. Tauris, 2008).

14. Charles Kurzman, "Critics Within: Islamic Scholars' Protests Against the Islamic State in Iran," *International Journal of Politics, Culture, and Society*, volume 15, 2001, pp. 350–351.

15. Abdul-Karim Soroush, "The Evolution and Devolution of Religious Knowledge," in Kurzman, ed., *Liberal Islam*, pp. 244–251. Much of Soroush's work is available online in English and Persian at drsoroush.com.

16. Barry Rubin, *The Tragedy of the Middle East* (Cambridge, England: Cambridge University Press, 2002), p. 184. Tamara Cofman Wittes, "The Promise of Arab Liberalism," and Jon B. Alterman, "The False Promise of Arab Liberals," *Policy Review*, volume 125, June-July 2004, pp. 70, 83. Saba Mahmood, "Secularism, Hermeneutics, and Empire: The Politics of Islamic Reformation," *Public Culture*, volume 18, 2006, pp. 339, 346. Samuel Graham Wilson, *Modern Movements Among Moslems* (New York: Fleming H. Revell Company, 1916), p. 171.

17. *Crescent International* (London, England), March 1–15, 1989, quoted in Ziauddin Sardar and Meryl Wyn Davis, *Distorted Imagination: Lessons from the Rushdie Affair* (London, England: Grey Seal; Kuala Lumpur, Malaysia: Berita, 1990), p. 199. Bernard Lewis, "The Roots of Muslim Rage: Why So Many Muslims Deeply Resent the West and Why Their Bitterness Will Not Be Easily Mollified," *Atlantic Monthly*, September 1990, p. 60. For earlier references to the "class of/between civilizations," see also Bernard Lewis, *The Emergence of Modern Turkey* (London: Oxford University Press, 1961), p. 418, and Bernard Lewis, *The Middle East and the West* (Bloomington: Indiana University Press, 1964), p. 135. Samuel P. Huntington, "The Clash of Civilizations?," *Foreign Affairs*, Summer 1993, pp. 22–49; and *The Clash of Civilizations and the Remaking of World Order and The Clash of Civilizations and the Remaking of World Order* (New York: Simon & Schuster, 1996). Incidents of terrorism: Kristopher K. Robison, Edward M. Crenshaw, and J. Craig Jenkins, "Ideologies of Violence: The Social Origins of Islamist and Leftist Transnational Terrorism," *Social Forces*, volume 84, 2006, p. 2015.

18. *Crescent International*, June 16–30, 1999.

19. *Sada al-Jihad*, number 27, 2008, p. 26. Zawahiri: *Al-Ansar*, number 91, 1994, cited in Thomas Hegghammer, "Deconstructing the Myth about al-Qa'ida and Khobar," *CTC Sentinel*, February 2008, p. 22.

20. *Gallup Poll of the Islamic World, 2002.*

21. Ronald Inglehart, *World Values Survey*, worldvaluessurvey.org. John L. Esposito and Dalia Mogahed, *Who Speaks for Islam? What a Billion Muslims Really Think* (New York: Gallup Press, 2007), p. 48.

22. Pew Global Attitudes Project, *Spring 2007 Survey: Survey of 47 Publics: Final 2007 Trends Topline*, October 4, 2007, p. 16.

23. *World Values Survey*; Pippa Norris and Ronald Inglehart, "Islamic Culture and Democracy: Testing the 'Clash of Civilizations' Thesis," *Comparative Sociology*, volume 1, 2002, p. 250; Mansoor Moaddel, "The Saudi Public Speaks: Religion, Gender, and Politics," *International Journal of Middle East Studies*, volume 38, 2006,

p. 86; Amaney Jamal and Mark Tessler, "Attitudes in the Arab World," *Journal of Democracy*, volume 19, 2008, p. 98; Asia Foundation, *Afghanistan in 2007: A Survey of the Afghan People* (Kabul, Afghanistan: Asia Foundation, 2007), pp. 75–78. Comparisons within divided societies: Yılmaz Esmer, "Is There an Islamic Civilization?," *Comparative Sociology*, volume 1, 2002, pp. 294–295; Steven Ryan Hofmann, "Islam and Democracy: Micro-Level Indications of Compatibility," *Comparative Political Studies*, volume 37, 2004, pp. 652–676; Richard Rose, "How Muslims View Democracy: Evidence from Central Asia," *Journal of Democracy*, volume 13, 2002, pp. 106–107. *Pew Global Attitudes Project, 2002.*

24. Zawahiri: Moataz A. Fattah and Jim Butterfield, "Muslim Cultural Entrepreneurs and the Democracy Debate," *Critique: Critical Middle Eastern Studies*, volume 15, 2006, pp. 54, 63. "Al-Sahab Releases Video of Interview With Abu-Yahya al-Libi," World News Connection, September 12, 2007, document GMP20070912637001. Abu Basir Tartusi, "Limadha Kaffartu Yusuf al-Qaradawi?," November 1, 2008, pp. 13–16, abubaseer.bizland.com; see also MEMRI Special Dispatch No. 2162, December 24, 2008, memri.org. For more Islamist critiques of democracy, see Farhad Khosrokhavar, "The Jihadist View of Democracy," in *Inside Jihadism* (Boulder, Colo.: Paradigm Publishers, 2009), pp. 103–151.

25. Noorhaidi Hasan, *Laskar Jihad: Islam, Militancy and the Quest for Identity in Post-New Order Indonesia*, doctoral dissertation, Universiteit Utrecht, p. 151. Masykuri Abdillah, *Responses of Indonesian Muslim Intellectuals to the Concept of Democracy, 1966–1993* (Hamburg, West Germany: Abera Verlag, 1997), pp. 69–71. Survey: Saiful Mujani and R. William Liddle, "Politics, Islam, and Public Opinion," *Journal of Democracy*, volume 15, 2004, p. 114. Election results: International Parliamentary Union, *Parline Database*, www.ipu.org.

26. Charles Kurzman and Ijlal Naqvi, "Islamic Party Performance in Parliamentary Elections," United States Institute of Peace Working Paper, 2009. Islamic parties in Palestine and Turkey won a majority of seats in parliament, though less than 50 percent of votes. Daniel Brumberg, "Islam, Elections, and Reform in Algeria," *Journal of Democracy*, volume 2, 1991, p. 64. Belhadj: Ricardo Rene Larement, *Islam and the Politics of Resistance in Algeria, 1783–1992* (Trenton, N.J.: Africa World Press, 2000), p. 206; see also M. Al-Ahnaf, B. Botiveau, and F. Frégosi, *L'Algérie par ses islamistes* (Paris, France: Éditions Karthala, 1991), pp. 87–98.

27. Kurzman and Naqvi, "Islamic Party Performance"; Michael Herb, *Kuwait Politics Database*, Georgia State University, gsu.edu.

28. Kurzman and Naqvi, "Islamic Party Performance."

29. Kurzman and Naqvi, "Islamic Party Performance"; "Barnamij Hizb al-Ikhwan al-Muslimin: al-Isdar al-Awwal," August 25, 2007, p. 103, islamonline.net; Nathan J. Brown and Amr Hamzawy, "The Draft Party Platform of the Egyptian Muslim Brotherhood: Foray into Political Integration or Retreat into Old Positions?," Carnegie Endowment for International Peace, January 2008; Ayman Zawahiri, "Al-Liqa' al-Maftuh ma' al-Shaykh Ayman Zawahiri: Al-Halqa al-Thaniya," As-Sahab Media, April 2008, pp. 19–26.

30. Ronald Inglehart and Pippa Norris, *Rising Tide: Gender Equality and Cultural Change Around the World* (Cambridge, England: Cambridge University Press, 2003). Gallup: Dalia Mogahed, "Perspectives of Women in the Muslim World," Gallup World Poll, 2006; Frank Newport, "The Issue of Women in Government in Islamic Countries," Gallup News, March 30, 2006; Magali Rheault, "Majorities Support Women's Rights in North Africa," Gallup News, November 6, 2007; Magali Rheault, "Saudi Arabia: Majorities Support Women's Rights," Gallup News, December 21, 2007. Pew Global Attitudes Project, *World Publics Welcome Global Trade—But Not Immigration: 47-Nation Pew Global Attitudes Survey,* October 4, 2007.

31. For examples in Egypt and Lebanon, see Omayma Abdellatif and Marina Ottaway, "Women in Islamist Movements: Toward an Islamist Model of Women's Activism," Carnegie Middle East Center, number 2, 2007, and Omayma Abdel-Latif, "In the Shadow of the Brothers: The Women of the Egyptian Muslim Brotherhood," Carnegie Middle East Center, number 13, 2008, carnegieendowment.org.

32. *Pew Global Attitudes Project, 2002*; Charles Kurzman, "Tropes and Challenges of Islamic Toleration," in Ingrid Creppell, Russell Hardin, and Stephen Macedo, eds., *Toleration on Trial* (Lanham, Md.: Lexington Books, 2008), pp. 153–167.

33. Katherine Meyer, Helen Rizzo, and Yousef Ali, "Islam and the Extension of Citizenship Rights to Women in Kuwait," *Journal for the Scientific Study of Religion,* volume 37, 1998, pp. 138–140; Helen Rizzo, Katherine Meyer, and Yousef Ali, "Women's Political Rights: Islam, Status and Networks in Kuwait," *Sociology,* volume 36, 2002, p. 653; Katherine Meyer, Helen Rizzo, and Yousef Ali, "Changed Political Attitudes in the Middle East: The Case of Kuwait," *International Sociology,* volume 22, 2007, p. 307; Helen Mary Rizzo, *Islam, Democracy, and the Status of Women: The Case of Kuwait* (New York: Routledge, 2005); Mary Ann Tétreault, "A State of Two Minds: State Cultures, Women, and Politics in Kuwait," *International Journal of Middle East Studies,* volume 33, 2001, pp. 203–220. On women's suffrage globally, see Pamela Paxton and Melanie M. Hughes, *Women, Politics, and Power: A Global Perspective* (Los Angeles, Calif.: Pine Forge Press, 2007), pp. 59–62.

34. Majelis Ulema Indonesia, "Keputusan Fatwa: Pluralisme, Liberalisme dan Sekularisme Agama," July 29, 2005, www.mui.or.id. Al-Fawzan: *Al-Jazirah* (Riyadh, Saudi Arabia), June 26, 2007, www.al-jazirah.com.

35. Fauzi M. Najjar, "Islamic Fundamentalism and the Intellectuals: The Case of Nasr Hamid Abu Zayd," *British Journal of Middle Eastern Studies,* volume 27, 2000, pp. 177–200; Raymond William Baker, *Islam Without Fear: Egypt and the New Islamists* (Cambridge, Mass.: Harvard University Press, 2003), p. 263. See also Nasr Abu Zaid, *Voice of an Exile* (Westport, Conn.: Praeger, 2004); Nasr Abu Zayd, *Rethinking the Qur'an: Towards a Humanistic Hermeneutics* (Utrecht, Netherlands: University of Humanistics, 2004); Nasr Abu Zayd, *Reformation of Islamic Thought* (Amsterdam, Netherlands: Amsterdam University Press, 2006).

36. Hamid Algar, *Mirza Malkum Khan* (Berkeley: University of California Press, 1973); M. Şükrü Hanioğlu, *Bir Siyasal Düsünür Olarak Doktor Abdullah Cevdet ve Dönemi* (Istanbul, Turkey: Üçdal Neşriyat, 1981); Michaelle Browers, *Democracy and Civil Society in Arab Political Thought* (Syracuse, N.Y.: Syracuse University Press, 2006).

37. Muslim American blogger: Samir Khan, *Inshallah Shaheed,* July 4, 2007, inshallahshaheed.wordpress.com; *New York Times,* October 15, 2007. *Jakarta Post,* December 24, 2002.

38. Convention resolutions: Tahaffuz-e-Pakistan Ulama-o-Mashaykh Convention, hosted by the Minhaj-ul-Quran Ulama Council, Lahore, Pakistan, May 2009, minhaj.org; Ulama and Mashaikh Convention, organized by the Jamiat Ulema-e-Pakistan, Islamabad, Pakistan, May 2009, reported in *Dawn* (Karachi, Pakistan), May 18, 2009, dawn.com. International Islamic University: *Dawn,* October 21, 2009. Sufi leaders in Pakistan: Altaf Hussain, leader of the Muttahida Qaumi Movement, speaking by telephone to the Ulema and Mashaikh Convention, Karachi, Pakistan, April 2009, reported in the *Nation* (Lahore, Pakistan), April 20, 2009, nation.com.pk. Al-Durri: *New York Times,* September 15, 2008.

39. Julia Day Howell, "Modulations of Active Piety: Professors and Televangelists as Promoters of Indonesian 'Sufisme,'" and James B. Hoesterey, "Marketing Morality: The Rise, Fall, and Rebranding of Aa Gym," in Greg Fealy and Sally White, eds., *Expressing Islam: Religious Life and Politics in Indonesia* (Singapore: Institute of Southeast Asian Studies, 2008), pp. 40–62 and 95–112; Ayşe Öncü, "Becoming 'Secular Muslims': Yaşar Nuri Öztürk as a Super-Subject on Turkish Television," in Birgit Meyers and Annelies Moors, eds., *Religion, Media and the Public Sphere* (Bloomington: Indiana University Press, 2006), pp. 227–240. Amr Khaled, *A Call for Coexistence,* episode 1, 2007, amrkhaled.net. On Amr Khaled: Muhammad Baz, *Du'at fi al-manfa: Qissat 'Amr Khalid wa al-du'at al-judud fi-Misr* (Cairo, Egypt: Dar al-Faris li'l-Nashr wa al-Tawzi', 2004); Sophia Pandya, "Religious Change Among Yemeni Women: The New Popularity of 'Amr Khaled," *Journal of Middle East Women's Studies,* volume 5, 2009, pp. 50–79; Lindsay Wise, "Amr Khaled: Broadcasting the Nahda," *Transnational Broadcasting Studies,* number 13, 2004, tbsjournal.com.

40. Susan Friend Harding, *The Book of Jerry Falwell: Fundamentalist Language and Politics* (Princeton, N.J.: Princeton University Press, 2000), p. 22. See also Jeffrey K. Hadden and Anson Shupe, *Televangelism, Power, and Politics on God's Frontier* (New York: H. Holt, 1988); and David Edwin Harrell, Jr., *Pat Robertson: A Life and Legacy* (Grand Rapids, Mich.: William B. Eerdmans, 2010). Critics of Amr Khaled: Brother Mujahid, January 8, 2008, islamicawakening.com; al-Taliban Akabir, September 30, 2006, aljazeerahtalk.net.

41. *Al-Masry al-Youm,* June 3, 2009, almasry-alyoum.com. Gilles Kepel, *Muslim Extremism in Egypt: The Prophet and Pharaoh,* 2nd ed. (Berkeley: University of California Press, 2003), p. 213.

42. Oprah comparison: *Independent* (London, England), January 4, 2006.

43. *New York Times,* November 28, 2003, and March 7, 2004; *Washington Post,* July 22, 2007.

44. *Washington Post,* October 7, 2005; *New York Times,* August 22, 2009; Mark LeVine, *Heavy Metal Islam* (New York: Three Rivers Press, 2008), pp. 249–250; J. Michael Waller, "Muslim Pop Artists Lead Youthful Resistance to Islamic Extremism," *Serviam,* January-February 2008, serviammagazine.com.

CHAPTER 5

1. Darren W. Davis and Brian D. Silver, "Americans' Perceptions of the Causes of Terrorism: Why Do They Hate Us?," 2004, msu.edu/~bsilver.

2. *This Day* (Lagos, Nigeria), July 10, 2003; *Lancet* (London), June 5, 2004; World Health Organization, *Global Polio Eradication Initiative: Annual Report 2008,* 2009, polioeradication.org.

3. Majelis Ulama Indonesia, "Penggunaan Vaksin Polio Khusus (IPV)," October 8, 2002, mui.or.id; International Union for Islamic Scholars, statement of December 31, 2005, iumsonline.net; Muttehida Majlis-e-Amal, February 26, 2007, IslamOnline.net.

4. Mao Tse-tung, "U.S. Imperialism Is a Paper Tiger," July 14, 1956, *Selected Works of Mao Tse-tung,* volume V, marxists.org; see also Mao Tse Tung, *Quotations from Mao Tse Tung* (Beijing, China: Foreign Languages Press, 1966), pp. 72–75. Bin Ladin interview with John Miller, *ABC Nightline,* June 10, 1998. On al-Qaida's use of non-Islamic precedents for strategy and tactics, see chapter 3. Leonard Peikoff, "What to Do about Terrorism," May 1, 1996, aynrand.org.

5. Bernard Lewis, "The Revolt of Islam," *New Yorker,* November 19, 2001, p. 63.

6. *Wall Street Journal,* February 3, 2004. Bernard Lewis, *The Middle East and the West* (Bloomington: Indiana University Press, 1964), p. 115; Bernard Lewis, *The Muslim Discovery of Europe* (New York: W. W. Norton, 1982), p. 60; Bernard Lewis, *What Went Wrong?* (New York: Oxford University Press, 2002), pp. 158, 100.

7. *World Values Survey;* Charles Kurzman, ed., *Liberal Islam: A Sourcebook* (New York: Oxford University Press, 1998).

8. Bernard Lewis, *The Emergence of Modern Turkey,* 3rd ed. (New York: Oxford University Press, 2001), pp. xx, 424.

9. *Wall Street Journal,* February 3, 2004; Bernard Lewis, "The Revolt of Islam," p. 63; Charlie Rose, "A Conversation with Author Bernard Lewis," December 20, 2001, charlierose.com

10. Barry M. Blechman and Tamara Cofman Wittes, "Defining Moment: The Threat and Use of Force in American Foreign Policy," *Political Science Quarterly,* volume 114, 1999, p. 5. Black Hawk Down: Mark Bowden, *Black Hawk Down* (New York: Atlantic Monthly Press, 1999).

11. Project for the New American Century, "Statement of Principles," June 3, 1997, www.newamericancentury.org.

12. Project for the New American Century, "Letter to President Clinton on Iraq," January 26, 1998, newamericancentury.org. Iraq planning, January 2001: Ron Suskind, *The Price of Loyalty* (New York: Simon & Schuster, 2004), pp. 129, 354.

Iraq planning on hold: Michael DeLong, *Inside CentCom* (Washington, D.C.: Regnery, 2004), pp. 21, 63.

13. Tenet: Bob Woodward, *Bush at War* (New York: Simon & Schuster, 2002), p. 26. Afghanistan: Mozhdeh, *Afghanistan va Panj Sal-e Solteh-ye Taleban*, p. 74. Kabul press conference: Kathy Gannon, *I Is for Infidel* (New York: Public Affairs, 2005), pp. 87–88. Saudi and Pakistani delegations: Wright, *The Looming Tower*, pp. 288–289. "Authorization for Use of Military Force Against Terrorists," House Joint Resolution 64/Senate Joint Resolution 23, passed September 14, 2001, signed into law by President Bush on September 18, 2001.

14. Claire Sterling, *The Terror Network* (New York: Holt, Rinehart, and Winston, 1981). Bob Woodward, *Veil: The Secret Wars of the CIA, 1981–1987* (New York: Simon & Schuster, 1987), pp. 99–100.

15. George W. Bush, "Statement by the President in His Address to the Nation," September 11, 2001, whitehouse.gov; Woodward, *Bush at War*, pp. 30–31; Douglas J. Feith, *War and Decision* (New York: Harper, 2008), p. 7; DeLong, *Inside CentCom*, pp. 21–22. On definitions of state sponsorship, see also Daniel Bynum, *Deadly Connections: States that Sponsor Terrorism* (Cambridge, England: Cambridge University Press, 2005); and Jeffrey M. Bale, "Terrorists as State Surrogates or Proxies: Separating Fact from Fiction," unpublished paper, 2010.

16. Peace movements after 9/11: Gregory M. Maney, Lynne M. Woehrle, and Patrick G. Coy, "Harnessing and Challenging Hegemony: The U.S. Peace Movement after 9/11," *Sociological Perspectives*, volume 48, 2005, pp. 357–381. Charles Kurzman, "Understanding the Attack on America," September 17, 2001, unc.edu/~kurzman.

17. Jerry L. Martin and Anne D. Neal, *Defending Civilization: How Our Universities Are Failing America and What Can Be Done About It* (Washington, D.C.: American Council of Trustees and Alumni, 2001), pp. 1, 26–27. Charles Tilly, "Predictions," September 15, 2001, essays.ssrc.org/sept11.

18. Donald N. Wilber, *Overthrow of Premier Mossadeq of Iran* (Langley, Va.: Clandestine Service Historical Paper No. 208, 1969), appendix E, pp. 21–22, posted at nytimes.com. Domestic effects: *New York Times*, December 25, 1977; see also Christopher Simpson, *Blowback: America's Recruitment of Nazis and Its Effects on the Cold War* (New York: Collier Books, 1988), p. 5.

19. Chalmers A. Johnson, *Blowback: The Costs and Consequences of American Empire* (New York: Metropolitan Books, 2000), pp. 10–13, 30.

20. Johnson, *Blowback*, pp. 10–11.

21. Chalmers Johnson, "US Stumbles into Yet Another Futile War," *Canberra Times*, October 11, 2001.

22. *Global Terrorism Database.* I compared September 11, 2000–September 10, 2001, with September 12, 2001–September 11, 2002. Research assistant Stephen Kirsch and I coded the attackers as Islamist based on the group identified in the database as the perpetrator. Since almost half of the perpetrators during this period were unspecified, we imputed the Islamist category for all unidentified perpetrators in Muslim-majority countries, plus Israel and Thailand. This method

overcounts Islamist terrorism in these countries, since not all attacks were Islamist, but is unlikely to bias the estimate of trends.

23. *Washington Post,* November 30, 2001.

24. Yousef Ibrahim, "Bush's Iraq Adventure Is Bound to Backfire," *International Herald Tribune,* November 1, 2002; *New York Times,* October 25, 2002; TomPaine.com. Abu 'Azzam al-Ansari, "Shukran, Ayyatuha al-Sahyusalibiyya," *Sada al-Islam,* October-November 2006, pp. 13–17. Terrorist attack data from the *Global Terrorism Database.*

25. Dalton Fury, *Kill Bin Laden: A Delta Force Commander's Account of the Hunt for the World's Most Wanted Man* (New York: St. Martin's Press, 2008), pp. 233–234. George W. Bush, "We're Fighting to Win—And Win We Will," speech in Norfolk, Virginia, December 7, 2001, georgewbush-whitehouse.archives.gov.

26. George W. Bush, "President Bush Delivers Farewell Address to the Nation," January 15, 2009, georgewbush-whitehouse.archives.gov. Terrorist attack data from the *Global Terrorism Database.*

27. *Los Angeles Times,* December 23, 1996. This report is based on a CIA memorandum describing a conversation in which the imam told an Iranian diplomat about his conversation with the American diplomat. Both the imam and the American diplomat denied that any such conversation took place—House International Relations Committee, *Final Report of the Select Subcommittee to Investigate the U.S. Role in Iranian Arms Transfers to Croatia and Bosnia ("The Iranian Green Light Subcommittee"),* October 10, 1996, pp. 470–477. American public opinion: Richard Sobel, "Portraying American Public Opinion Toward the Bosnia Crisis," *Harvard International Journal of Press/Politics,* March 1998, pp. 16–33. Clinton decision and weapons flow: Cees Wiebes, *Intelligence and the War in Bosnia, 1992–1995* (Münster, Germany: Lit Verlag, 2003), pp. 158–198.

28. *Washington Post,* May 13, 1994. Yugoslav Telegraph Service, May 14, 1994. United States Congress, "National Defense Authorization Act for Fiscal Year 1995," October 5, 1994, section 1404(f). Bombing Serb positions: Robert C. Owen, ed., *Deliberate Force: A Case Study in Effective Air Campaigning* (Maxwell Air Force Base, Ala.: Air University Press, 2000).

29. Instant experts: Jaafar Abdulmahdi Saheeb, "Arab Views on Balkans' Moslems," *Politikologija Religija,* volume 2, 2008, pp. 65–76. Fund-raisers: Muhammad I. Ayish and Ali Qassim, "Direct Satellite Broadcasting in the Arab Gulf Region," *International Communication Gazette,* volume 56, 1996, p. 25. Organization of the Islamic Conference: 21st Conference of the Foreign Ministers, "Final Communiqué," Karachi, Pakistan, April 25–29, 1993; Seventh Islamic Summit Conference, "Declaration on Bosnia and Herzegovina," Casablanca, Morocco, December 13–15, 1994. International Crisis Group, "Bin Laden and the Balkans," ICG Balkans Report Number 119, November 9, 2001, crisisgroup.org; Evan Kohlmann, *Al-Qaida's Jihad in Europe: The Afghan-Bosnian Network* (Oxford, England: Berg, 2004); John R. Schindler, *Unholy Terror: Bosnia, Al-Qa'ida, and the Rise of Global Jihad* (St. Paul, Minn.: Zenith Press, 2007); Shaul Shay, *Islamic Terror and the Balkans* (New Brunswick, N.J.: Transaction, 2009).

30. *Crescent International*, July 1–15, 1995. Lawrence, *Messages to the World*, p. 40.

31. Turkey: Monti Narayan Datta, "The Decline of America's Soft Power in the United Nations," *International Studies Perspectives*, volume 10, 2009, pp. 265–284, and supplementary data kindly provided by Professor Datta.

32. Pew Global Attitudes Project, *Global Public Opinion in the Bush Years (2001–2008)*, December 18, 2008.

33. George W. Bush, "Address to a Joint Session of Congress and the American People," September 20, 2001, georgewbush-whitehouse.archives.gov. Lawrence, *Messages to the World*, p. 239.

34. Surveys: Norris and Inglehart, "Islamic Culture and Democracy." Muslims on apostasy: "'Wir haben abgeschworen!' Warum die Kampagne des Zentralrats der Ex-Muslime ein Tabu bricht," 2007, ex-muslime.de; "Manifesto of the Council of Ex-Muslims of Britain," 2007, ex-muslim.org.uk. American cultural conservatives: Andrew R. Murphy, *Prodigal Nation: Moral Decline and Divine Punishment from New England to 9/11* (New York: Oxford University Press, 2009).

35. Giacomo Chiozza, *Anti-Americanism and the American World Order* (Baltimore, Md.: Johns Hopkins University Press, 2009), pp. 74, 98. The Middle East countries are Egypt, Jordan, Lebanon, and Turkey; seven other Muslim-majority countries in Africa and Asia are considered separately. The Muslim societies in the second set of surveys are Egypt, Indonesia, Iran, Kuwait, Lebanon, Pakistan, Saudi Arabia, and the United Arab Emirates. For another statistical analysis of the Pew Global Attitudes Project, see Michael G. Elasmar, *Through Their Eyes: Factors Affecting Muslim Support for the U.S.-Led War on Terror* (Spokane, Wash.: Marquette Books, 2007). See also Peter J. Katzenstein and Robert O. Keohane, eds., *Anti-Americanisms in World Politics* (Ithaca, N.Y.: Cornell University Press, 2007). Algeria and Jordan: Mark A. Tessler and Michael D. H. Robbins, "What Leads Some Ordinary Men and Women in Arab Countries to Approve of Terrorist Acts against the West," *Journal of Conflict Resolution*, volume 51, 2007, p. 322. Nine countries: *Gallup Poll of the Islamic World, 2002*. Telhami, *2008 Annual Arab Public Opinion Poll*, pp. 71–73; Telhami, *2009 Annual Arab Public Opinion Survey*, p. 15.

36. Hypocritical: WorldPublicOpinion.org, "Public Opinion in the Islamic World on Terrorism, al Qaeda, and US Policies," February 25, 2009, p. 18. Gallup poll: Esposito and Mogahed, *Who Speaks for Islam?*, p. 83. Shibley Telhami, *2005 Annual Arab Public Opinion Survey with 2004 Comparisons*, p. 34; Telhami, *2006 Annual Arab Public Opinion Survey*, p. 34; Telhami, *2008 Annual Arab Public Opinion Poll*, p. 74; Telhami, *2009 Annual Arab Public Opinion Survey*, p. 17; Telhami, *2010 Arab Public Opinion Poll*, p. 12. Kano grocer: Agence France Presse, July 10, 2003.

37. Telhami, *2005 Annual Arab Public Opinion Survey with 2004 Comparisons*, p. 39; Telhami, *2006 Annual Arab Public Opinion Survey*, p. 17; Telhami, *2008 Annual Arab Public Opinion Poll*, pp. 89–91; Telhami, *2009 Annual Arab Public Opinion Survey*, p. 39; Telhami, *2010 Arab Public Opinion Poll*, p. 62. Pew Global Attitudes Project, *A Rising Tide Lifts Mood in the Developing World*, July 24, 2007, pp. 46–47. Pakistan: Terror Free Tomorrow, "Pakistanis Strongly Back Negotiations with Al Qaeda and Taliban over Military Action; Public Support for Al Qaeda Gaining

Ground," July 2009, pp. 8–9, terrorfreetomorrow.org; WorldPublicOpinion.org, "Pakistani Public Opinion on the Swat Conflict, Afghanistan, and the US," July 1, 2009, p. 4.

38. Pew Global Attitudes Project, *Islamic Extremism: Common Concern for Muslim and Western Publics,* July 14, 2005, p. 34, and associated datasets. Telhami: *Annual Arab Public Opinion Poll,* 2005–2010; see also WorldPublicOpinion.org, "Muslim Public Opinion on US Policy, Attacks on Civilians and al Qaeda," April 24, 2007, p. 6. Spread Christianity, humiliate Muslims: WorldPublicOpinion.org, "Public Opinion in the Islamic World on Terrorism, al Qaeda, and US Policies," February 25, 2009, pp. 11–12, 17.

39. Public diplomacy: U.S. Government Accountability Office, *U.S. Public Diplomacy: Key Issues for Congressional Oversight,* May 2009, gao.gov; Peter Krause and Stephen Van Evera, "Public Diplomacy: Ideas for the War of Ideas," *Middle East Policy,* October 2009, pp. 106–134. War on Islam: Joas Wagemakers, "Framing the 'Threat to Islam': Al-Wala' wa al-Bara' in Salafi Discourse," *Arab Studies Quarterly,* Fall 2008, p. 13; Abid Ullah Jan, *War on Islam?* (United Kingdom: Maktabah al-Ansar, 2002). Crusade: George W. Bush, "Remarks by the President Upon Arrival," September 16, 2001, georgewbush-whitehouse.archives.gov. Bush comments on Islam: "Backgrounder: The President's Quotes on Islam," undated, georgewbush-whitehouse.archives.gov. Graham: NBC Nightly News, November 16, 2001. Tancredo: Tom Tancredo, "Bigger Sins than Offending," *Denver Post,* July 24, 2005; Chris Dorsey, "Tancredo Says Threat of Attack on Holy Sites Would Deter Terrorism," IowaPolitics.com, July 31, 2007.

40. Spring 2008 surveys: Pew Global Attitudes Project, *Global Public Opinion in the Bush Years,* p. 15; Telhami, *2008 Annual Arab Public Opinion Poll,* p. 78. Surveys after Obama took office: Telhami, *2009 Annual Arab Public Opinion Survey,* pp. 6, 10, 13; *2010 Arab Public Opinion Poll,* pp. 6, 7, 10. (See also WorldPublicOpinion. org, "Pakistani Public Opinion on the Swat Conflict, Afghanistan, and the US," pp. 9–10.) Duplicate: *Sada al-Jihad,* December 2008, pp. 7–9.

41. Telhami, *2009 Annual Arab Public Opinion Survey,* p. 16; *2010 Arab Public Opinion Poll,* p. 11. Barack Obama, speech to the American Israel Political Action Committee, June 4, 2008, transcript at aipac.org.

42. "The Nobel Peace Prize 2003," October 10, 2003, nobelprize.org; IRNA, October 12, 2003. Shirin Ebadi, "Nobel Lecture," Oslo, Norway, December 10, 2003, nobelprize.org. Iranian accusations against Ebadi: *Kayhan,* January 16, 2005; *Siyasat-e Ruz,* July 23, 2005; translations by BBC Worldwide Monitoring.

43. George Washington, "Farewell Address," September 17, 1796, avalon.law.yale.edu.

44. Gingrich covert funding: *Wall Street Journal,* October 27, 1995; *New York Times,* January 26, 1996. Bush administration: Seymour M. Hersh, "Preparing the Battlefield: The Bush Administration Steps Up Its Secret Moves Against Iran," *New Yorker,* July 7, 2008, p. 61. Iranian attitudes toward the United States: *Gallup Poll of the Islamic World,* 2002. Iranian attitudes on relations with the United States: "Most Tehranis Favor Iran-US Negotiations," Islamic Republic News Agency, September 22, 2002; Terror Free Tomorrow, "Polling Iranian Public

Opinion: An Unprecedented Nationwide Survey of Iran," 2007, p. 6, and "Ahmadinejad Front Runner in Upcoming Presidential Elections; Iranians Continue to Back Compromise and Better Relations with US and West: Results of a New Nationwide Public Opinion Survey of Iran before the June 12, 2009 Presidential Elections," pp. 12–13, terrorfreetomorrow.org.

45. Charles Kurzman, "Soft on Satan: Challenges for Iranian-U.S. Relations," *Middle East Policy*, June 1998, pp. 63–72; *Hamshahri*, August 5, 1999; "The 'Grand Bargain' Fax: A Missed Opportunity?," *Frontline*, October 23, 2007, pbs.org.

46. Agence France Presse, April 6, 2009; Associated Press, April 6, 2009.

47. Obama before Iranian election: Press conference of May 18, 2009, whitehouse. gov. Obama after Iranian election: Press conference of June 15, 2009, whitehouse. gov; see also Obama's interview with CNBC, June 16, 2009, cnbc.com, in which Obama commented that "the difference between Ahmadinejad and Mousavi in terms of their actual policies may not be as great as has been advertised," and that "the easiest way for reactionary forces inside Iran to crush reformers is to say it's the US that is encouraging those reformers."

48. Obama's rivals in Washington: Eric Cantor, "Cantor on Iran, Election Protests and Administration's Silence," June 15, 2009, republicanwhip.house.gov; Radio Free Europe/Radio Liberty, June 16, 2009, rferl.org. Everyone understands: Babak Sarfaraz, "Iran's New Revolutionaries," *Nation*, July 13, 2009. Ebadi: *Washington Post*, June 17, 2009.

49. Fars News, August 2 and August 25, 2009, farsnews.ir; Islamic Republic News Agency, August 25, 2009, irna.ir.

50. *Washington Post*, October 15, 2009; numerous YouTube videos of November 4, 2009.

51. Yarro, "Chera Tarh-e Obama bara-ye Bar-Qarari-ye Rabeteh-ye Addi ba Iran Naf'-e Demokrasi dar Iran Ast?," November 11, 2009, yarro.blogspot.com, reproduced at mowjcamp.com, November 13, 2009.

52. Greg Mortenson and David Oliver Relin, *Three Cups of Tea* (New York: Penguin, 2006), p. 97, 219.

53. William J. Lederer and Eugene Burdick, *The Ugly American* (New York: W. W. Norton, 1958), pp. 205–232.

54. Helen B. Hunerwadel, *Our Burma Story*, unpublished manuscript, 1979; Otto K. Hunerwadel, Jr., "Hunerwadel Family," Beersheba Springs Historical Society, Tennessee, June 2008, grundycountyhistory.org. The Hunerwadels are also profiled in James A. Michener, *The Voice of Asia* (New York: Random House, 1951), pp. 223–226.

55. W. Morgan Shuster, *The Strangling of Persia* (New York: Century, 1912); Robert A. McDaniel, *The Shuster Mission and the Persian Constitutional Revolution* (Minneapolis, Minn.: Bibliotheca Islamica, 1974); Kurzman, *Democracy Denied*, pp. 182, 229–231.

56. Nicholas J. Cull, *The Cold War and the United States Information Agency: American Propaganda and Public Diplomacy, 1945–1989* (Cambridge, England: Cambridge University Press, 2008), pp. 190, 196.

57. Colin Powell, remarks at NetDiplomacy conference, September 6, 2001, usinfo. org. Charlotte Beers, testimony before the Committee on International Relations, U.S. House of Representatives, October 10, 2001, foreignaffairs.house.gov.

58. Sam Cherribi, "U.S. Public Diplomacy in the Arab World: Responses to Al-Jazeera's Interview with Karen Hughes," *American Behavioral Scientist,* volume 52, 2009, p. 762. Karen Hughes, "'Waging Peace': A New Paradigm for Public Diplomacy," *Mediterranean Quarterly,* volume 18, 2007, pp. 18–36; Strategic Communication and Public Diplomacy Policy Coordinating Committee, *U.S. National Strategy for Public Diplomacy and Strategic Communication,* June 2007, state.gov.

59. Petraeus and Mullen: CNN, August 28, 2009. Required reading: U.S. Army Combined Arms Center, Ft. Leavenworth, "Pre-Deployment Afghanistan Reading List," August 4, 2009, usacac.army.mil. Kolenda: *Washington Post,* May 1, 2008; *New York Times,* July 13, 2008, and July 18, 2010; American Forces Press Service, May 19, 2009; *Christian Science Monitor,* December 4, 2009.

CHAPTER 6

1. *Times Higher Education,* May 29, 2008.

2. Martin and Neal, *Defending Civilization,* p. 6.

3. Martin Kramer, *Ivory Towers on Sand: The Failure of Middle Eastern Studies in America* (Washington, D.C.: Washington Institute for Near East Policy, 2001), pp. 57, 55.

4. "International Studies in Higher Education Act of 2003," Report to Accompany House Resolution 3077, U.S. House of Representatives, October 8, 2003. Representative Howard Berman, *Congressional Record,* October 21, 2003, p. H9757; Stanley Kurtz testimony at the hearing on "International Programs in Higher Education and Questions of Bias," Subcommittee on Select Education, Committee on Education and the Workforce, U.S. House of Representatives, June 19, 2003, published at nationalreview.com (the page containing the second quotation is missing from the official Government Printing Office edition, Serial No. 108-21, between pages 76 and 77).

5. Stanley Kurtz, "UCLA Tests Congress," National Review Online, March 3, 2009, nationalreview.com; U.S. Congress, "Higher Education Opportunity Act," Public Law 110–315, August 14, 2008, p. 3336.

6. Defense Advanced Research Projects Agency, *Fiscal Year (FY) 2004/FY 2005 Biennial Budget Estimates,* February 2003, p. 80, and DARPA press release canceling the program, July 29, 2003, darpa.mil; *New York Times,* July 29, 2003. The Policy Analysis Market website, which was quickly removed from the Internet, is archived at cryptome.org.

7. U.S. Department of Homeland Security, "Broad Agency Announcement: Initial University-Based Center of Excellence," July 23, 2003, dhs.gov; Robert M. Gates, U.S. secretary of defense, speech announcing the Minerva Initiative, April 14, 2008, defense.gov. Websites for these programs are located at hsuniversityprograms.org and minerva.dtic.mil.

8. Jeffrey Heath, *From Code-Switching to Borrowing: Foreign and Diglossic Mixing in Moroccan Arabic* (London, England: Kegan Paul International, 1989), p. 122; Muhammad Hasan Amara and Bernard Spolsky, "The Diffusion and Integration of Hebrew and English Lexical Items in the Spoken Arabic of an Israeli Village," *Anthropological Linguistics*, volume 28, 1986, p. 48; *Washington Post*, May 31, 2009.

9. Roger Hsiao et al., "Optimizing Components for Handheld Two-Way Speech Translation for an English-Iraqi Arabic System," Ninth International Conference on Spoken Language Processing, Pittsburgh, Pennsylvania, September 17–21, 2006, p. 766; Tactical Language and Culture Training System, advertising video, November 7, 2007, tacticallanguage.com.

10. Sean O'Brien, "Computational Social Science," DARPATech Symposium, Anaheim, California, August 8, 2007; Robert Popp, "Utilizing Social Science Technology to Understand and Counter the 21st Century Strategic Threat," DARPATech Symposium, Anaheim, California, August 9–11, 2005, p. 107, darpa.mil. National Science and Technology Council, Subcommittee on Social, Behavioral, and Economic Sciences, *Combating Terrorism: Research Priorities in the Social, Behavioral and Economic Sciences*, 2005, pp. 6, 7, 13, whitehouse.gov.

11. Auguste Comte, "Considérations philosophiques sur les sciences et les savants" (1825), in *Système de politique positive*, volume 4 (Paris, France: self-published, 1854), appendix pp. 150–151, 172.

12. Bruce Bueno de Mesquita, "Forecasting Policy Decisions: An Expected Utility Approach to Post-Khomeini Iran," *PS*, volume 17, 1984, p. 233; *Predicting Politics* (Columbus: Ohio State University Press, 2002), p. 69; *The Predictioneer's Game* (New York: Random House, 2009), p. xix; "U.S. Policy Towards Iran," public lecture, Duke University, January 15, 2009; "What Will Iran Do?," TED lecture series, February 2009, minute 8, ted.com.

13. Bueno de Mesquita, "What Will Iran Do?," minute 16. U.S. Congress, "National Defense Education Act of 1958," September 2, 1958.

14. Bueno de Mesquita, "What Will Iran Do?," minute 15; *The Predictioneer's Game*, pp. 200–201, 240.

15. *New York Times Magazine*, August 16, 2009, pp. 20–25; Bueno de Mesquita, "Forecasting Policy Decisions," p. 233; *Predicting Politics*, p. 75; "U.S. Policy Towards Iran."

16. David Hunt, *On the Hunt: How to Wake Up Washington and Win the War on Terror* (New York: Crown Forum, 2007), p. 67. Jarret Brachman cites dozens of examples of al-Qaida's attention to counterterrorism (CT) research in "Mining Our Business: AQ's Love-Hate Relationship with Western CT Research, RAND, et al.," February 4, 2010, jarretbrachman.net.

17. Kurzman, *The Unthinkable Revolution in Iran*, p. 133.

18. *Crime in the United States, 2009*; Internet Crime Complaint Center, *2009 Internet Crime Report* (Glen Allen, Va.: National White Collar Crime Center, 2010).

19. Edward Jay Epstein, *The Hollywood Economist: The Hidden Financial Reality Behind the Movies* (Brooklyn, New York: Melville House, 2010).

20. Walter Laqueur, "The Terrorism to Come," *Policy Review* 126, 2004: pp. 49–64.

21. Pew Global Attitudes Project, *Muslims in Europe: Spring 2006 15-Nation Survey*, data downloaded from pewglobal.org. Europol, *TE-SAT 2010: EU Terrorism Situation and Trend Report*, 2010, p. 21, europol.europa.eu.

22. Edward W. Said, *Orientalism* (New York: Vintage Books, 1979), pp. 308–309.

23. Rafael Patai, "On Culture Contact and Its Working in Modern Palestine," *American Anthropologist, Memoir Series*, number 67, 1947, pp. 1–48. Examples of critiques of Said by fans of his: Sadiq Jalal al-Azm, "Orientalism and Orientalism in Reverse," in Jon Rothschild, ed., *Forbidden Agendas: Intolerance and Defiance in the Middle East* (London, England: Al Saqi Books, 1984), pp. 349–376; Aijaz Ahmad, *In Theory: Classes, Nations, Literatures* (London, England: Verso, 1992), pp. 159–220; Gyan Prakash, "*Orientalism* Now," *History and Theory*, volume 34, 1995, pp. 199–212; Daniel Martin Varisco, *Reading Orientalism: Said and the Unsaid* (Seattle, Wash.: University of Washington Press, 2007).

24. Norvell B. De Atkine and Daniel Pipes, "Middle Eastern Studies: What Went Wrong?," *Academic Questions*, volume 9, 1995–1996, p. 61. De Atkine's career: Norvell B. De Atkine, "The Political-Military Army Officer: Soldier Scholar or Cocktail Commando?," *American Diplomacy*, volume 4, number 1, 1999, unc.edu/depts/diplomat; Norvell B. De Atkine, "It's an Information War," *U.S. Naval Institute Proceedings*, January 2004, pp. 64–65. Norvell B. De Atkine, "Foreword," in Raphael Patai, *The Arab Mind* (Long Island City, N. Y.: Hatherleigh Press, 2007), p. xv. Command and General Staff College, Ft. Leavenworth, "CAC Commander's Cultural Awareness Reading List," viewed May 2010, cgsc.edu (this list also includes books by scholarly critics of Patai, such as John Esposito). Abu Ghraib: Tony Lagouranis and Allen Mikaelian, *Fear Up Harsh: An Army Interrogator's Dark Journey Through Iraq* (New York: NAL Caliber, 2007), pp. 17–19. On the popularity of *The Arab Mind* among neoconservatives, see Seymour Hersh, "The Gray Zone," *New Yorker*, May 24, 2004, p. 42. For another military manual that cites *The Arab Mind*, albeit sparingly, see Lt. Col. William D. Wunderle, *A Manual for American Servicemen in the Arab Middle East: Using Cultural Understanding to Defeat Adversaries and Win the Peace* (New York: Skyhorse Publishing, 2008). *The Arab Mind* is also included on Fort Carson's "Brave Rifles Reading List for Operation Iraqi Freedom," November 1, 2004, smallwarsjournal.com, with the caveat that "the author portrays the Arabs too stereotypically and may over generalize."

25. De Atkine, "Foreword," p. x; De Atkine and Pipes, "Middle Eastern Studies," pp. 60, 70; De Atkine e-mail to the Carolina Seminar in Comparative Islamic Studies, January 15, 2004.

26. Norvell B. De Atkine, "Foreword" (November 2001), in Rafael Patai, *The Arab Mind* (Long Island City, New York: Hatherleigh Press, 2002), p. x; De Atkine, "Foreword" (2007), pp. xvi–xvii.

27. Patai, *The Arab Mind* (2007 edition), p. 33.

28. Robert A. Pape, *Dying to Win: The Strategic Logic of Suicide Terrorism* (New York: Random House, 2005); Donald Black, "The Geometry of Terrorism," *Sociological Theory*, volume 22, 2004, pp. 14–25.

29. Terrorism experts: Lisa Rachel Stampnitzky, "Disciplining an Unruly Field: Terrorism Studies and the State, 1972–2001," Ph.D. dissertation, Department of Sociology, University of California, Berkeley, 2008. Economists' paper: Alan Krueger and Jitka Maleckova, "Education, Poverty, and Terrorism: Is There a Causal Connection?," *Journal of Economic Perspectives*, volume 17, number 4, 2003, pp. 119–144.

30. Fear of SARS: TNS Intersearch/ABC News/Washington Post Poll #2003–923, April 3, 2003. In another survey, 40 percent of respondents said they were concerned about their family's exposure to SARS while 31 percent said they were concerned about their family's exposure to terrorism. Gallup/CNN/USA Today Poll #2003–27, April 22–23, 2003. Both surveys are archived at the Roper Center for Public Opinion Research, University of Connecticut. Avoiding public places: Robert J. Blendon et al., "The Public's Response to Severe Acute Respiratory Syndrome in Toronto and the United States," *Clinical Infectious Diseases*, volume 38, 2004, p. 927. Nigeria and other countries: Pew Global Attitudes Project, *21 Population Survey*, May 2003, pewglobal.org. SARS cases by country: World Health Organization, "Cumulative Number of Reported Probable Cases of SARS," July 1, 2003, who.int. Nigerian health officials announced one death from SARS a day after the Pew survey had finished, but the case was later reclassified as not being SARS: Associated Press, May 12, 2003. Nigerian public health announcements: Edetaen Ojo, "Nigeria: Ten Weeks of Government Secrecy—No Questions Asked—Panic All-Round," OpenDemocracy.net, June 25, 2003.

31. Richard Schabas, "SARS: Prudence, Not Panic," *CMAJ* (Canadian Medical Association Journal), May 27, 2003, pp. 1432–1434; Lawrence O. Gostin, Ronald Bayer, and Amy L. Fairchild, "Ethical and Legal Challenges Posed by Severe Acute Respiratory Syndrome Implications for the Control of Severe Infectious Disease Threats," *JAMA* (Journal of the American Medical Association), volume 290, 2003, pp. 3229–3237. Julie Gerberding, director of the Centers for Disease Control and Prevention, "Update on Severe Acute Respiratory Syndrome (SARS)," April 22, 2003, cdc.gov.

32. Intelligence assessments on smallpox and Iraq: *New York Times*, September 8 and December 3, 2002; *Washington Post*, November 5, 2002. Turned out to be false: Joseph Cirincione et al., *WMD in Iraq: Evidence and Implications* (Washington, D.C.: Carnegie Endowment for International Peace, 2004), pp. 33–36; United States Senate Select Committee on Intelligence, *Report on the U.S. Intelligence Community's Prewar Intelligence Assessments on Iraq*, July 7, 2004, pp. 146–161, 166–174. George W. Bush, "President Delivers Remarks on Smallpox," December 13, 2002, georgewbush-whitehouse.archives.gov. Fear of smallpox attack: Gallup/CNN/USA Today Poll #2003-05, January 23–25, 2003. Fear of getting smallpox: ICR/Harvard Poll #2003-SARS1, April 11–15, 2003. Public health officials relieved: *Science*, December 20, 2002, pp. 2312–2316.

33. Analogy with virus: Richard N. Haass, assistant secretary of state for planning, "The Bush Administration's Response to September 11th—and Beyond,"

October 15, 2001, www.cfr.org. *New York Times Magazine*, September 11, 2005, p. 44; see also Ruth Mayer, "Virus Discourse: The Rhetoric of Threat and Terrorism in the Biothriller," *Cultural Critique*, number 66, 2007, pp. 1–20.

34. Robert Wuthnow, *Be Very Afraid: The Cultural Response to Terror, Pandemics, Environmental Devastation, Nuclear Annihilation, and Other Threats* (New York: Oxford University Press, 2010).

35. Homeland Security Council, *National Planning Scenarios: Created for Use in National, Federal, State, and Local Homeland Security Preparedness Activities*, Draft Version 20.1, April 2005, washingtonpost.com. Terrorist fatalities of the past 40 years: *Global Terrorism Database*. Steven D. Levitt and Stephen J. Dubner, *SuperFreakonomics* (New York: William Morrow, 2009), p. 65.

36. Ron Suskind, *The One Percent Doctrine: Deep Inside America's Pursuit of Its Enemies since 9/11* (New York: Simon & Schuster, 2006), p. 62

37. Rolf Mowatt-Larssen, *Al Qaeda Weapons of Mass Destruction Threat: Hype or Reality?* (Cambridge, Mass.: Belfer Center for Science and International Affairs, Harvard Kennedy School, 2010). U.S. Department of Transportation, Fatality Analysis Reporting System, *2008 Data Summary*, nhtsa.dot.gov. Federal Bureau of Investigation, *Crime in the United States*, "Expanded Homicide Data Table 10: Murder Circumstances by Relationship," 2009, fbi.gov.

38. Obama campaign positions: Democratic National Convention Committee, *The 2008 Democratic National Platform: Renewing America's Promise*, August 25, 2008, democrats.org. CBS News Poll, "Where America Stands," May 20–24, 2010, cbsnews.com; Washington Post Polls, November 2, 2005, through March 23–26, 2010, washingtonpost.com. In polls from 2002 and 2003, respondents trusted Republicans twice as often as Democrats to do a better job against terrorism.

INDEX

Abd al-Rahman, Umar, 63
Abd al-Raziq, Ali, 102–103
Abdulmutallab, Umar Farouk, 171, 203
Abou El-Fattouh, Abdel Monem, 124
Abu Hudhayfa, 76
Abu Jandal, 33
Abu Qatada, 82
Abu Zayd, Nasr Hamid, 119
Abu Zubayda, 82
Afghanistan, 5, 9–10, 12, 14, 16, 18, 25, 31,
    33, 44, 45, 47, 52, 55–56, 57–58, 59,
    64, 71, 72, 73, 74, 75–83, 88, 99, 108,
    109, 110, 136–138, 140–147, 162,
    168
Africa, 54, 107, 130, 151
Ahmad Khan, Sayyid, 101
Ahmadinejad, Mahmud, 157, 158, 159, 162,
    182
Aisha, 50
Akhundzada, Fath Ali, 119
Al-Absi, Shakir, 90–91
Al-Adl, Sayf, 50, 57
Al-Afghani, Jamal al-Din, 62
Al-Awlaki, Anwar, 34
Al-Azhar, 43, 53, 56, 63, 67, 103
Al-Azm, Sadik, 26–27
Al-Banna, Hasan, 61
Al-Durri, Fouad Ali Hossein, 121
Al-Fawzan, Salih, 118–119
Al-Hakayma, Muhammad Khalil, 62–63
Al-Husayn ibn Ali, 68
Al-Jazeera, 10, 12, 25, 80, 167

Al-Libi, Abu Yahya, 111
Al-Muhajiroun (Great Britain), 10, 33
Al-Muqrin, Abdulaziz, 59
Al-Nabhani, Taqiuddin, 82
Al-Nogaidan, Mansour, 125–126
Al-Qaida, 7, 8, 9, 10, 11, 12, 13, 16, 17, 18,
    19–20, 25, 29, 31, 33, 34, 35, 36, 38,
    39, 40, 43, 44, 45, 47, 48, 50, 54, 57,
    58, 59–64, 67–68, 71, 73, 75–91, 93,
    109, 111, 115, 127, 132, 136–138,
    142–144, 151–153, 169–170, 171,
    172, 184, 194, 198, 201–202, 204
Al-Qaradawi, Yusuf, 43, 111
Al-Saoub, Habis Abdulla, 52
Al-Saud, Abd al-Aziz, 68
Al-Suri, Abu Musab, 9
Al-Zarqawi, Abu Musab, 62, 84
Algeria, 6, 41, 43, 59, 84, 108, 109, 113,
    124–125, 150
An-Na'im, Abdullahi, 103
Army of Islam (Gaza), 89
Asian Muslim Action Network (Thailand),
    106
Atkins, Homer, 163–164
Atta, Muhammad, 19
Australia, 32
Ayyash, Yahya, 81–82
Azerbaijan, 47, 119
Azzam, Abdullah, 9–10, 74–75, 82, 85, 90

Bahrain, 118
Bahri, Mohammed, 126

Bangladesh, 40, 43, 109, 114, 151
Basayev, Shamil, 30
Bazargan, Mehdi, 157
Beers, Charlotte, 166–167
Belhadj, Ali, 113
Bin Ladin, Usama, 7, 10, 16, 19–20, 28–32,
        33, 35, 36, 37, 38–39, 42, 45, 47, 48,
        51, 54, 60, 62, 63, 67–68, 70, 75–79,
        83, 88, 103, 132, 137, 141–142, 144,
        147, 149, 177, 187
Black, Donald, 194
Blowback, 140–145
Bosnia, 59, 98, 110, 145–147
Boubekeur, Amel, 34–35
Brachman, Jarret, 34, 184
Brazil, 195
Buddhism, 74
Bueno de Mesquita, Bruce, 181–183
Bukhara, 99
Burma, 164
Bush, George W., 64, 78, 128, 133, 135, 136,
        138, 143, 144, 148, 149, 150, 151,
        152, 153, 157, 166–167, 196–197,
        200, 202

California, 41, 66, 162
Canada, 92–94, 196
Carter, Jimmy, 46, 153, 157
Casey, William, 137–138
Center for the Study of Islam and
        Democracy (U.S.), 106
Central Asia, 99, 110, 117, 163, 188
Central Intelligence Agency, 12, 46, 126,
        136–138, 140–141, 159, 181
Cevdet, Abdullah, 119
Chapel Hill, 3–6, 13, 17, 23, 138–139
Charlotte, 17
Chechnya, 30, 88
Cheney, Dick, 136, 172, 197, 201
Cheney, Lynne, 172–173
China, 52, 79, 132, 185, 186, 195
Chiozza, Giacomo, 150
Christians, 22, 30, 60, 70, 96, 98, 100, 116,
        123, 147, 149, 150, 152, 153
Clinton, Bill, 78, 136, 145
Columbine, 17
Comte, Auguste, 180–181
Cuba, 82, 83, 155, 165, 166

Dadullah, Mansur, 80
Dadullah, Mulla, 9, 80

De Atkine, Norvell B., 190–193
Democracy, Muslim attitudes toward, 20,
        29, 33, 36, 37, 38, 41, 42–43, 88,
        94–107, 110–118, 124–125, 131,
        134–135, 149–151, 155–156,
        158–162
Derwish, Kamal, 58
Dhani, Ahmad, 127

Ebadi, Shirin, 154–156, 159
Edgar, Iain, 38
Egypt, 9, 25, 34, 38, 41, 42, 43, 47, 48, 54,
        58, 61–62, 63, 64, 67, 83, 84, 87, 98,
        101, 102–103, 108, 109, 115–116,
        119, 122–124, 127, 143, 148, 191
Elliott, Andrea, 55
Ethiopia, 116
Europe, 24, 30, 32, 34, 44, 60–61, 86, 96,
        100, 119, 145, 159, 188–190, 198

Falwell, Jerry, 123
Faraj, Abd al-Salam, 9, 61–62
Fatah, 58
Federal Bureau of Investigation, 6, 13
Felicity Party (Turkey), 114
Fouda, Yosri, 12
France, 6, 27, 34–35, 46, 70, 86, 87, 178
Friedman, Thomas, 64, 94

Gallup, 27–28, 109, 116, 150, 151
Gandhi, Mahatma, 138
Gaza, 11, 81, 83, 89, 90
Germany, 11, 40
Gibson, Mel, 30
Germany, 137, 198
Gingrich, Newt, 157
Graham, Franklin, 153
Great Britain, 10, 27, 31–32, 33, 34, 36, 46,
        50, 68, 70, 71, 80, 82, 87, 88,
        107–108, 135, 159, 171, 178, 198
Greece, 27, 60
Guantánamo, 82, 83, 155
Guevara, Che, 19–20, 30, 31–32, 45
Gulf War, 17, 24
Gustave, Dawood, 31
Gymnastiar, Abdullah, 121

Hamas (Palestine), 11, 20, 43, 58, 81,
        83–91, 111
Hanafi, Hassan, 103
Haqqani, Maulvi Mohammad, 80–81

Harakat al-Ansar (Pakistan), 40
Harakat ul-Mujahideen (Pakistan), 8
Hashemi Rafsanjani, Akbar, 157
Hashish, Issam, 124
Hathout, Maher, 41
Hijab, 37, 39, 69, 72, 116–117
Hindus, 65, 70
Hiroshima, 28
Hizb ut-Tahrir al-Islami, 82
Hizbullah (Lebanon), 47–48, 58, 89–91
Holland, 24
Hughes, Karen, 167
Hunerwadel, Helen and Otto, 164, 165
Hunt, David, 184
Huntington, Samuel, 108
Husayn, 40
Hussein, Saddam, 132–133, 136, 142

Ibn Abd al-Wahhab, Muhammad, 69
Ibn Masud, 56
Ibn Taymiyya, 69
Ibrahim, Saad Eddin, 63
Ilyas, Muhammad, 39
India, 15–16, 36, 39, 63, 65, 98
Indonesia, 29, 32, 48, 64, 65, 101, 103, 106,
    109, 111–112, 117, 118, 121, 127,
    134, 147–148, 151
Internet, 6, 8, 10, 16, 26, 31, 32, 34, 37–38,
    46, 47, 51–52, 54, 56, 57, 59, 71, 94,
    109, 123, 171, 176, 185
Iran, 17, 19, 46, 47, 49–50, 63, 65, 70,
    72–73, 87, 91, 98–100, 103–109,
    113–114, 119, 140, 141, 154–162,
    164–165, 181–185
Iraq, 5, 14, 17, 18, 19, 33, 36, 43, 44, 45, 47,
    52–55, 70, 80, 83, 84, 88, 90, 114,
    121, 132–133, 135–137, 142,
    143–145, 147, 177, 178–179, 191,
    192, 197
Islam 21 (Great Britain), 106
Islamic Constitutional Movement (Kuwait),
    114
Islamic Jihad (Egypt), 84
Islamic Liberation Party, 82
Islamic Salvation Front (Algeria), 113,
    124–125
Islamic Thinkers Society (U.S.), 94–95
Islamic Unity Front (Bangladesh), 114
Israel, 5, 32–33, 43, 44, 46, 47, 71–72,
    81–90, 149, 151, 153–154, 176, 189
Italy, 11, 60

Jamaat-e-Islami (Bangladesh), 43, 114
Jamaat-e-Islami (Pakistan), 43, 44
Jannati, Ahmad, 73
Japan, 28, 137, 198
Jeepo, 164
Jemaah Islamiya (Southeast Asia), 64, 84
Jesus, 60
Jews, 18, 33, 70, 82, 87, 98, 99, 149, 154,
    159, 189
Johnson, Chalmers, 141–142
Jordan, 29, 35, 47, 81, 87, 109, 110, 143,
    150, 191
Justice and Development Party (Turkey),
    114

Karbala, 40
Karnataka, 15–16
Kashmir, 121
Katzenstein, Peter, 147
Kazakhstan, 110
Kemal, Namık, 101
Kenya, 31, 78, 90, 142
Keohane, Robert, 147
Khaled, Amr, 122–124
Khalifa, Rashad, 19
Khamenei, Ali, 72, 108, 162, 183
Khan, Sayyid Ahmad, 101
Khan, Samir, 120
Khatami, Muhammad, 104, 157–158
Khayr al-Din, 96–97, 101
Khiva, 99
Khomeini, Ruhollah, 63, 72, 107, 108, 183
Kolenda, Christopher, 167–168
Kotkin, Joel, 198–199
Kramer, Martin, 173–174, 177
Krauthammer, Charles, 143
Kurds, 36
Kuwait, 17, 28, 70, 114, 118, 150, 193

Laqueur, Walter, 18, 187–189
Lashkar Jihad (Indonesia), 111–112
Lebanon, 47–48, 87, 89–91, 135, 149, 191
Lewis, Bernard, 108, 132–135
Liberal Islam, 20, 41–42, 95–127
Liberal Islam Network (Indonesia), 106,
    120
Libya, 54, 83

Madani, Abbassi, 113, 125
Madi, Abu'l-Ela, 124
Madjid, Nurcholish, 103

Mahmutćehajić, Rusmir, 103
Malaysia, 43, 103, 106
Malkum Khan, 119
Mao Zedong, 58, 132
Maryland, 49
Massoud, Ahmad Shah, 78
Maudoodi, Abu'l-Ala, 63, 66
McCants, William, 51
McVeigh, Timothy, 18
Mead, Margaret, 14
Media, 6, 12, 15–16, 23, 25–29, 43, 47, 60,
    75–77, 80, 83, 90, 104, 121–124, 132,
    135, 140, 146, 150–153, 158,
    166–167, 184
Mexico, 15
Moaddel, Mansoor, 36
Mohammed, Khalid Sheikh, 11–12, 77, 193
Montazeri, Hossein Ali, 183
Moosa, Ebrahim, 13
Morocco, 29, 35, 43, 48, 55, 70, 126–127, 178
Mortenson, Greg, 162–163, 165, 167–168
Mossadeq, Mohammed, 140
Moses, 123–124
Mueller, Robert, 13
Muhammad, 9, 38, 50, 56, 60, 66, 67, 68, 97,
    102
Muhammad, Nek, 59
Mullen, Mike, 167
Murrow, Edward R., 166
Musavi, Mir Hossein, 158
Musawah (Malaysia), 106
Muslim Association of Canada, 93
Muslim Brotherhood (Egypt), 42–44, 61,
    83, 89, 115–116, 124
Muslim Canadian Congress, 93
Muslim Communities Union, 43

Naeemi, Sarfraz, 120–121
Nafar, Tamer, 32–33
Nagasaki, 28
Namık Kemal, 101
Naqvi, Ijlal, 37, 114
Nasir, Kamilu, 151
Nasr, Vali, 63
Nasrullah, Hasan, 48
National Awakening Party (Indonesia), 112
National Counterterrorism Center, 14
Nawaz, Aki, 31–32
Nazis, 18, 24, 33
New York, 6, 23, 24, 25, 57–58, 94, 128,
    139, 198–199, 203

Nigeria, 47, 110, 130, 151, 195–196
Nixon, Richard, 145
North Carolina, 3–6, 13, 17, 23, 120,
    138–139, 163, 191, 192
Northern Ireland, 11
Nuri, Abdullah, 104–106
Nuri, Shaykh Fazlullah, 99–100

Obama, Barack, 22, 153–154, 158–160,
    162, 202–203
Oklahoma City, 17, 18
Oman, 118
Oregon, 52
Ottoman Empire, 64, 66–68, 87, 96–100,
    119
Öztürk, Yaşar Nuri, 121–122

Pahlavi, Shah Mohammad Reza, 107
Pakistan, 8, 11–13, 14, 18, 29, 31, 34,
    35–45, 48, 52, 54, 58, 59, 64, 65, 70,
    73, 79–81, 83, 84, 90, 100–101, 109,
    120–121, 127, 143, 148, 151–152,
    154, 162–163, 188, 193, 201
Palestine, 11, 16, 26, 27, 29, 32–33, 44, 72,
    81–91, 110, 149, 153–154, 176, 178,
    189
Palestine Liberation Organization, 89
Pape, Robert, 193
Patai, Raphael, 189–193
Peraino, Kevin, 54
Petraeus, David, 167
Pew Global Attitudes Project, 28–29, 35, 49,
    110–111, 117, 151, 152, 153, 188
Philippines, 52, 165
Picot, François Georges, 87–88, 90
Pipes, Daniel, 192
PKK (Turkey), 45
Powell, Colin, 166

Qatar, 43, 118
Quran, 4, 17–19, 34, 44, 66, 88, 97, 101,
    102, 103, 112, 119–123, 127
Qutb, Sayyid, 9, 61

Radical sheik, 29–35
Rafsanjani, Akbar Hashemi, 157
Raslan, Mustafa, 124
Reagan, Ronald, 137, 157
Reid, Richard, 38–39
Renan, Ernest, 86
Robertson, Pat, 123

Rose, Charlie, 135
Rumsfeld, Donald, 64, 136
Russia, 27, 30, 98, 119, 140, 165, 195, 196

Sadat, Anwar, 9, 124, 191
Sadr, Muqtada, 114
Sageman, Marc, 57
Said, Edward, 189–191
Salafist Group for Preaching and Combat
    (Algeria), 84
Salahuddin, Dawud, 49–50
Salam, Khaled, 124
SARS, 195–196
Saudi Arabia, 5, 8, 30, 39, 41, 42, 51,
    54, 58, 59, 62, 63, 64, 67, 68, 70,
    73, 75, 78–79, 85, 87, 94, 110,
    118–119, 125–126, 142, 148,
    149, 153, 194
Schanzer, David, 13
September 11 attacks, 21, 23, 24, 25–28, 31,
    40, 43, 44, 45, 46, 47–49, 63, 71, 84,
    90, 94, 111, 128, 132, 133, 136–142,
    148, 149, 156, 169–170, 171, 172,
    173, 177, 186, 187, 193, 197, 198,
    199, 200
Serbia, 137, 145–147
Shahzad, Faisal, 23, 203
Shakur, Tupac, 31
Sheikh Mohammed, Khalid, 11–12, 77, 193
Shia Islam, 19, 36, 40, 42, 47–48, 58, 67,
    89–91, 98, 107, 109
Shuster, Morgan, 165
Sick, Gary, 48–49
Silverman, Ira, 50
Singapore, 98
Smallpox, 196–197
Somalia, 13, 59, 132, 135
Soroush, Abdolkarim, 103–104, 107, 119
South Asia, 100, 130
Southeast Asia, 64, 84, 117
Soviet Union, 9–10, 11, 74, 108, 137, 140,
    141–142, 146
Spain, 11, 59, 90
Sterling, Claire, 137–138
Stern, Jessica, 32
Sudan, 70, 103, 142
Sufism, 31, 121
Suharto, 112
Sunni Islam, 19, 36, 40, 54, 89–91, 107, 109,
    121
Suskind, Ron, 201

Sweden, 149
Sykes, Mark, 87–88, 90
Syria, 40, 83, 87, 111

Tablighi Jamaat, 39–40, 42
Taheri-Azar, Mohammad, 3–6, 17–19,
    23–24, 32, 58, 203
Tajbakhsh, Kian, 159
Takfir, 41
Taliban, 12–13, 16, 20, 37, 39, 51, 52, 54,
    56, 59–60, 64, 68–81, 84, 91, 109,
    121, 137–138, 152
Tancredo, Tom, 153
Tantawi, Muhammad, 53
Tanzania, 31, 78, 90, 142
Tatarstan, 98
Televangelism, 121–124
Telhami, Shibley, 48, 150, 151, 152, 153
Temple-Raston, Dina, 58
Tenet, George, 136
Thailand, 52–53, 106
Tilly, Charles, 140
Top, Noordin, 84
Truman, Harry, 65
Tunisia, 96, 97
Turkey, 31, 37, 43, 45–46, 48, 58, 64, 66–68,
    87, 111, 117, 121, 134, 147–148, 151,
    194

Ugly American, 163–165
Umar, 97
Umar, Muhammad, 16, 68, 74, 75–80
United Development Party (Indonesia),
    112
United Iraqi Alliance (Iraq), 114
United States
    armed forces, 11, 55, 76, 138, 167–168,
        176–177, 178–180, 191–192
    domestic terrorism, 3–6, 11, 13–14, 34,
        49, 94, 120
    fear of terrorism, 21–22, 195, 197–204
    foreign policy, 4, 20, 45–46, 65,
        128–168, 204
    military operations, 17, 18, 19, 28, 33,
        36, 44, 45, 47, 52, 53–54, 70, 75,
        78–79, 82–83, 90, 109, 132, 135,
        141–142, 144–147, 149, 154, 155,
        160, 168, 177, 178, 191, 193–194
    Muslim attitudes toward, 109, 128–168
    Muslim-Americans' opposition to
        terrorism, 14, 41, 94–95

United States (*continued*)
  target of terrorism, 11–13, 38–39, 44, 48,
    63, 76, 78, 80, 89–91, 169–171, 177,
    180
University of North Carolina, 3–6, 17, 175
Uzbekistan, 117

Vahdeti, Derviş, 99–100
Victory of Islam (Lebanon), 90
Vietnam, 135

Wadud-Muhsin, Amina, 103
Wahhabism, 42
Wahid, Abdurrahman, 112
Wali-Allah, Shah, 69
Washington, D.C., 5, 25
Washington, George, 156
Wickham, Carrie Rosefsky, 43
Winfrey, Oprah, 124

Wolfe, Tom, 29
Women's rights, 37, 38, 39, 69, 72, 84,
    114–117
World Health Organization, 14
World Public Opinion, 152
World Values Survey, 41, 109, 110, 113, 116
Wuthnow, Robert, 199

X, Malcolm, 19–20, 30

Yasin, Ahmad, 83–84
Yassine, Abdessalam, 70
Yemen, 33, 34, 54, 71, 120, 171
Yousafzai, Sami, 81
Yusufzai, Rahimullah, 76

Zammar, Muhammad Haydar, 40
Zawahiri, Ayman, 7–8, 34, 43, 47, 48, 62,
    68, 85, 88–90, 109, 111